COMMUNICATION AND POWER IN ORGANIZATIONS: DISCOURSE, IDEOLOGY, AND DOMINATION

PEOPLE, COMMUNICATION, ORGANIZATION

LEE THAYER, Series Editor

University of Wisconsin, Parkside

Associate Editors

Charles Conrad

University of North Carolina, Chapel Hill

Gerald M. Goldhaber

State University of New York, Buffalo

W. Charles Redding

Purdue University

Organization ←→ *Communication: Emerging Perspectives I,* edited by Lee Thayer

Organization ←→ *Communication: Emerging Perspectives II,* edited by Lee Thayer

Communication and Power in Organization: Discourse, Ideology, and Domination, by Dennis K. Mumby

Studying Human Communication: Evaluating Method and Data, edited by Nancy J. Wyatt and Gerald M. Phillips

in preparation

Responsive Institutions: A Communication Order withoiut Control, by Joseph Pilotta, John W. Murphy, Tricia Jones, and Elizabeth Wilson

Television and Organizational Life, edited by Leah R. Ekdom and Nick Trujillo

COMMUNICATION AND POWER IN ORGANIZATIONS: DISCOURSE, IDEOLOGY, AND DOMINATION

Dennis K. Mumby
Rutgers, The State University of New Jersey

ABLEX PUBLISHING CORPORATION
NORWOOD, NEW JERSEY

Library of Congress Cataloging-in-Publication Data

Mumby, Dennis K.
　　Communication and power in organizations.

　　(People, communication, organization)
　　Bibliography: p.
　　Includes index.
　　1. Communication in organizations. 2. Corporate culture. 3. Organiza-
tional　　behavior.　　4. Power　　(Social　　sciences)　　I. Title. II. Series.
HD30.3.M86 1988　　　　　　　　　302.3′5　　　　　　　　88–3356
ISBN 0–89391–480–0

Ablex Publishing Corporation
355 Chestnut Street
Norwood, New Jersey 07648

CONTENTS

INTRODUCTION TO THE SERIES

PREFACE

1 THE PROCESS OF ORGANIZING: THE CULTURAL PERSPEC-
  TIVE ON ORGANIZATIONAL COMMUNICATION   1
  Perspectives on Organizational Culture   6
  Sense-making and Organizing   9
  Culture and Organizational Symbolism   12
  Toward an Alternative Perspective
    on Organizational Culture   19
  Summary and Conclusion   21

2 HUMAN INTERESTS, KNOWLEDGE FORMATION,
  AND ORGANIZATIONAL CULTURES   23
  A Theory of Interests   24
  Critical Theories of Organizing   31
  A Critique of Habermas's Critical Theory   39
    The Problem of "Interests"   39
    Psychoanalysis and the Critique of Ideology   42
    Systematically Distorted Communication as Ideology   44
    The Ideal Speech Situation and Ideology   45
  Implications for Organizational Cultures   47
  Rethinking Power and Ideology   51
  Summary and Conclusion   52

3 POWER, INTERESTS, AND ORGANIZATIONAL
  CULTURE   55
  The Concept of Power   56
  Power in Organizations   61
  Summary and Conclusion   68

4   IDEOLOGY AND ORGANIZATIONAL CULTURES   *71*
Ideology and Consciousness   *72*
Louis Althusser: Ideology and the State   *74*
Göran Therborn: Ideology as Subjection-Qualification   *78*
Anthony Giddens: Ideology and Structuration   *82*
Organizational Culture and Ideology   *89*
Summary and Conclusion   *93*

5   IDEOLOGY AND ORGANIZATIONAL SYMBOLISM   *95*
The Ideological Function of Organizational Narratives   *102*
Narrative Politics   *105*
Organizational Narrative as Ideology: An Application   *115*
Summary and Conclusion   *124*

6   IDEOLOGY, EPISTEMOLOGY, AND TRUTH   *127*
Theories of Knowledge   *129*
Radical Conversation   *138*
Radical Methodology   *144*
Two Modes of Inquiry   *148*
Summary and Conclusion   *155*

7   CONCLUSION: INTERPRETATION AND DOMINATION   *157*
The Role of Interpretation   *159*
Conclusion   *166*

REFERENCES   *169*

AUTHOR INDEX   *181*

SUBJECT INDEX   *185*

To my parents,
Dennis and Grace.

Introduction to the Series

The main engine of Western civilization, as we know it, is at once the most indispensable and the least celebrated. It is not money, nor technology, nor even number. It is not science as such, nor ideology as such, nor even "industrialization" or "development" as such. Yet no aspect of Western civilization, as we know it, would be possible without it.

It is *organization*. Or better, perhaps the *idea* of organization.

All human civilization, as we know it, hinges upon some sort of "arrangement" between two or more people as to what role each will play in the pursuit of the larger good. The idea of kinship as central to all human civilization—as argued by Lévi-Strauss—is one example. A love relationship is another. Every business and every institution and every voluntary human enterprise is another. As the popular American song has it, "You do the cookin' honey/I'll pay the rent." Feminists or modernists may argue against *this* sort of arrangement; but they simply want to organize things in some *other* way.

Manifestiations of a given society's *ideas* of and about organization are so ubiquitous as to go unnoticed. Every society believes its way of organizing itself is "natural" or "God-given" or at least "right." To the members of every culture, the arrangements that exist for carrying out human enterprises in *other* cultures—from the domestic to the spiritual—may seem odd, or even bizarre. The main pretext for war, at least as we know it, has been that those odd and alien arrangements for doing things in other cultures were seen as a threat.

Human existence, as we know it, and the life of any society, as we know it, would be impossible without *some* idea as to how every human enterprise that involves two or more people is to be *organized*. Every mind emerges in the way it is trained to organize its grasp and its "understanding" of the world. We cannot exist apart from *some* way of organizing ourselves and the world in which we live.

Yet we know precious little about where our ideas about organizing ourselves and our world come from. We know still less, it would seem, about the *efficacy* of one way of organizing ourselves and our world vs. another (witness the never-ending quest, in our age, for the "best" or the ultimate way of organizing or managing a business enterprise, or of organizing the relationship between male and female). And we know still less, perhaps, about the long-range (or even the short-range) human *consequences* of this way or that way of organizing ourselves and the world in which we live—economically, politically, spiritually. The Navajo said, "Let it be done in beauty." Western man says, "Let it be done rationally." The consequences, even for our physical environment, are radically different.

We know so little about such matters of such great consequence to us, it may be, because any attempt to understand how we organize ourselves and our worlds is at the same time an attempt to understand how we understand. Trying to understand such things as make us human may be, as Alan Watts once suggested, a little like trying to bite one's own teeth.

But the ultimate "frontier" is not space. It is the way we come to be human, and all of the human artifacts we create and utilize to endow us with whatever humanity we may realize in our sojourn on earth. Of these, none is more central to our lives than the ways we have come to organize ourselves—whether for an affair or a space mission. It is those taken-for-granted arrangements between and among people engaged in one or another human enterprise that enable our lives and the life of our society. To understand them is to understand ourselves better. And to understand ourselves better is the only ground upon which we can stand to make better the conditions of our lives, now and for generations following, for us and for all of the peoples of the world.

To speak of organization is to speak of communication. The two may be more than merely coterminous. They may perhaps be two aspects of the same thing.

For if what another says is to have any meaning at all, one must have *some* sense of the nature of the human enterprise in which one is engaged with the other. And one must have *some* sense of the role one plays in that enterprise as that role relates to the role of the other. To "understand" what is going on and to participate in it in some way, one must already have understood how it is organized—whether it is a game, a conversation, a trip across town, or a board meeting. It is *that* understanding, that sense one has of how things are organized and how one fits into them, that makes human communication possible. And conversely. Wherever and whenever there has been evidence of the one, there has been evidence of the other. Paradoxically, to the Western mind, each is the precondition of the other. Each is interdependent with the other.

And thus the sense of the title of this book series: PEOPLE, COMMUNICATION, ORGANIZATION. Together, they comprise the enabling *system*, the inescapable *system*, which undergirds all human enterprise. As components of that system which undergirds *all* human enterprise, they are inextricably intertwined. To understand one is to understand the other. To be concerned about one necessarily invokes the other. Ultimately, we cannot understand people without taking into account how they communicate and the nature of the human organizations they get themselves into. We cannot understand human communication without taking into account the organized structures within which it occurs, and the nature of the people who assume or induce those social arrangements. And our understanding of human organization and of organizational life is going to be no better than our understanding of how people make each other, and how they are made, in communication. For it is *in* communication that we energize and give sense to the structures and the conditions of everyday life, those of human existence and of organizational life.

We *say* the structures and arrangements of our world into existence. And we have our lives, both within and without organizations, in the consequences of our saying-so. If there be defects or shortcomings, it is not to our enterprises and institutions to which we must look. If the arrangements by which we conduct the work and play of the world are not as we would have them, then we must look to the origin of those arrangements. We must look to the way in which we recreate them moment to moment, day to day, in what we say of them and think of them. They come into existence and evolve as they do because we *mind* them as we do. It is only as we come to mind them differently that "they" change. If one's marriage is not all that one had hoped; if one's business enterprise does not return all that it was expected to return; if the legal or other institutions of this society are not functioning as they "should"— then we must look to our ways of minding them—to *how* we understand them and speak of them.

Such social arrangements as bring us together in twos or eights or thousands are not born of necessity. They are born of human imagination—of *how* we can and do speak of the world, and of how we take it into account.

PEOPLE, COMMUNICATION, ORGANIZATION, each enables and constrains the other. How? What are the consequences of enabling ourselves in one way rather than another? Of minding the world one way rather than another? Of organizing ourselves one way rather than another? Of creating and practicing our humanity *in* communication in one form of organization rather than another? Of creating and practicing our humanity *in* organizations that constrain our ways of saying and seeing the world in one way rather than another? Of believing that any one is independent of the other?

This, then, is the charter for this series of books: To address the way we organize ourselves and our enterprises and our institutions as a result of the way we communicate with one another. And to address the way we communicate with one another as a result of how we have organized ourselves and our enterprises and our institutions. And what the human consequences are, or may be.

In doing so, we will want to speak to the thoughtful "practitioner" as much as to the grounded "philosopher," to the practical as much as to the abstract, to the layman as much as to the expert. For there is nothing esoteric about the subject; no one's life falls outside of the intellectual concerns which will guide us here. In this arena of life, unless all gain in understanding, no one does. That is in the nature of what we join here to think about and explore.

Lee Thayer
Series Editor

PREFACE

The intellectual origins of this book go back 10 years to my time as an undergraduate student at Sheffield City Polytechnic in England. It was there that I was first exposed to contemporary European social theory, and in particular to important thinkers such as Antonio Gramsci, Louis Althusser, and Stuart Hall. In addition, the eclecticism of my undergraduate degree allowed me to develop a sense of the prevailing issues in the various disciplinary areas of literary criticism, sociolinguistics, psycholinguistics, and mass communication. It was from this broad background that I derived my initial interest in language and, in particular, the relationship between language and meaning.

I was encouraged to pursue this interest, however poorly focused it might have been, when I began my graduate studies at Southern Illinois University in Carbondale. Here, under the tutelage of scholars such as Stan Deetz, Richard Lanigan, and Tom Pace (who, if pressed, might define themselves respectively as "hermeneutic," "semiotic," and "existential" phenomenologists) I spent the greater part of 4 years struggling with the various forms of phenomenology, and attempting to articulate for myself a view of the relationship between language and meaning, experience, reality, etc., with which I was comfortable. My early work as an undergraduate has sensitized me to the political and potentially repressive qualities of language, while my later work as a graduate student made me highly aware of the great philosophic tradition associated with the study of communication. In a very real sense I think that this book represents a marriage between these two aspects of my own personal intellectual heritage. And so even though ostensibly the book is about organizational communication, I see it more as a treatise on the relationship between communication and meaning and the attendant consequences of examining this relationship from a political perspective. The fact that I came to organizational studies very late in my graduate career is testament to this focus. I might therefore say that the focus on organizational cultures essentially provides me with an appropriate and convenient vehicle for examining the communication–domination relationship.

The first chapter therefore takes up the basic issue of what it means to conceptualize organizations as cultures. Questions of sense-making, meaning, and symbolic forms are taken up, and it is argued that the relationship between organizational communication and meaning formation can only be adequately studied through a conceptual assimilation of issues of power and domination. I suggest that organizational meaning, although formed intersubjectively, does not arise spontaneously, but is the product of various power interests that are part of the deep structure of organizational behavior.

Chapter 2 develops this theme by focusing on the question of interests and critically examining the work of Jurgen Habermas. Habermas has become more familiar to communication scholars in recent years, but the complexity and difficulty of his work appears to have restricted the application of his philosophy of communication in our field. I therefore provide a critical overview of his project, and then suggest how his theory of knowledge-constituting interests and his universal pragmatics might inform the study of communication and domination in organizational cultures. In essence, I argue that his theory of interests demonstrates how communication can function in both a repressive and emancipatory capacity, and that an adequate theory of organizing must examine the link between communication and both of these possibilities.

Chapter 3 directly addresses the concept of power. I examine several views of power and look at the application of this concept to the process of organizing. Traditionally, power has been treated as a legitimate product of organizing and has not been viewed in terms of its iteration as a means of repression and domination. I therefore argue for a conception of power-as-domination in which power is exercised by virtue of the structuring of certain group interests into organizational activity. In other words, domination occurs when particular organizational interests come to define the process of organizing.

The means by which organizational interests come to be structured is taken up in chapter 4 with a development of the concept of ideology. I argue against conceiving of ideology as purely ideational (i.e., as consisting simply of individual beliefs and values), and suggest that it is rooted in the everyday practices of social actors. I conceive of ideology as the process by which social actors are interpellated (addressed) and the means by which their sense of consciousness of the social world is constituted. Ideology functions to articulate a sense of the world in which contradictions and structures of domination are obscured, and the particular interests of dominant grouups are perceived as universal interests and hence actively supported, even by oppressed groups (Gramsci's concept of "hegemony"). I further argue that ideology manifests itself and is expressed principally through various discursive practices, and that the analysis and critique of ideology must make explicit the connection between relations of domination and systems of signification.

Chapter 5 takes up just this issue by closely examining the way in which one particular form of signification—organizational narrative—can function ideologically. I suggest that there is nothing intrinsically ideological about the act of storytelling, but rather that the structure of narrative lends itself well to the maintenance and reproduction of certain meaning formations. When such meaning formations function to reproduce the interests of particular groups to the exclusion of others, then narrative functions ideologically. I thus examine the nature of narrative per se, and discuss how this particular discursive practice is not simply a neutral purveyor of information; rather, the act of storytelling is a political act that has consequences for the reproduction of organizational reality. In an application of my theoretical stance I take a single organizational story and analyze it in terms of its ideological functioning. While analyzing a single story out of context obviously has serious limitations, it does provide a strong sense of how such an analysis might help us to rethink the relationship between organizational communication and organizational meaning.

Chapter 6 raises some of the metatheoretical issues that the previous chapters inevitably raise. If we make problematic the relationship between language and meaning, then how are we to know what constitutes 'truth?'' Following thinkers such as Rorty and Gadamer, I argue against foundationalist epistemologies in which truth is judged in terms of an isomorphism between language and reality. A more fruitful concept of truth regards theories as different discourse, each vying for position in the conversation of humankind. The most successful theories are judged not on their ability to reflect an objective reality, but on the extent to which they challenge us to engage in self-reflection and hence emancipation from conditions of discursive closure. Addressing the issues of ideology and domination thus requires that we go beyond the parameters of traditional positivist social theory to questions regarding the relationship between theory and power.

Finally, chapter 7 concludes my argument by briefly addressing the question of interpretation and examining the problematic issue of the validity of the interpretive act. I argue that the evaluation of interpretation, whether it be of a novel, a movie, a story, and so forth, should not be based on questions of author intent, discovery of essences, or any other foundational criteria. An interpretation is more appropriately validated if it exploits the disjuncture that exists between the reader/listener and the text. The interpretive act is one of deconstruction and resistance, struggling against the framing of the world that the text tries to impose on one. The dialectic between reader/listener and text that produces meaning is therefore fundamentally political, as is the act of interpretation. It is through the interpretive process that we make sense of our world, and it is through this same process that our social world is reproduced. Meaning and interpretation, domination and discourse, are thus inextricably linked.

The writing of this book has inevitably required the help, support, and understanding of several people. Its foundation was laid in a doctoral dissertation completed at Southern Illinois University, Carbondale, under the direction of Stan Deetz. Stan has played several roles for me over the last 7 years—mentor, colleague, friend, confidant—and has been supportive and sympathetic in each. The clarity and depth of his thinking and the steadiness of his guidance have been a source of inspiration. I am grateful to Richard Lanigan and Tom Pace who, in different ways, gave me insight into the problem of language and meaning. Gordon Nakagawa and Julie Williams, my "surrogate parents," have been close friends over the last few years, providing both intellectual and emotional support when it was much needed. Thanks to my colleagues in the Department of Communication at Rutgers University for providing the collegial atmosphere that has helped stimulate this work. Finally, I want to express my appreciation to Christina Gonzalez for her love and support during much of the writing of this book.

Dennis Mumby

New Brunswick, NJ
July 1987

1

THE PROCESS OF ORGANIZING: THE CULTURAL PERSPECTIVE ON ORGANIZATIONAL COMMUNICATION

The issue of power and theories of organizational communication have maintained a somewhat uneasy relationship in recent years. For the most part, questions about power have been defined largely from what might loosely be termed a "managerial" perspective. In other words, power is recognized as a relevant issue only when viewed as a legitimate aspect of the management process. Organizational research is thus replete with studies of superior-subordinate interaction, compliance-gaining strategies, decision-making processes, and so forth, all of which tend to look at organizations through managerial glasses. Treatments of power which circumvent this managerial frame of reference are fairly rare, although work by theorists such as Clegg (1981; Clegg & Dunkerley, 1980), Conrad (1983), and Frost (in press), have begun to pose questions about the relationship between communication and power-as-domination in organizations. Such an alternative view of power is heretical to many organizational managers, insofar as it assumes that organizational practices can be characterized as something other than "rational" in the strict sense of the term. The "myth of rationality" (Cohen, March, & Olsen, 1972; Conrad, 1985a; March & Olsen, 1976; Weick, 1979) embodies the belief that the process of organizing can be characterized principally by the rational assimilation of available information, and the subsequent setting of appropriate, carefully selected goals. In this context the communication process serves as an information conduit—the better the organization's communication network, the more accurate the transmission of information and hence the better the decision-making process. Pfeffer (1981) reports one such expression of this organizational myth:

Managers aren't politicians, I was told. They are rational, interested in efficiency and effectiveness, hardworking and engaged in the serious business of resource allocation and strategy formulation in major enterprises that control vast sums of wealth and energy. They certainly are not politicians, engaged in conflict and dispute, subject to various pressures and responding to constituencies which could promise them the most votes or money. (p. 369)

I would argue that the very notion of managers as individuals motivated by rational decision making is in itself a political position, and is intrinsically tied up with issues of power. The myth of rationality perpetuates a view of organizations principally as sites where technical issues are the main concern—questions of efficiency, productivity, resource allocation, expertise, and so forth. This view allows managers to assume a dominant position by articulating all issues within this rational frame. Managers maintain power by framing everything within a technorational context, and systematically excluding other organizational perspectives. For example, exclusion of other organization members from participation in the decision making process is justified on the ground that few people have the technical expertise or adequate access to information to make important decisions. The ideology of technical rationality thus provides a means by which the existing structure of power is maintained and reproduced.

Most organizational research implicitly adopts this managerial bias, not simply because it is more interested in the managerial perspective, but largely because the so-called value-neutrality of scientific research is easily co-opted by dominant managerial interests. Research questions thus get framed from a managerial perspective, and findings are couched in managerial language (Goodall, 1984). The issue of rationality as a defining concept of organizing takes on limited applicability at best. As Weick (1979,p. 21) suggests, "rationality is best understood as in the eye of the beholder," and as "bounded" by the individual's perceptual and information processing limitations. Furthermore, ostensibly rational organizational behavior is often made sense of and deemed "rational" only in retrospect; that is, there is no (or at most a limited) pre-existing rationale which frames and directs organizational activity. Thus "organizations are often reluctant to admit that a good deal of their activity consists of reconstructing plausible histories after-the-fact to explain where they are now, even though no such history got them to precisely this place" (Weick, 1979,p. 5). Much of the process of organizing therefore involves simply figuring out what organizing *is*, and adapting one's behavior accordingly. If such behavior is demonstrated to be "rational" then so much the better.

Given the myth of rationality, then, what is a more appropriate way to characterize the organizing process and its products? The theory of organizing that I propose in this book is radical in that it focuses directly on the relationship between communication and power-as-domination (hegemony). I will argue that this relationship is closely connected to the question of organizational interests. Simply put, power is exercised in an organization when one group is able to frame the interests (needs, concerns, world view) of other groups in terms of its own interests. In other words, the group in power can provide the frame of reference for all organizational activity. As such, the exercise of power is intimately connected with organizational sense-making, which in turn is largely delimited by the communication process. It is the unpacking of this relationship between communication, power, and organizing, which is the project of the rest of this book.

At this point, however, we need to do a little backtracking in order to focus on the notion of "sense-making." This concept has provided the impetus for the development of a relatively new paradigm in organizational research, commonly referred to as the "interpretive" or "organizational culture" approach (Carbaugh, 1982a; Frost et al., 1985; Putnam & Pacanowsky, 1983). This approach conceptualizes organizations as cultures in order to examine the ways in which organization members engage in the creation of a shared sense of organizational reality. Such research generally takes organizational symbolism — myths, stories, legends, jokes, rites, logos — as the most clearly visible articulation of organizational reality.

While this research has only come to the fore in the last few years, it clearly offers a perspective on organizations and organizational communication that is distinct from well-established approaches to analyzing the organizing process. Indeed, I do not think it would be an overstatement to suggest that the notion of organizational cultures offers an alternative theoretical paradigm through which to view organizations. While exponents of "organizational culture" would certainly not claim to resolve all fundamental problems, nor clarify all obscure organizational issues, they certainly *can* stake a claim to providing an original and powerful conceptual device for examining organizational behavior. My initial purpose here is to explain the emergence of this approach, but more importantly I intend to lay out a more conceptually sound and far-reaching theoretical framework than has so far been articulated under the rubric of "organizational culture."

To this end, three questions can be initially posed, and at least partial answers provided. First, what was the impetus behind the emergence of a cultural approach to organizations? Second, what are the underlying theoretical tenets of this approach? Finally, do theories of organizational culture provide an adequate conceptualization of the relationship between communication and the process of organizing?

In relation to the first question, one of the great ironies of the current interpretive-functionalist debate in organizational communication is that the two paradigms have, to a point, a common intellectual heritage. Max Weber's writings on bureaucracy provide the cornerstone on which functionalists have built their models of organizational rationality. On the other hand, Weber's model of social science research, with his emphasis on *Verstehen* (understanding) as an epistemological device, pre-dates the attempts of modern interpretivists to build an alternative analytical framework for examining organizations. Unfortunately for the field, considerably more attention has been paid to the functionalist's rather one-sided reading of Weber, a state of affairs largely attributable to Parsons's interpretation of his work. In any event, functionalism has become firmly ensconced as the "received view" of organizational behavior. It is only with the encroachment of the European tradition into American social science, along with the rediscovery of the American symbolic tradition[1] that this intellectual hegemony has been challenged. Now the work of Heidegger, Schutz, Gadamer, Habermas and others from the critical-interpretive tradition are increasingly finding a voice among disaffected American organizational theorists.

In a sense, it is the increasing dissatisfaction with the Parsonian functionalist approach to organizations that has rekindled interest in the interpretive tradition. Although familiar in other disciplines, it is certainly a new phenomenon in the field of communication. Indeed, Deetz's (1973) article addressing the application of the hermeneutic tradition to communication issues is arguably the first of its kind in this field. Now, however, the communication discipline is replete with articles exhorting its scholars to explore the alternative frame of reference that the interpretive approach offers and, significantly, it is the subdiscipline of organizational communication that is at the vanguard of this movement. Recent works by Pondy, Morgan, Frost, and Dandridge (1983), Frost et al. (1985), and special issues of *Journal of Management* (1985) and *Administrative Science Quarterly* (1983) certainly attest to the degree to which "organizational culture" has become a major theoretical rallying point.

What, then, can the interpretive approach offer to organizational scholars that more positivist, functional approaches cannot? I do not intend to engage here in a lengthy comparison of these two paradigms,

---

[1] For example, see Rorty's (1979, 1982) discussion of the works of James and Dewey and their attempt to develop epistemological alternatives to positivism.

as there are many excellent reviews available in the communication literature.[2] Interpretivists, however, would argue that the positivist predilection for developing neutral observation language, prediction and control, and developing law-like generalizations, provides an unnecessarily restricted view of the human actor. Such a conception of knowledge is unable to account for the process by which actors *make sense* out of their humanly constructed social reality. Understanding an organization's culture, for example, does not depend on the accurate re-presentation of an independent, externally existing reality. Rather, the task is one of showing why and how certain organizational practices are intersubjectively meaningful for its members. In other words, how does one make sense out of the process called "organizing?"

Conrad (1985b) usefully characterizes the principal differences between traditional (functionalist) and interpretive approaches to organizational study by evoking three continua along which organizational research can be evaluated. The first continuum deals with the way in which the communication process has been conceptualized in formal organizations. One pole of this continuum conceives of communication as a process of information exchange, while the opposite pole sees communication as the creation and maintenance of symbolic meaning systems. Traditionally, organizational research has been dominated by studies examining the process of information exchange; it is only with the rise of the interpretive paradigm that the symbolic use of communication has received real attention from organizational scholars. The second continuum deals with researchers' assumptions about the kinds of communicative interaction that one should focus on. Traditional research has consistently focused on interaction at the individual level, studying superior-subordinate relations, for example. Such research seems closely tied with concern for the process of information flow in organizations. At the other extreme, recent research has drawn on contemporary social theorists such as Giddens, Bernstein, and Clegg (along with reinterpretations of Weber, see above) to examine more macro-issues, such as the relationship between organizations and their environments. Concentrating on broader social concerns places greater focus on issues such as power, the influence of group interests on meaning formation, and the use and manipulation of organizational symbol systems to support such interests. Finally, Conrad's third continuum focuses on "the relationship between researcher-theorists and the symbolic actions that they examine" (1985b, p. 192). Traditional

---

[2] The reader is directed to the following sources: Burrell and Morgan (1979), Morgan (1980, 1983a), Putnam (1983), Morgan and Smircich (1980). An excellent critique of positivist social science research is provided by Gergen (1978), amongst others.

research has adopted a policy of objectivity á la natural science, while current interpretive approaches favor active engagement with the subject of study, and styles of presenting research results which blur the distinction between art and science. Pacanowsky's (1983) quasifictional account of a small-town police force is perhaps the most extreme example of this.

While not exhaustive, these three continua represent the main differences between the functionalist and interpretive paradigms, and it is the latter which I intend to explore as a framework for examining organizations. For the purposes of this work, the functionalist approach is viewed as inherently conservative both theoretically and politically, unnecessarily delimiting the parameters for organizational research. An approach from the functionalist perspective is unable to provide an adequate characterization of the relationship among communication, meaning, and power-as-domination.

What, then, are the underlying theoretical tenets of the cultural approach to organizations? Drawing heavily on ethnographic approaches (Geertz, 1973; Sanday, 1979), cultural views of organizing embrace the notion that organization members continually engage in the production, maintenance and reproduction of a shared sense of organizational reality. From this perspective, researchers are interested in the ways in which sense-making and the production of a coherent, consensual organizational reality are brought together by organization members. Focus is placed on the emergent, ongoing, and often precarious nature of organizational reality. Organization members are perceived not as completely rational actors with relatively straightforward needs and clear-cut goals, but as people who are continually engaged in the process of coping with an ambiguous information environment (Louis, 1980). Such a conception of organizations provides insight into the ways in which organization members, as *social actors*, behave in organizational environments and, in addition, it provides a positive view of organizations as sociocultural milieux (Louis, 1983). In the following section I will take a more detailed look at the concept of culture, examining some of its underlying assumptions and suggesting the implications of each. Finally, I want to adopt a more critical position vis-à-vis culture, and suggest ways in which the concept might be more fruitfully employed in an organizational context.

PERSPECTIVES ON ORGANIZATIONAL CULTURE

Much of the literature on organizational cultures takes as one of its principal tasks, explication of the relationship between "organizing" and "culture." The term organizing (as opposed to "organization") is adopted to reflect the ongoing, spontaneous, processual nature of organizational life. Through the process of organizing, members actively construct their environment. The term "organization," on the other hand, suggests a more static, structured, and finished quality of organizations which cultural theorists wish to avoid. Although by no means mutually exclusive (as we shall later see), the two terms imply very different perceptions of organizational communication.

Broadly speaking, the literature on organizational culture can be divided into two camps, each reflecting a different relationship between organization and culture. The first camp can be called "cultural pragmatists" (Martin, 1985, p. 95) in the sense that they espouse and actively promote the management and change of organizational culture. This explicitly managerial orientation views culture as an organizational variable (something an organization *has*) which can be manipulated to best suit the needs of the organization—normally the rationale for change lies with efficiency, productivity, and worker morale. Manipulation of organizational culture is seen as a road to more effective management (Kropowski, 1983). Peters and Waterman's *In Search of Excellence* (1982), with its "seven easy steps" to corporate success, is simply the pop version of this orientation. The often opportunistic bent of this approach is nicely manifested by Sathe when he says, "The challenge for leaders is to harness culture's benefits while remaining alert to the dangers of perpetuating a culture that is out of tune with the needs of the business, the organization, and its members" (1983, p. 22).

This treatment of culture as an organizational variable is rooted in a means-end, purposive-rational approach to organizations, laying heavy emphasis on environmental control. Such control over organizational culture is perceived as an important way for managers to remain sensitized to the "social undercurrents" that pervade corporate life. In order for organizations to maintain optimal efficiency and productivity, managers are required to identify "the taken for granted and shared meanings that people assign to their social surroundings" (Wilkins, 1983a, p.25), and assess the degree to which such shared meaning systems are detrimental or beneficial to the organization's climate.

Much of this pragmatic approach to organizational culture seems to have a distinct marketing orientation, and appears to reflect a greater need for accountability from a managerial perspective. One could argue that the cultural approach to organizations has become popular from a functional standpoint because it provides managers with an effective way to deal with the current pluralistic climate of many organizations. In this sense, the issue of "culture" has not simply emerged spontaneously, but is rather very much a product of a particular market economy in which many corporations are feeling pressure from several quarters: foreign competition, shareholders, disaffected workforces, technology, and so forth. The management of organizational climate thus allows managers to pay closer attention to "quality of life" issues in the workplace, and to design a culture that is suited to the needs of the particular organization (Sathe, 1985).

Such a view implies that there exists an homogeneous culture which frames the activity of all organization members. While this may be true of some organizations, most managers would probably agree that one of the main products of the process of organizing is the coexistence of inconsistent and divergent sets of organizational beliefs and values ("Those R&D boys don't seem to appreciate the notion of accountability.") Many cultural pragmatists recognize this principle, and strive to develop complex and sophisticated models to account for organizational complexity. Krefting and Frost (1985) exemplify this approach:

> We believe that efforts to change an organization by managing its culture will yield evolving solutions rather than those that are imposed, and that such efforts will produce outcomes that are equifinal. Because some of the consequences of managing culture are often unanticipated, the process of working with organizational culture involves risk. The challenge is magnified by the presence of multiple subcultures in a single organizational setting. Therefore, the management of culture ought to be carefully considered and cautiously undertaken. (p.156)

From this perspective, culture cannot be easily manipulated to serve the purposes of managerial interests. It rather exists as a complex web of socially constructed experiences which embodies various and heterogeneous organizational meaning structures. Managers therefore cannot impose certain forms of corporate culture; they can only attempt to tease out and develop the full capacities and potential of an already existing culture.

The second position on organizational culture, adopted by the "cultural purists" (Martin, 1985, p.95), does not make a separation between organization and culture. From this point of view an organization does not *have* a culture, it *is* a culture. The socially constructed nature of organizational reality is just that—*socially* constructed. Organizations are not deemed to have any existence independent of the shared values and meaning systems that are generated by organization members. As such, cultural purists deem it inappropriate to talk about changing and manipulating organizational culture, both because the bifurcation of organizations and culture is questionable from a conceptual viewpoint, and because of the questionable ethics that lie behind attempts at cultural manipulation. From the cultural purist perspective, organizations are variously defined as follows:

A set of understandings or meanings shared by a group of people. The meanings are largely tacit among members, are clearly relevant to the particular group, and are distinctive to the group. Meanings are passed on to new group members. (Louis, 1983, p.5)

Culture as a root metaphor promotes a view of organizations as expressive forms, manifestations of human consciousness. . . . The understanding of organizations as cultures . . . is strikingly similar to the notion of paradigm as it is applied in scientific communities. In other words, paradigms and cultures both refer to world views, organized patterns of thought with accompanying understanding of what constitutes adequate knowledge and legitimate activity. (Smircich, 1983b, pp.347–350)

Smircich's equation of culture with the scientific notion of paradigm is particularly evocative in the sense that it gets at one of the most basic of concerns of the interpretive approach; a focus on the degree to which an organization member's enmeshment in a set of social practices affects his or her construction of reality. By treating organizations as cultures, organizational researchers attempt to explicate the system of rules, beliefs values, and so forth, that individuals generally take for granted as members of a particular organization. However, being an organization "member" is not simply a question of taking on a particular set of values and beliefs; it is more than that. It is the active participation in, and creation of, a particular mode of existence; it involves the creation of a particular way of looking at the world which frames and gives sense to organizational behavior. Studies from this perspective, whether conceptual or empirical, are largely concerned with demonstrating the intersubjective and negotiated character of organizational reality. As such, there is frequently an explicit rejection of the idea that organizations are prestructured and have a reality that exists independently from their members. In addition, it is often suggested that traditional positivist research does little to illuminate the world view of the social actor, and must therefore be complemented or replaced by more naturalistic methods (Evered & Louis, 1981; Jick, 1979; Van Maanen, 1979). Thus at the very heart of the notion of "culture" is a focus on the sense-making process in organizations, i.e., what is it that allows organization members to engage in behavior that can be consensually identified as "meaningful" or "appropriate?" This issue is taken up in more detail in the next section.

SENSE-MAKING AND ORGANIZING

In examining the notion of sense-making, researchers are interested in the ways in which certain behaviors and practices take on meaning in a given context. An organization member does not arrive at a completely subjective, arbitrary interpretation of organizational practices; rather, the process by which an event becomes meaningful is rooted in and framed by intersubjectively shared patterns of discursive and behavioral practices (Pacanowsky & O'Donnell-Trujillo, 1983). Such patterns become inscribed as an organization's text (Deetz, 1982), ensuring the culture's continued reproduction.

The notion of intersubjectivity is crucial to an understanding of the sense-making process in organizations (or any social collectivity), but at the same time it is probably one of the most abused terms in social theory. A common mistake is to treat intersubjectivity as a special case of subjectivity, i.e., as the objectification of a subjective point of view in which an individual experience becomes shared by others. In reality, the conception of meaning as intersubjectively created circumvents the traditional subject-object split that has dominated Western thought since Descartes. Rooted in the phenomenology of Husserl and Heidegger, and more recently in Gadamer's hermeneutics, the notion of intersubjectivity recognizes that meaning arises in the interaction *between* subject and object. Meaning is not a product of individual consciousness, nor is it waiting to be discovered in the object of study. Both phenomenology and hermeneutics recognize that meaning arises because social actors maintain a certain intentionality toward the world, and also because that intentionality requires consciousness *of* an object of study that has its own autonomy and integrity. In other words, the possibility of consciousness requires consciousness *of* something that presents itself to the social actor as a potentially meaningful phenomenon.

Applied to organizational behavior, the notion of intersubjective meaning recognizes that organization members are constantly confronted with an information environment that challenges their perceptions of the organizing process. Dealing with this information environment involves developing consensual meanings among members, such that there is a shared sense of organizational reality. A taken-for-granted social reality is created in an organization through the continuous movement back and forth between sense and non-sense. In other words, social actors must frame ambiguous information in terms of what they already know "makes sense." This ambiguous information, in turn, subtly changes an actor's perception and definition of "organizational reality." Weick's (1979; Kreps, 1982, 1986) notion of organizations as "equivocality reducing mechanisms" recognizes this to-and-fro process, demonstrating the degree to which predictability is a necessary component of a successfully functioning organization.

Implicit, then, in the concept of sense-making is the idea that the relationship between members of an organization and their organizational culture is fundamentally reciprocal. Members' behavior both frames and is framed by organizational reality (Berger & Luckmann, 1971). As Jelinek, Smircich, and Hirsch (1983, p.331) state, "Culture – another word for social reality – is both product and process, the shaper of human interaction and the outcome of it, continually created and recreated by people's ongoing interactions." The process of sense-making is therefore partial and ongoing, rather than complete and fully constituted. What is considered "real" is contingent upon the constantly shifting relationship between social actor and organizational environment.

What is also clear, however, is that the whole sense-making process creates a very objective and tangible structure for organization members. The sense of "organizational consciousness" that every formal organization develops is not simply something that is in the heads of its members; it manifests itself in the everyday practices of the organization. These everyday practices, although imbued with meaning by organization members themselves, come to take on a significance that is objectified and apparently independent from those members. Social members respond to what is real for them – not to what they think is a creation of their consciousness.

An example might clarify this issue. Smith and Eisenberg (in press) provide an interesting analysis of the metaphors used by Disneyland employees to talk about their organization. They show, for example, that frequent use of the "drama" metaphor embodied the function of the park in providing "a show, an escape from the real world" (p. 8). Thus "roles" at Disneyland are carefully "scripted," and dress codes are viewed as costuming. Smith and Eisenberg show that the theme of Disneyland as family entertainment gradually became incorporated into employees' own perceptions of the organization, so that the role of employee became one of family member. When Disneyland hit a financial crisis, prompting the cutting of employees' wages and benefits, many workers were shocked that management could adopt such a business orientation. For these workers, the concept of Disneyland as a family wasn't simply a way of talking about the organization – it rather constituted the organizational *reality* for them. It was how they *experienced* the organization. Interestingly enough, management attempted to circumvent this clash of perspectives by trying to co-opt the family metaphor in explaining the cutbacks:

> According to management, family life was sometimes hard, and truly close families must make sacrifices if they are to survive. This attempt at co-optation never really caught on, and more and more it became clear

to management that the financial exigencies they faced would require some permanent changes in the park. (Smith & Eisenberg, p. 12)

This example emphasizes the importance of locating discussions of the process of sense-making in the real world (the *raison d'être* of Disneyland notwithstanding). The everyday activities of organization members are the medium and product of organizational reality. Organizations make sense to their members because these activities both "fit" the perception of what reality is, and at the same time are visible and practical articulations of that reality. Organizations thus exist through the text of members' behavior, and talk about that behavior.

In the next section of this chapter I want to focus on the process of organizational communication. From the perspective of organizational culture, communication is an intrinsic part of the process through which organizational reality is created; in a real sense, communication *is* culture. In keeping with the research in this area I will talk about organizational *symbolism* rather than organizational communication. While a definition of the symbolic aspect of communication is not simple, it certainly refers to more than the exchange of information. I take the "symbolic" to refer to the ability of a sign of some kind (whether verbal, behavioral, or material) to refer to something other than itself. The significance of a particular symbol system is conventionally derived through the ability of a particular language community to develop consensual meaning. At a later point I will also show that "symbolic" is not to be equated with "abstract." Important to my thesis is the idea that organizational symbolism, especially discourse, has a material reality that plays an active role in the constitution of human subjectivity (consciousness).

CULTURE AND ORGANIZATIONAL SYMBOLISM

The significance of symbolic structures in the creation of organizational cultures is, by and large, well accepted (Daft & Wiginton, 1979; Frost et al., 1986; Pondy et al., 1983). Much of the current research into organizational cultures is based upon the premise that organization members, as social actors, actively participate in the construction of organizational reality through organizational symbolism, in its various forms. The rules, beliefs, attitudes, values, etc., that both regulate and constitute the process of organizing are maintained and reproduced largely through the use of organizational symbolism. Dandridge, Mitroff, and Joyce (1980), for example, state:

The term "organizational symbolism" refers to those aspects of an organization that its members use to reveal or make comprehendable [sic] the unconscious feelings, images, and values that are inherent in that organization. Symbolism expresses the underlying character, ideology, or value system of an organization. In making this character comprehendable [sic], symbols can reinforce it or can expose it to criticism and modification. (p.77)

This view is fairly representative of the position taken on the relationship between the symbolic and the process of organizing. The above quotation, however, belies some of the complexities that are inherent in this relationship. One of the main issues, for example, concerns the degree to which organizational symbolism can be said to be an intrinsic part of organizational reality. Is there an organizational reality that exists independently of its symbolic structure, or are organizational reality and its symbolic representation basically synonymous? This question has important implications for this book because it determines the importance and centrality of organizational symbolism in the creation of meaning systems, power structures, and so forth, in organizations.

The prevailing sentiment seems to be in favor of a representational view of the relationship between the symbolic and reality; that is, symbols are conceived as largely descriptive in nature, simply representing a reality that already exists independently of its symbolic form. From this perspective, the role of the symbolic is largely one of predisposing social actors to a certain interpretation of reality, organizing attitudes, beliefs, values, etc., in a particular way, and generally playing a role in establishing the relationship between social actors and the social system in which behavior takes place.

One of the products of this perspective—at least in the communication discipline—is the tendency to talk about communication as a symbolic activity, and then to view information as the product of this activity. In other words, the communication process is seen as involving two distinct activities: the mechanics of communicating, and the process of gathering the information provided therein. In a recent organizational communication text, for example, (Kreps, 1986) implicitly adopts this perspective when he states:

Communication is a symbolic activity that people engage in to help interpret and influence their social worlds. Through communication, they gather raw data from their environments and process these data into information, an interpretive outcome of communication that helps them understand diverse phenomena and increase the predictability of life. . . .

Information is relevant data that is gained from the meanings that people create. (p.13)

Kreps emphasizes this separation with a tripartite, hierarchical model that distinguishes between communication, information, and organization respectively. Such a model relies heavily on the notion that the process of communication itself is somehow separate from—or at least only a part of—the means by which understanding and meaning formation take place. Again, the view is one which conceives of symbolic activity (communication) as playing a representational role in the creation of meaning.

What I would like to argue is that this frequent bifurcation of communication and information is a basically arbitrary distinction, which diverts attention from a more central issue that requires examination; that is, the intrinsic relationship between symbolic activity and the process of interpretation and meaning formation. While most organizational theorists would readily accept a connection between symbolism and meaning, most, like Kreps, insist on maintaining a careful distinction between the act of communication and the process of creating meaning; in most instances communication is seen as a conduit *for* information (meaning being attached in the head of the receiver), rather than as the *site* of meaning creation (Reddy, 1979).

My alternative conception of communication-as-symbolic is rooted in the hermeneutic and phenomenological traditions and has been articulated in the work of scholars such as G. H. Mead (1967) and Hugh Duncan (1968). It provides a more clearly focused and much needed examination of the degree to which the process of organizing and the communication process are interrelated. In addition, the perspective that I offer places considerable emphasis on the relationship between symbolic forms and the articulation of power structures in organizations. Again, the relationship between the symbolic, meaning, and power is a neglected area of research. I want to focus directly on the relationship between communication-as-symbolic and the production, maintenance, and reproduction of organizational reality. My most basic premise is that *meaning is produced in communication*. That is, meaning is neither conveyed *through* communication, nor is it the product of individual interpretation or an objectively existing entity outside of social interaction. In an organizational context, communication is the process through which meaning is created and, over time, sedimented. Communication—as an institutional form—articulates meaning formations which, when habitualized over time, provide the background of common experience that gives organization members a context for their organizing behavior. Communication is thus not simply the vehicle for information, but rather is the very process by which the notion of organizing comes to acquire consensual meaning. Organizing is therefore continuously created and recreated in the act of communication among organization members.

Deetz (1982) clearly articulates the centrality of communication in the process of organizing:

> Of all institutional forms, language has a special position. All other institutional forms may be translated into language. . . . Further, every perception is dependent on the conceptual apparatus which makes it possible and meaningful, as this conceptual apparatus is inscribed in language. Talk and writing are thus much more than the means of expression of individual meanings; they connect each perception to a larger orientation and system of meaning. The conceptual distinctions in an organization are inscribed in the systems of speaking and writing. *Speaking and writing are thus epistemic.* (p.135)

Although language and communication are not completely synonymous, I take speaking and writing to be the principal modes of communication in an organizational context. As such, it is the spoken and written forms that are the main focus of analysis in this book. In later chapters I will deal explicitly with organizational narrative as one of the principal symbolic structures that shapes reality for organization members.

Let me now give a brief overview of the kind of research that is currently being conducted in the area of organizational symbolism, after which I will outline how the symbolic aspect of organizational communication fits into my overall theoretical framework.

The general approach to organizational symbolism in the literature is to adopt a largely descriptive stance, and to investigate the shared systems of symbols that are revealed in organization members' routine behavior. The major premise behind this approach conceives of symbol systems as the most visible manifestation of organizational structure— they reflect the unconscious, taken-for-granted rule system that enables an organization to function coherently.

For example, Skopec (1982) argues that the clearest indication of the existence of a culture (as opposed to an arbitrary cluster of individuals) is the use of "unique or idiosyncratic patterns of rhetoric." Skopec suggests that such "rhetorical manifestations of organizational culture" can be discerned at three distinct levels of rhetoric: discourse, meaning, and interpretation. In other words, an organizational culture minimally requires a characterizing mode of discourse; a second, and stronger, indication of a culture is that organization members assign particular and consensually validated meanings to such discourse; finally, the degree to which interpretation of organization events by outsiders elicits uniformity of response from members is the strongest evidence of the existence of organizational culture.

One of the tasks of the literature has been to delineate the boundary conditions of the relationship between symbolism and organizational culture—what organizational artifacts can be said to have legitimate symbolic value? The consensus among theorists is that to have some kind of symbolic significance such artifacts must have a shared, consensual meaning among at least a portion of the organizational membership. Carbaugh (1982b, p.10), for example, suggests that the guiding question of the cultural approach to organizations must ask, "what *shared* system of symbols and meanings are constituted and revealed in workers' routine communicative life?" (emphasis his). Other researchers adopt a similar approach (Manning, 1979; Pettigrew, 1979; Smircich, 1983a; Wilkins, 1983a, b). Thus Smircich's (1983a) ethnographic study of an insurance company attempts to illustrate "how organizations exist as systems of shared meanings and to highlight the ways in which shared meanings develop and are sustained through symbolic processes" (p. 55).

Of course, the notion of "the symbolic" is a generic term which does little to explicate the complex nature of the symbolic systems that characterize most organizations. Following Weick's law of requisite variety, the level of structural complexity of an organization is complemented by its level of symbolic complexity. Discussions of organizational symbolism must therefore reflect this complexity. Dandridge, Mitroff, and Joyce (1980), for example, develop a symbolic matrix that incorporates both the type and function of symbols. The three types of symbols are: *verbal*, which include myths, legends, stories, slogans, jokes, and rumors; *actions*, involving rituals, parties, meals, breaks, and rites; and *material*, including status symbols, products, logos, awards, pins, and so forth. Each of these types of symbols functions at the levels of description, energy control, and system maintenance. Thus a story that is continually related as an expression of a particular aspect of organizational life might perform a descriptive function (providing information and vicariously sharing experiences), an energy controlling function (increasing or decreasing tension among members), or promote system maintenance through its use as a justification for certain actions (mergers, redundancies, etc.).

Similarly, Martin, Feldman, Hatch, and Sitkin's (1983) examination of organizational stories clearly demonstrates how the complexities and contradictions/tensions of organizational life are at least partly handled through the rich corpus of stories that organization members create in making sense of organizational activity. For example, the structuring of most organizations embodies a contradiction between equality and inequality—organizations are often hierarchical, authoritarian structures that function within a society that places a high value on equality. Such a contradiction is often managed by organization members through the relating of stories which depict low-status employees either (a) solving difficult problems against considerable odds; (b) rising meteorically up the organization; or (c) winning out in a confrontation with a superior. For example:

> At the age of 12 Deupree had left school in Covington, Kentucky, to work as an insurance agency's office boy at $1 a week. He did this out of economic necessity and moved on to a couple of other jobs before applying for work at P&G. Hired in 1905 as an office boy in P&G's Treasury Department at $4.50 per week, he soon was promoted to a cashier's cage. It was there that he caught the attention of Thomas H. Beck, head of what was then P&G's newly organized Bulk Soap Sales Division. Beck was struck by Deupree's pleasant nature. "You're the first cashier I've known who ever smiled when paying out money," he said. Beck remembered the amiable young man in 1909 when his division needed another salesman. From this point on, Deupree's rise was rapid, and by 1917 Cooper Proctor had appointed the 32-year-old Deupree to be P&G General Sales Manager. (Martin et al., 1983, p.442)

What this Horatio Alger and other kinds of organizational stories do is to provide members with a sense of organizational lore—a feeling for what is possible (if not probable) within the organization. In essence, stories help provide members with a set of boundary conditions for organizing; they create a context in which choices can be made about appropriate and inappropriate kinds of organizational behavior. In the case of the tension between equality and inequality, stories like the one above help members to come to terms with the day-to-day inequalities that they may experience in the course of their jobs. Such stories highlight the *possibility* of advancement, while at the same time legitimating the inequities that characterize work situations. Of course, not all stories have a positive moral imperative ("work hard and you'll go far") and, as Martin et al. point out, many stories directly exploit the negative aspects of an organization, predisposing members toward a pejorative sense of organizational reality:

> Harry was a mid-level bureaucrat with the imposing title of "Head of Administration and Budgeting" in the policy division of a large government agency. When new top management came in, a reorganization of the division occurred. When the dust settled, Harry was found at his new

job—reading newsclippings and underlining parts of the paper which were relevant to the institution's business. (Martin et al., 1983, pp. 442-443)

The main point to emphasize about both—indeed all—kinds of stories is that they should not simply be conceived as an information conduit for organization members. Stories do not simply tell people about what goes on in their organizations; rather, they should be examined in terms of their role in creating perceptual environments for organization members. In other words, they play a fundamental role in the creation and reproduction of organizational reality.

An important aspect of the studies cited above is that they closely tie organizational reality to the type and function of symbolic usage—different symbol systems will shape organizational reality in different ways. In recent years the study of metaphor has provoked a lot of interest in the "fit" between organizational language and organizational culture (Deetz, 1986; Koch & Deetz, 1981; Deetz & Mumby, 1985; Pondy, 1983; Smith & Eisenberg, 1985). Current studies of metaphor recognize that it is not simply a stylistic embellishment of literal language, but actually shapes the experience of social actors (Lakoff & Johnson, 1980a, b). Deetz (1986) and Deetz and Mumby (1985) argue that certain metaphor use in organizations may encourage certain forms of organizational structuring. To oversimplify this relationship, military metaphors can characterize highly structured, formal organizations, while family and organism metaphors might exemplify more flexible systems. In any event, it is argued that a reciprocal relationship exists between metaphors and organizational structuring. That is, a particular organization may talk about itself using certain metaphors, but at the same time these metaphors serve to produce and reproduce the organizational structure that they describe. Thus symbols both regulate *and* constitute organizational reality. What is nearly always more accurately the case is that different and often conflicting metaphor structures vie for acceptance as expressions of the dominant view of the organization. With this in mind, control of an organization's symbol system becomes of paramount importance for the power interests in organizations.

Pondy (1983) clearly articulates the importance of studying the metaphoric structure of organizational language when he states:

The central hypothesis [of the study] is that the use of metaphors in organizational dialogue plays a necessary role in helping organization participants to in-fuse their organizational experiences with meaning and to resolve apparent paradoxes and contradictions, and that this infusion of meaning or resolution of paradox is a form of organizing. In this sense, the use of metaphors helps to couple the organization, to tie its parts together into some kind of meaningful whole; that is, metaphors help to organize the objective facts of the situation in the minds of the participants. An alternative hypothesis is that the very creation of the objective facts of the organization is guided by underlying root metaphors. That is, metaphors serve both as models *of* the situation and models *for* the situation. (p.157)

The resolving of "apparent paradoxes and contradictions" is a central role of metaphor in the process of organizing. Metaphors do not act simply as an "equivocality reducing mechanism," but in addition perform the task of bringing certain aspects of an organization into sharper relief, while making other aspects experientially and cognitively more peripheral. In this way, the potentially bewildering complexities of organizational structure are ordered, greatly facilitating the sense-making processes of organization members. The earlier discussion of the "uniqueness paradox" demonstrates that stories can play a similar role: complex and potentially contradictory organizational issues can be resolved through the application of a relatively straightforward and highly adaptable narrative "template," via which members can structure their perceptions.

While both metaphors and stories possess this simplifying quality, they also perform the function of transforming organizational meaning systems into objective structures. The notion of organizational hierarchy, for example, is a widely accepted organizational "given" even though it is a social *construct* which need not necessarily be an intrinsic part of organizational structuring. The objective, taken-for-granted nature of such constructs, however, is created and reinforced by the way in which organizational talk is structured. Thus the predominance of a metaphor such as *organization as military unit*, with strong perceptual biases toward chain of command, obeying orders and following rules, tends to reify the notion of hierarchy, predisposing people toward experiencing it as a defining characteristic of the process of organizing. With this perception in place, hierarchy becomes a material structure that exists independently from those who function within it. Such a perception of a human construct necessarily limits the scope of organizational change.

TOWARD AN ALTERNATIVE PERSPECTIVE ON ORGANIZATIONAL CULTURE

The perspective adopted in this book involves an interpretive, meaning-centered approach to social phenomena. Such an approach is a defining characteristic of research on organizational cultures (despite its many variations), and will remain central to the thesis developed in the rest of this book. Below, I want to provide an explication of the way in which this meaning-centered approach will be contextualized in the theoretical perspective that this book develops.

One of the main problems of the interpretive approach to organizations is that it tends, by and large, to be descriptive, often lacking a critical element. The principal goal of interpretive research is to generate a sense of the way in which people create and maintain a shared sense of social reality. In other words, why is an organization's modus operandi meaningful to the people who work in it? From this central issue other concerns arise, such as the degree to which an organization's culture is mutable, how a culture should be studied, the ethics of researcher intervention in a culture, and so forth. From my own perspective, all of these issues are appropriate, but need to be contextualized in terms of what might be called the "deep structure" of organizational culture.

The notion of deep structure provides a way of examining the relationship between symbolism and power in an organization. Basically, "deep structure" refers to a social collective's underlying system of rationality; it is that part of an organization which provides members with a sense of what is appropriate and inappropriate organizational behavior. In short, it is the logic-in-use which frames members' perceptions. Conrad (1983, p.187) connects deep structure and power by stating that "Deep structures of power are the limits that define and solidify a society or an organization. They *are* the power-related reality of an organization. Without them there can only be groups of individuals, not social collectives whose members act in stable, predictable, and synchronized ways."

What I would like to suggest is that deep structure is not so much an identifiable organizational phenomenon, but is rather a relationship between two organizational levels. Figure 1 diagrams this relationship. The surface level represents the everyday, ongoing activity of organization members; it is at this level that organizational meaning structures

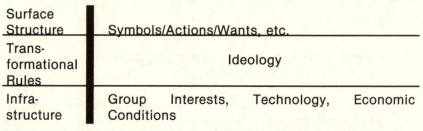

Surface Structure	Symbols/Actions/Wants, etc.		
Trans-formational Rules	Ideology		
Infra-structure	Group Interests, Technology, Economic Conditions		

Figure 1   Ideological Mediation between Surface Structure and Infastructure

manifest themselves in the form of stories, jokes, rituals, actions, etc. The organizational infrastructure is constituted by the various power interests within the organization, the system of technology that it utilizes, the availability and health of economic resources, and the structure of labor relations within the organization.

In this context, the notion of deep structure functions in a mediatory capacity beween these two levels—it provides the means through which congruence develops between organizational interests, technology, etc., and the way this structure is expressed symbolically. The earlier example of the metaphoric structure of discourse at Disneyland demonstrates this point. The use of the drama and family metaphors performs the double function of expressing the organizational ideology/mode of rationality and simultaneously acts as a means by which that ideology is constituted and framed. As such, the continual and ongoing maintenance and reproduction of organizational rationality allows a "fit" to develop between organizational power interests and the way the organization is talked about—the family metaphor helps to maintain a rather paternalistic power structure (with Walt as the head of the family), while the drama metaphor articulates the importance of the role that workers play in maintaining the illusion that Disneyland creates (an illusion that the company's continued success and profitability is dependent upon).

SUMMARY AND CONCLUSION

This chapter has examined the issue of organizational culture, and has explored ways in which a meaning-centered approach to organizing provides insight into the phenomenon of organizational structuring. It has been suggested that an adequate theory of the relationship between communication and organizing must move beyond a view which treats communication, information, and organization as conceptually discrete. Rather, communication must be conceived as the means by which organizational structure and reality is produced and reproduced. In other words, organizations are constructed through the articulation of meaning as produced in communication.

It was further argued that the relationship between communication-as-symbolic and organization is mediated by the structure of power in organizations. Power interests frame the way in which organizations construct reality; communication functions to both construct this reality, and to reproduce the extant organizational power structure. In this sense, a reciprocal relationship exists between communication and the ongoing structure of organizational power interests.

The remaining chapters in this book will therefore explore in detail the concept of organizational culture, focusing not on a description of the surface features of culture, but rather providing an in-depth explication of the relationship between organizational communication as symbolic, ideology, and the structuring of power interests. What should emerge is a perspective of organizations that stays true to the cultural approach (with its focus on interpretive practices), but that broadens its scope to recognize the pervasive effect of ideology and power on the production of organizational realities. The impetus for this perspective is derived from the critical tradition in contemporary social thought; the work of theorists such as Jürgen Habermas, Louis Althusser, Stuart Hall, and Anthony Giddens will pervade the theoretical approach that is laid out in subsequent chapters.

My immediate concern in chapter 2 is to discuss the notion of interests. Relying principally on Habermas's work, I will develop a position that argues for the fundamentally social basis of knowledge. That is, the degree to which actors develop a sense of social reality is overdetermined by the structuring of human interests. This relationship, and its implications for a theory of organizational cultures, will be taken up in detail in chapter 2.

2

HUMAN INTERESTS, KNOWLEDGE FORMATION, AND ORGANIZATIONAL CULTURES

Communication is the basis for social formation, transformation and legitimation. This chapter will explore the implications of this assertion for organizational cultures in the context of the writings of Jürgen Habermas. Habermas's project, although a complex and diffuse one, has become more familiar to communication scholars in recent years (Burleson & Kline, 1979). His philosophical position, grounded in a theory of communication, can be applied to the question of organizational meaning formation in several different ways. First, he shows that knowledge does not exist as an independent entity, but is derived from knowledge-constituting interests—technical, practical, and emancipatory—each of which frames both everyday knowledge and the knowledge produced by social inquiry in a different way. Second, his theory of interests is developed as a grounding for the critique of ideology and domination.[1] He argues, for example, that the emphasis of late-capitalist society on technical-rational knowledge subverts the social actor's active participation in the political decision-making process by reducing all knowledge questions to the issue of technique, resulting in the cult of "the expert." Third, his critique of ideology and domination is elaborated through a theory of communicative competence, which expresses the emancipatory interest (Habermas, 1970b, 1979). Communicative competence realizes the capacity of the individual to be emancipated from objectifying political conditions through self-reflection. Such reflection is anticipated in the ideal speech situation (Habermas, 1970a, b, 1972, 1975, 1979) which provides the context for the discursive generation of claims to truth (validity). Finally, Habermas's critique of ideology

---

[1] The concept of ideology will be discussed fully in chapter 4.

(referred to as "systematically distorted communication") through his theory of interests allows him to examine the process of legitimation in capitalist society, and to argue that generalizable interests have become subordinated to privatized needs. The result is a politically apathetic society, producing false consensus and legitimation through domination.

All of these themes are essential to Habermas's construction of a critical theory of society and, as such, are applicable to organizational cultures in the sense that the latter are both microcosms of societal structure, and function as an integral part of society. In contrast to the literature discussed in chapter 1, Habermas's work allows us to examine organizational cultures in terms of the mediation of social knowledge through power interests. I will therefore explicate Habermas's project in some detail, and then assess his work as it applies to the issues of ideology and power in organizational settings, giving specific attention to the question of representation of interests.

A THEORY OF INTERESTS

Habermas's theory of cognitive (knowledge-constituting) interests is developed out of a recognition of the natural propensities that characterize the sociocultural form of life of human beings. That is, humans engage in control and manipulation of their environment (work), and encounter other speaking and acting subjects (interaction). These two largely invariant aspects of existence correspond to the technical and practical interests, and to a large degree guide knowledge-constitution in society.

> These two viewpoints [technical control and interaction] express anthropologically deep-seated interests, which direct our knowledge and which have a quasi-transcendental status. . . . the technical and practical interests of knowledge are not regulators of cognition which have to be eliminated for the sake of objectivity of knowledge; instead, they themselves determine the aspect under which reality is objectified, and can thus be made accessible to experience to begin with. They are the conditions which are necessary in order that subjects capable of speech and action may have experience which can lay a claim to objectivity. (Habermas, 1974, pp.8–9)

The technical and practical interests are the domain of the empirical-analytic and hermeneutic sciences respectively. Each guides knowledge in a different manner. The empirical-analytic sciences are principally concerned with prediction and technical control of the environment.

They seek to provide observation statements that are commensurable with an objectively given and pre-existing reality. Prediction and control are therefore achieved by making knowledge claims that can be directly (or potentially) tested through scientific procedure, i.e., hypothesis testing via deductive methods. By and large it is this approach to knowledge that has dominated the social sciences since Comte's articulation of a positivist philosophy in the late 19th century. The hermeneutic sciences, on the other hand, are concerned with the notion of understanding (*Verstehen*) as the principal motivation for knowledge generation. Such knowledge is derived through intersubjectively negotiated meaning, mediated through ordinary language. Reality, then, is interpreted within the framework of "action-orienting mutual understanding" (1972, p.195), which is possible, insofar as humans share a language system.

Habermas refers to the technical and practical interests as "quasi-transcendental," because they deal not with pure theoretical reason, but with "methodological rules for the organization of processes of inquiry" (1972, p.194). In this sense they have a transcendental function, but at the same time are embedded in the actual structures of human life. Habermas contrasts the two interests in the following manner:

> Both categories of investigations are embedded in systems of actions. Both are set off by disturbances of routinized intercourse whether with nature or with other persons. Both aim at the elimination of doubt and the re-establishment of unproblematic modes of behavior. The emergence of a problematic situation results from disappointed expectations. But in one case the criterion of disappointment is the failure of a feedback-controlled, purposive-rational action, while in the other it is the disturbance of a consensus, that is the non-agreement of reciprocal expectations between at least two acting subjects. Accordingly, the intentions of the two orientations of inquiry differ. The first aims at replacing rules of behavior that have failed in reality with tested technical rules, whereas the second aims at interpreting expressions of life that cannot be understood and that block the mutuality of behavioral expectations. Experiment refines the everyday pragmatic controls of rules of instrumental action to a methodical form of corroboration, whereas hermeneutics is the scientific form of everyday life. (1972, p.175)

In *Knowledge and Human Interests*, Habermas's task is to provide a "rational reconstruction" of the logic that underlies the technical and practical interests in order to show that a third interest, the emancipatory, provides an impetus for knowledge formation. The emancipatory interest differs from the other two in its incorporation of the process of critique through self-reflection. Habermas lays the ground for this move by providing critiques of Hegel and Marx. Both, he argues, developed theories of knowledge that contained possibilities for the development of a critical, reflexive move, but both ultimately failed for different reasons. Hegel's position is considered inadequate because he lapses into an absolutism in which the mind finally constitutes all knowledge. Marx recognizes this problem in Hegel, asserting that consciousness arises materially through the development of forces of production and class struggle. Habermas considers this critique of Hegel to be lacking, however, in that Marx conflates labor and interaction, reducing self-formation (consciousness) to an aspect of the process of production. Habermas points out that Marx even goes so far as to assert that the economic laws of modern society are natural laws. In other words, Marx argues for a "natural science of man" which can predict the demise of capitalism and the rise of socialism.

As Habermas (1972) suggests, the positivist overtones of such a position render impossible the "element of reflection that characterizes a critique investigating the natural-historical process of the self-generation of the social subject" (p. 46). Marx's failure to grasp the significance of a *critical* theory of society sets the stage for the positivist appropriation of social science and philosophy, in which reason becomes equated with scientific reason alone.

Habermas therefore recognizes the need to redress both Hegel's idealism and Marx's historical determinism by distancing critical theory from an exclusive preoccupation with either philosophy (Hegel) or science (Marx):

> Because of its reflection on its own origins, critique is to be distinguished from science as well as from philosophy. For the sciences focus away from their constitutive contexts and confront the domain of their subject matter with an objective posture; while, obversely, philosophy has been only too conscious of origins as something that had ontological primacy. (1974, p.2)

Habermas provides a rational reconstruction of both idealism and historical materialism by developing a "theory of society conceived with a practical intent" (1974, p.3). This move is accomplished through the elaboration of an emancipatory interest, in which self-reflection is conceived in an intersubjective (as opposed to monadological) context. From this perspective truth, or reality, arises out of the discursive generation of a rational consensus, worked out by communicatively competent participants.

Like the technical and practical interests, the emancipatory interest constitutes knowledge, but in a way that is neither idealist nor objectivist. Rather, its focus is the formation of reason itself as it occurs through interaction. Such a move is emancipatory in that it links critical reflection with practical reason; that is, it locates self-formation in the context of socially enacted human relations. Self-reflection, reason, and emancipation thus become inextricably linked:

> The experience of reflection articulates itself substantially in the concept of a self-formation process. Methodically it leads to a standpoint from which the identity of reason with the will to reason freely arises. In self-reflection, knowledge for the sake of knowledge comes to coincide with the interest in autonomy and responsibility (*Mündigkeit*). For the pursuit of reflection knows itself as a movement of emancipation. Reason is at the same time subject to the interest in reason. We can say that it obeys an emancipatory cognitive interest, which aims at the pursuit of reflection. (Habermas, 1972, p.197–198)

Through the process of self-reflection the emancipatory interest is conceived as the means by which individuals can escape the seemingly natural constraints that institutional structures provide for people. For Habermas, emancipation through self-reflection can deconstruct the predominance of the technical interest, which fetishizes scientific method and obscures the self-reflective move in knowledge formation. By locating the criteria for conducting social life in purposive-rational action, technocratic consciousness collapses the distinction between the technical and practical interests. The latter reflects an essential condition for human self-formation, placing primacy on its intersubjective nature. However, "Technocratic consciousness makes this practical interest disappear behind the interest in the expansion of our power of technical control" (1970c, p.133). The technical interest is thus ideological in the sense that it distorts the nature of social relations by reducing them to issues of prediction and control.

The issue of the pervasiveness of the technical interest in society is, of course, becoming more and more central in critical social studies as technology is increasingly accepted as the panacea for many of society's problems. The layperson's concern that people are being replaced by machines translates—from a social science/cultural studies perspective—into attempts to assess the impact of the technological revolution on the ways in which humans communicate with one another. Such research runs the gamut from a largely uncritical perspective that hails the arrival of each new technical innovation, to a position which expresses deep concern with the way in which technology is perceived to be dominating the structuring of human consciousness.

While Habermas does not deal directly and explicitly with forms of technology, he is obviously critical of the easy acceptance of technological advancement, considering it to be a form of ideological domination. He explicitly develops a critique of ideology and domination through a theory of communicative competence, which assumes a capacity for the individual to be emancipated from objectifying political and ideological constraints through discursively produced self-reflection. The theory of communicative competence brings the emancipatory interest to fruition. It is the means by which "ideologically frozen relations of dependence" (1972, p.310) can be reconstructed, releasing the individual from the domination of illegitimately "naturalized" social processes. It is only in the context of an interest in emancipation that communication can be nonauthoritarian and undistorted, producing "universally practiced dialogue from which our . . . idea of true consensus [is] always implicitly derived" (1972, p.314).

The normative grounding for Habermas's theory of communicative competence resides in the development of a universal pragmatics (1979, pp.1–68). Habermas uses the term "universal" insofar as his attempt is to provide a conception of rationality that is more comprehensive than any previously identified. It must incorporate practical reason and at the same time expand theoretical reason beyond reduction to the scientific method. In this sense, the task of a universal pragmatics is to "identify and reconstruct universal conditions for possible understanding" (1979, p.1).

Habermas's point of departure in this task is an explication of the notion of the "double structure of speech," introduced by Austin (1962) and further developed by Searle (1969). This recognizes that every utterance communicates at two levels of meaning, each of which must be understood by the interactants if a speech act is to be performed successfully. The first level is propositional content, in which utterances make certain claims about the ontological status of the world (i.e., a logical claim to truth). Second, at the level of illocutionary force, a particular relationship is established between participants which helps them to come to an understanding of each other. Thus in Searle's famous example of making a promise (e.g., "I promise to return the book to you tomorrow.") the act of promising simultaneously performs a relational and referential function: it commits one person to another in a particular fashion, and it communicates the factual nature of a certain state of affairs in the world (in this case, the future act of returning a book).

Habermas appropriates the double function of speech to articulate four claims to validity, each of which must be fulfilled for an utterance to be free from distortion. The first two relate directly to the two functions outlined above; that is, at the level of propositional content a statement makes a logical claim to truth, while at the level of illocutionary force a normative claim is made for rightness, i.e., the establishment of legitimate interpersonal relationships. An example of an utterance that fulfills the first validity claim but not the second might be the issuing of an order by a sergeant to a captain in the military. The command "Straighten your tie" might well make a correct claim to truth (the crookedness of the captain's tie), but it certainly would not fulfill a claim to rightness, given its violation of the established relationship between a sergeant and a captain.

The third validity claim involves truthfulness in the sense of being sincere about one's utterances. Such speech, according to Habermas, discloses the speaker's subjectivity and is characterized by expressive language (use of the first person, etc.). Thus, "truthfulness guarantees the transparency of a subjectivity representing itself in language" (1979, p.57). Finally, the fourth validity claim is fulfilled through the comprehensibility of the speakers in addressing one another. This fourth claim requires not only that the two participants speak roughly the same language, do not mumble, and so forth, but also that both interlocutors abstain from engaging in jargon that is deliberately intended to mystify or assert dominance over another person. For example, a violation of this validity claim occurs with doctors who intentionally use jargon with patients in order to mislead them, or place them in positions of subordination by simply refusing to engage in discourse about a patient's condition.

It is these four validity claims that, taken together, form Habermas's universal conditions for rationality. In this context, truth emerges and is accepted not through a correspondence with an empirical reality, but rather is produced consensually through discursively generated, constraint-free testing of its claims to validity. The product of this "ideal speech situation" is a rational will that represents common and generalizable, rather than particular interests:

> The interest is common because the constraint-free consensus permits only what *all* can want; it is free of deception because even the interpretation of needs in which *each individual* must be able to recognize what he wants become the object of discursive will-formation. The discursively formed will may be called "rational" because the formal properties of discourse and of the deliberative situation sufficiently guarantee that a consensus can arise only through appropriately interpreted, generalizable interests, by which I mean needs *that can be communicatively shared*. (1975, p.108).

It should be noted, of course, that in developing this discursive model of rationality which expresses the emancipatory interest, Habermas does not completely negate the technical and practical interests; indeed, both are essential for knowledge formation. Instead, he reconstructs them, incorporating them both into his discursive model. Thus the claim to truth corresponds to the objective reality of the external world (technical interest), while the claim to rightness incorporates the socially constructed world (practical interest). By reframing those interests within a more comprehensive view of rationality, Habermas can make strong claims for the discursive redemption of truth, thereby transcending both idealism and scientism. Thus although his ideal speech situation is, by definition, ideal (and thus not reproducible in the real world), nevertheless:

> No matter how the intersubjectivity of mutual understanding may be deformed, the *design* of an ideal speech situation is necessarily implied in the structure of potential speech, since all speech, even of intentional deception, is oriented toward the idea of truth. This can only be analyzed with regard to a consensus achieved in unrestrained and universal discourse. . . . On the strength of communicative competence alone, however, and independent of the empirical structures of the social system to which we belong, we are quite unable to realize the ideal speech situation; we can only anticipate it. (1970b, p.372).

The ideal speech situation can be anticipated, if not realized, insofar as Habermas's conception of rationality is universally applicable, i.e., is implied in all instances of communication.

Undistorted communication thus arises out of the ability of each (communicatively competent) speaker to test rigorously the justifiability of each validity claim put forward by redeeming it discursively. In contrast, systematically distorted communication occurs when the universal, pragmatic norms of the ideal speech situation become subordinated to privileged interests, producing asymmetrical power relationships and resulting in a false consensus about the validity claims made. In *Legitimation Crisis*, Habermas argues that the state maintains an asymmetrical relation with members of society through the imposition of claims to validity that are largely untestable. In other words, it replaces generalizable interests with particular interests. On a societal level only norms based on a rational consensus express generalizable interests, otherwise they are based on force, and are thus ideological. In the latter case Habermas uses the term "normative power" to identify ideologically structured norms.

> A social theory critical of ideology can, therefore, identify the normative power built into the institutional system of a society only if it starts from

the *model of the suppression of generalizable interests* and compares normative structures existing at a given time with the hypothetical state of a system of norms formed, ceteris paribus, discursively. Such a counterfactually projected reconstruction . . . can be guided by the question (justified, in my opinion, by considerations from universal pragmatics): how would the members of a social system, at a given stage in the development of productive forces, have collectively and bindingly interpreted their needs (and which norms would they have accepted as justified) if they could and would have decided on organization of social intercourse through discursive will-formation, with adequate knowledge of the limiting conditions and functional imperatives of their society? (1975, p.113)

Given that one of my basic premises is that organizational cultures are produced and reproduced through various forms of discursive practices, let us now examine the application of Habermas's model of discursive rationality to an organizational context. As I have indicated in chapter 1, organizational sense-making and meaning formation is accomplished by social actors through symbolic processes. Generally, however, the literature on organizational culture stops short of examining the way in which certain interests are legitimated through the structuring of symbolic practices. Normative power exists within an organization when communicative action is distorted through the imposition of interests particular to a certain group.

CRITICAL THEORIES OF ORGANIZING

One of the problems inherent in applying a critical perspective such as Habermas's to an analysis of organizational communication is that there is a fundamental incompatibility between such a critical orientation and management notions about the process of organizing. How many managers, for example, would readily accept the notion that organizational interests are unfairly biased in favor of a fairly limited, managerial definition of how an organization should operate? How many organizations would readily embrace the idea of a more democratically structured, participative version of organizing? It is true that most organizational research maintains a distinct management orientation, but this often has little to do with the ideological predisposition of the researcher; in most cases more pragmatic concerns prevail, such as the fact that funding for research is often provided by the organization concerned, or that the organizational problem has been predefined by management, and the researcher is hired to provide the solution. In any case, a researcher who demonstrates a perspective that is sympathetic to management definitions of organizing is more likely to gain access to research contexts.

Despite this problem, critical studies of organizational communication are beginning to emerge. What is even more surprising in a sense is that some of the most enthusiastic supporters of such an approach are people who are located in fairly traditional management programs. To be sure, many of the researchers and theorists who expound the virtues of the organizational culture approach view it principally as a new tool for management (in the traditional sense), but there are also several researchers who use the approach in a more critical manner to suggest alternative ways of conceptualizing the organizing process.

In a practical application of Habermas's universal pragmatics, Forester (1981, 1982) examines the way in which discursive rationality can be used to examine the production and reproduction of political relationships in organizations. Forester states:

> The argument of this essay, in effect, is that Habermas's notion of systematically distorted communication may be developed and made concretely, organizationally and politically practical by locating it within the fundamental communicative reproduction of social relations constituting any social organization. The dimensions of that reproduction (relations of knowledge, consent, trust and attention) are rooted in Habermas's analysis of the structure of ordinary communicative action and speech, his so-called "universal pragmatics" (1982, p.13).

Writing from the perspective of an organizational planner, Forester argues that planners not only seek certain goals and produce certain results for organizations, but that they also should reproduce those social and political relations best suited to an organization's ends. Formally speaking, a planner's goals are purely instrumental, or technical, in nature. However, technical judgments are themselves structured by social rules and conventions. To this extent, technical judgments are respected and given legitimacy insofar as they are rendered in an appropriate institutional context. Therefore "technical judgments can yield instrumental results . . . because the institutional roles of the technically skilled and those who need them are socially and politically reproduced" (Forester, 1982, p.6). As Habermas (1970c) has pointed out, however, the practical (social) nature of such technical-rational decisions is obfuscated by the ideology of technology. Technical judgments are legitimate only because the technical interest is derivative of the practical. Technology as ideology, however, inverts this relationship, making the practical appear to be derived from the technical interest.[2]

Forester (1981, 1982) takes up Habermas's four validity claims in slightly reformulated terms and attempts to link them directly and explicitly to the issues of power and legitimation in organizations. From this perspective, organizations are viewed as structures of practical communicative interaction that attempt to reproduce particular social relations through relations of knowledge (truth), consent (rightness), trust (truthfulness), and attention (intelligibility). Each of these relations must be managed appropriately to assure reproduction of certain power structures both inside and outside the organization.

For example, corporations often need to monitor carefully the kind of public image that they are presenting. To this end, they may wish to suppress certain organizational characteristics that may not fit comfortably with the projected corporate image. This is achieved principally through the control of information flow, which dictates both internal and external organizational knowledge, both of which may be very different. IBM, for example, conducts advertising campaigns which focus heavily on the organization's humane qualities, with its concern for helping the ordinary business person (embodied by the Chaplin figure seen in much of its advertising). Such an image, however, is produced mainly for external consumption, and serves the market needs of IBM. In-house knowledge is more oriented toward organizational efficiency and adherence to a strict code of behavior (embodied by the ubiquitous IBM "uniform" of dark suit and white shirt)

Similarly, McDonald's is particularly skilled at using television to articulate a corporate image that draws heavily on traditional American values such as family, friendship, and honest hard work. While most of us recognize that the reality that McDonald's produces on television is very different from the actual experience of eating in one of their franchises, this does not wholly negate the ability of their commercials to create a symbolic reality that makes us feel warm inside.[3]

---

[2] The prioritizing of the technical over the practical interest manifests itself in contemporary society in various ways. Certainly in Western culture "the expert" has practically attained the status of a deity. Many human problems are couched in terms that suggest some kind of technical solution, whether this involves solving a communication problem in an organization, or curing sexual impotence. Such a privileging of the technical over the practical seems to ignore the degree to which humans place themselves at the mercy of a technocratic elite. As Deetz and Kersten (1983, p.153) state, "Technical rationality and instrumental reason have come to eclipse practical concern for liberation and life."

[3] Here, of course, we are straying into the extremely complex and problematical area of the relationship between the television viewer and the television message. While I do not want to engage in any lengthy discourse on this particular topic, I would like to point out that we need to conceive of this relationship in more than simple "effects," or "uses and

I include these examples because they represent ways in which organizational power can manifest itself discursively. All of these companies engage in systematically distorted communication because they engage in discourse that, in Habermas's sense, is not fully redeemable. Power is exercised in each instance because the organizations are able to impose a particular kind of structure on the discourse that they engage in without having the veracity of this discourse challenged. This is not to say that any of these companies lies in its commercials, but rather that they are able to construct discursively a certain kind of reality that goes largely unchallenged by virtue of the basically unidirectional flow of information on television. In this context, Forester makes an explicit connection between discursive validity claims and the exercising of power:

> Power may be understood not as a possession of an actor working mysteriously upon another actor, but rather as a normative relationship binding the two actors together, a relationship which structures one agent's *dependence* on the other's information, *deference* to the other's supposed authority, *trust* in the other's intentions, and consideration of the other's claim to attention. (1982, p.12)

In the context of systematically distorted communication, the issue of legitimacy involves the ability to institutionalize meaning structures not through a rationally derived consensus, but through the *imposition* of claims to truth, rightness, and so forth, that cannot be discursively redeemed. Power thus resides with those interest groups that are best able to make truth claims that are most secure against discursive redemption. Furthermore, such normative power is enhanced considerably if accepted as unproblematic by those against whom the power is exercised.[4] For example, dependence for information of one organizational group on another will produce systematically distorted communication if the latter group chooses to deliberately control access to important information that would assist the dependent group. Such a normatively constituted relationship can be seen by the dependent

---

gratifications" terms. Television exists in a complex relationship with many other variables, not least of which is the sociopolitical and economic environment that strongly influences what makes it onto the television screen. If we add to this equation the viewer's ability to decode TV messages in a variety of ways (perhaps but not necessarily including the intended message), then we have indeed set ourselves a massive analytical task. My own perspective on these issues has been best informed by the Marxist cultural studies approach (see Becker, 1984, for a review of this work).

[4] The notion of the constitution and ongoing structuring of power will be explored more fully in the next chapter. The whole concept of power is a problematic one, and I will explicate it in terms of its relationship to the ideological structuring of meaning formations.

group as either problematic and in need of change, or else as simply "the way things are," i.e., as the natural structure of organizational behavior.

These normative relationships are not simply the product of interaction between the interest groups concerned, but are also a result of the structural aspects of the process of organizing. That is, the meaning structures that are articulated by the various groups come to have a substantive quality to them by virtue of the way in which they are manifested in material organizational behavior. This behavior, in turn, is framed by the meaning structures that provide a sense of organizational reality for members (Giddens, 1979). The notion of systematically distorted communication must therefore be considered not as a purely discursive (i.e., rhetorical) phenomenon, but rather as very much a *material* aspect of the process of organizing.

A critical approach to organizational culture thus moves beyond the surface issue of sense-making to examine the means by which certain meaning structures come to be more pervasive and widely accepted (i.e., more legitimate) than others. In other words, from a critical perspective the concern is to examine the ways in which *vested* interests can potentially limit discursive choices and thus produce a false, rather than a rational, consensus. Organizations, as the site of vested interests, distort and constrain communication in such a way that those interests are maintained and reproduced.[5] In such a context the role of critical theory, as conceived by Habermas, is one of social reconstruction; that is, the restoring of a rational consensus through the critique of systems of ideology and domination, along with the self-reflection and self-formation that occurs as a result of such critique.

Some theorists have tentatively begun to embrace the possibility of a critical theory of organizational communication. Frost (1980, p.503), for example, suggests that "Critical organization science should attempt a combination of theory and revolutionary action aimed at making individuals fully aware of the contradictions and injustices in their organizational existence and at assisting them to find a path out of their contradictions." Such a position expresses Habermas's notion of a critical theory with a practical intent. Deetz (1982) and Deetz and

---

[5] I do not intend to imply here that the whole process of domination and legitimation is born out of some Machiavellian conspiracy by certain groups to structure organizations to support their own interests (although there is often a definite intent to perpetuate certain power structures). Rather, I want to suggest in this and later chapters that the process of legitimating certain structures of reality is achieved through the articulation of ideological meaning structures, the "natural order" of which is just as readily accepted by the dominant groups as by the subordinate groups. To paraphrase Althusser (1971), ideology does not stand up and shout "I am ideological;" it is rather in the very nature of ideology to disguise itself against being seen as ideology.

Kersten (1983) put this idea in a slightly different framework when they state that critical theory's pursuit of social reconstruction should involve the three tasks of understanding, critique ,and education. Here, understanding refers to the ability of social actors to engage in "discursive penetration" (Giddens, 1979) and recognize the human, social origin of those factors that create and sustain organizational reality. Critique involves the examination and questioning of the process by which these meaning structures become accepted as legitimate. Finally, education recognizes the need for organization members to engage actively in the process of self-formation through the building of an alternative organizational reality that is discursively built through a coercion-free consensus.

An illustration of the three stages of this process can be observed in the example of the Disneyland conflict described in the previous chapter. The process of understanding is visible in the members' recognition that management has attempted to redefine what it means to be a member of the Disneyland organization (i.e., a redefinition from "family member" to "employee"). Critique occurs in that members are able to question the legitimacy of management's actions in laying off workers and introducing cutbacks. Education occurs in the workers' ability to develop actively a vision of the organization that is different from the one expressed by management, and which resulted in the practical action of an attempt to disseminate this alternative reality to members of the public.

The most important element in any critical theory of organizing is the incorporation of the critical move itself—a move that allows for reflection upon one's conditions of existence. This process of self-reflection is absent from more traditional approaches to examining organizational cultures insofar as the explication of the sense-making process is viewed as an end in itself.[6] While it is recognized that such meaning formations are socially constructed, the potential for a critical assessment of these meaning formations is severely limited because of the lack of a reflective turn; that is, extant theories of organizational culture do not generally endow organization members with the capacity for reconstructive thought. Instead, they are generally viewed as operating *within* social formations, even though they create and reproduce such formations themselves.

One can characterize the difference between the interpretive and critical approaches by invoking the notions of choice *in* context and

---

[6] Unless the research is conducted in the "cultural pragmatist" tradition of attempting to alter the organization's culture in order to improve organizational climate or increase productivity or both.

choice *of* context respectively. The former, characteristic of interpretive, naturalistic approaches, is generally limited to description of the surface structures of meaning that make up the day-to-day social practices of organization members; the concern here is to describe the organization based on in situ, member-generated concepts. The latter moves beyond simple description and focuses on the relationship between deep structure and surface structure, seeking to expose the constraints and blockages that distort the communication process. In this sense, choice *of* context attempts to probe beneath the surface meaning of organizations to create alternative ways of thinking about organizational behavior. For example, Burawoy's (1979) study of machine operators chose to invert received organizational logic by asking the question "Why do workers work as hard as they do?" rather than the more conventional managerial concern of "Why don't workers work harder?" This radical switch of conceptual focus allowed Burawoy to explore not only the workers' own organizational reality, but also the deep structure nature of organizational coercion and domination. Burawoy's choice *of* context thus allows him to avoid situating his research within a framework of meaning that is pre-articulated by dominant management ideology.

The whole process of critique that Habermas presents is grounded in Freudian discursive intervention, considered by Habermas to be the nearest thing to a concrete exemplification of the ideal speech situation. Freud is incorporated into Habermas's social theory insofar as "Psychoanalysis is relevant to us as the only tangible example of a science incorporating self-reflection" (1972, p.214). The professed aim of psychoanalytic theory is to emancipate the neurotic individual by removing the resistance that interdicts the public communication of repressed elements in the individual's unconscious. The dialectic between patient and therapist has, as its goal, self-reflection by the former so that repressed parts of the self may be reappropriated and subject to examination. It is the task of the analyst to assist the patient in "translating" those parts of the self that have been suppressed in privatized language, and to reformulate them in terms that can be communicated publicly. Thus, "The performance of the analyst in putting an end to the process of inhibition can therefore be understood as a process linked to desymbolization" (1970a, p.214).

Applied at a societal level, the psychoanalytic component of a critical theory takes as its object of analysis the collective neurosis of society as a whole. McCarthy (1982, p.194) states that Habermas uses "psychoanalytic concepts to establish a link between the institutional framework of society and individual psychology." The concept of neurosis translates into the ideological meaning systems that articulate forms of reality supporting particular power groups in society. This structuring of society can be maintained only if these ideological structures remain in place, blocking the expression of suppressed meaning systems. The task of a critical theorist is therefore to expose these ideological forms, presenting the possibility of a rational, coercion-free consensus of meaning. Validity claims based on false consensus (ideology) are rendered problematic by discursive testing, and emancipation is made possible through the discursive redemption of validity claims based on true consensus. Psychoanalysis is seen as a model for the critique of ideology. Emancipation is generalized from the individual to the social collective, and ideally produces a rational will that is free from the distorting influences of power and hegemonic processes.

Habermas does not apply his critical theory to specific institutional forms as such, but rather focuses on the issue of legitimation in later capitalism as a whole. Legitimation of ruling interests is becoming increasingly difficult, he argues, because of growing state intervention that is used to prop up an ailing free market economy. Because of this intervention conditions for the production of capital can no longer be viewed as natural, but as subject to control by the political apparatus. This intervention by the state is inherently contradictory in that "administratively socialized production" is used to maintain the "continued appropriation and use of surplus value." According to Habermas:

> In order to keep this contradiction from being thematized, then, the administrative system must be sufficiently independent of legitimating will-formation. The arrangement of formal democratic institutions and procedures permits administrative decisions to be made largely independently of specific motives of the citizens. This takes place through a legitimation process that elicits generalized motives—that is, diffuse mass loyalty—but avoids participation. This structural alteration of the bourgeois public realm provides for application of institutions and procedures that are democratic in form, while the citizenry, in the midst of an objectively political society, enjoy the status of passive citizens with only the right to withhold acclamation. (1975, pp.36–37)

Habermas addresses this depoliticization of social actors in terms of the dominance of the technical over the practical interest in society. System maintenance and means-end rationality is the dominant ideology of modern society. All forms of knowing are reducible to issues of technique. As such the knowing, self-reflecting, active subject is refined out of existence and replaced by an apolitical, nonparticipatory functionary who performs the tasks necessary for the reproduction of a social system that serves the interests of a small minority of the population.

Habermas provides us with a critical theory of society that attempts to reconstruct the relationship between the social actor and knowledge-constituting activity. This reconstruction involves a movement away from the ideology of technical rationality, and toward a view of social knowledge evolving from the practical understanding that is inherent in all domination-free discourse. The process of discursive testing (in the ideal speech situation) provides the means for a critique of ideology and domination as manifested in systematically distorted communication.

At this point I want to place in abeyance further explication of Habermas's social theory in order to examine a few of the caveats associated with his position. Our main concern so far has been to examine the degree to which Habermas's theory of communicative action provides insight into the structuring of meaning systems and the concomitant power relations in organizational cultures. His model gives considerable insight in that it allows us to reconstruct the role that discourse plays in structuring knowledge-constituting interests in organizations. However, there are four main areas in which Habermas's position is considered to be problematic: the first concerns his treatment of the relationship between technical-scientific rationality and ideology—the problem of cognitive interests; the second relates to his development of psychoanalysis as the model for the critique of ideology and domination; the third concerns his equation of systematically distorted communication and ideology; and the fourth involves the relationship between ideal speech and ideology. Each of these issues will be taken up in the next section.

A CRITIQUE OF HABERMAS'S CRITICAL THEORY

The Problem of "Interests"

As I have already indicated, Habermas views technical rationality as the dominant ideology of late capitalist society. The ideology of technique produces reason oriented toward avoiding risks and dangers to the system: "not, in other words, toward the *realization of practical goals* but toward the *solution of technical problems*" (Habermas, 1970c, p.103). Unlike Marcuse, Habermas posits that a critique of this "technocratic consciousness" requires not an alternative form of science and technology, but rather emphasis on another type of action; that is, communicative action. Until this is recognized, rationality will be conceptualized in the context of purposive-rational action.

Several scholars, however, have questioned Habermas's characterization of the relationship between science and ideology. Writing from a traditional Marxist perspective, for example, Larrain (1979) argues that Habermas's focus on technical rationality as the dominant form of ideology obscures the issue of class conflict in modern society. Larrain's position is that the class structure of society largely dictates the distribution of power within a given social system, and that the group(s) in power remain there as long as the dominant ideology supports the extant power structure. But Larrain argues that if ideology is equated with technical rationality, then the fundamentally class nature of the struggle for ideological domination is obfuscated; technique-as-ideology comes to exist as a form of rationality that is independent from its social/class origins. For Larrain, treating science *as* ideology is highly problematic:

> One may question whether science itself is the basis of depoliticization and the belief that the system cannot be challenged, or whether the main factor responsible for depoliticization is rather an ideology about science. It might be contended that this is exactly what Habermas is arguing, that technocratic ideology is an ideology which uses the name of science to hide itself. Yet there is a clear-cut difference. While Habermas affirms that the basis of that ideology is scientific-rational progress itself, one could argue against this that the basis of technocratic ideology is class contradiction and the appearance of scientificity is just a new ideological form which conceals these contradictions. (1979, p.209)

Larrain draws attention to the problem of conceiving of ideology as synonymous with scientific rationality: this position glosses over the fact that ideological meaning formations are inextricably bound up with the deep structure power relations that characterize institutional activity. If we view ideology as simply the product of a particular form of rationality, it becomes difficult to conceive of the former as an intrinsic component in the structural domination of one social group by another.

I therefore want to suggest my own reconstruction of the way in which Habermas conceives of the relationship between systematically distorted communication, ideology, power, domination, interests, and so forth. Rather than viewing the technical knowledge-constituting interest as *the* dominant ideological meaning formation, technical rationality must be interpreted as a particular kind of transformational rule that enables the reproduction of deep structure power relations at the surface level.[7] This allows us to obviate the problem that is encountered with Habermas's dual use of the term "interest" (i.e., cognitive, knowledge-constituting interests, and sectional, group interests); we can say that the former is one kind of ideological configuration, but that

---

[7] See Figure 1, chapter 1 for an explanation of the role that transformational rules play in my theoretical position.

it takes on significance only in the context of the latter notion of "interest."

We can therefore claim that technical rationality is ideological only when it is conceived as the dominant mode of thinking against which all action is measured, *and* when it is one of the means by which a particular power structuration is produced and reproduced to the detriment of certain social groups. In this context, systematically distorted communication is the discursive manifestation of this structuration process. At the same time, however, this "discursive manifestation" acts back upon the relations of power, redefining or reproducing them as the case may be.

Habermas is therefore correct in arguing that the technical interest is one of—if not *the*—dominant ideology in modern society but, as Larrain suggests, this ideological trans/formation of social knowledge is rooted in the socioeconomic configuration of Western industrial democracies. The rationality of science is not intrinsically ideological, but becomes so when appropriated as a tool to reinforce societal inequities. This issue is particularly germane when applied to organizational cultures, where the socialization of organization members is often conducted with a strong emphasis on the importance of efficiency, productivity, goal attainment, and so on, all of which are contextualized within the overarching framework of technocracy. Relational issues are subjugated to technical issues.

One of the interesting things about organizational life in general is that there is a fairly clear bifurcation of work (the technical interest) and interaction (the practical interest). The workplace is usually conceived of as an arena of our lives that is conducted by necessity rather than by choice; as such, the patterns of interaction created in this context are viewed as subject to the dictates of the organizationally defined roles that we take on. As a result we generally accept a different set of rules and strictures for organizational life than we would for our lives outside the organization. For example, the workplace is often structured in a way that is decidedly undemocratic when compared with other social structures (it is not usual, for example, for shop floor workers to be able to vote the company president out of office). This distinction that is created between the workplace and other aspects of our lives is ideological because it creates a *false* dichotomy between work and interaction; the implication is that the two are somehow separate spheres of our lives, which are governed by different modes of rationality. This allows technical rationality to dominate the workplace, justifying the institutionalization of undemocratic, nonparticipatory working conditions. The argument traditionally voiced by those in power to justify this situation is that worker participation and efficiency and high productivity are fundamentally incompatible. Such an argument, if accepted as valid, simply reinforces the status quo.

The question of interests, then, needs to be conceptualized in terms of social group or class interests. Giddens (1979, pp.188–196) speaks of the relationship between sectional and universal interests and their articulation in ideology – one of the principal functions of ideology is to represent sectional interests as universal. In other words, the dominant social groups can maintain their dominance only if their interests are accepted and appropriated universally, even if these interests merely confirm other groups in their subordinate position. Thus an authoritarian work environment is accepted as legitimate even by subordinate groups, because the dominant ideology suggests that such an environment is ultimately in the best interests of everyone by virtue of being the system that best maximizes profits.

Psychoanalysis and The Critique of Ideology

The question of ideology and its critique is the second problematic area of Habermas's social theory. Many critics have taken issue with his choice of psychoanalysis as the exemplar of the ideal speech situation through which ideology – in the form of systematically distorted communication – can be exposed to analysis and critique. The main point of contention is the issue of whether the psychoanalytic context can serve as a valuable heuristic device when applied to the neuroses experienced at a wider, social level. Critics have suggested that the application of the psychoanalytic model to the social context involves serious conceptual flaws, and McCarthy has stated that "there are a number of prima facie weaknesses in this analogy" (1982, p.211).

For example, the principal goal of psychoanalysis is to emancipate the patient from the repressions and delusions that he or she experiences. In the same way critical theory attempts to emancipate social groups from societal neuroses that systematically distort reality. McCarthy (1982, p.212) points out, however, that the key to the success of the psychoanalytic method is the patient's recognition of his or her suffering and the desire to be cured. The success of ideology at the societal level, however, is at least partly dependent on its ability to obscure relations of domination; it is therefore quite possible that repressed social groups do not experience dissatisfaction with their situation because they do not perceive themselves as subordinated to other groups, or else perceive the subordination as "natural." As Althusser (1971, p.175) states, "one of the effects of ideology is the practical *denegation* of the ideological character of ideology by ideology: ideology never says 'I am ideological'." In such cases, how does the critical social theorist enable the emancipation of oppressed social groups?

McCarthy (1982, p.212) also points out that an intrinsic part of the process of psychoanalysis involves forcing the patient to relive his or her suffering and that, furthermore, this suffering must not be terminated prematurely if a cure is to be effected. Again there is an obvious difficulty in applying this principle to social formations. While the therapist has institutionally sanctioned control over the relationship with his or her patient, the critical theorist has no such control over the social groups that he or she is attempting to emancipate. It is apparent that a cure cannot take place by virtue of the critical theorist subjecting social groups to various forms of privation in order that they may work through their ideological delusions. Indeed, one of the key elements of the psychoanalytic talking cure is the patient's resistance to the analyst, and the subsequent conflict that this produces. What form should this conflict take at a social level? The problem is exacerbated when one considers that a cure cannot be effected by simply informing patients of their delusions. Rather, the cure is achieved by the working through and reliving of the original conflict situation in the analytic context, where the therapist acts as interaction partner (the process of transference). Thus,

'If the critical theorist has not only to inform oppressed groups of their ideological self-deception but also has to overcome their "resistance," and if he has to do this not only outside of but in opposition to sustaining institutional authority, what are his chances of success? Of survival?" (McCarthy, 1982, p.212).

The psychoanalytic method does not therefore seem to possess direct, pragmatic application to the issues of ideology and domination at a social level. Giddens sums up the main difficulties:

The emancipatory goal of psychoanalysis, the expanded autonomy of the patient, is achieved through a process of self-understanding developed through the analyst-patient dialogue. Here there is a pre-existing consensual system, since analysis is entered into voluntarily by both parties; the participants share a mutual interest in the outcome, the betterment of the patient; the process of therapy is organised purely through symbolic communication; the achieving of reflexive understanding is the very medium of the extension of the analysand's autonomy of action; and the "domination" which the patient overcomes as a result of successful therapy is that of his or her own inner make-up, not the domination of others. None of these conditions seems to apply in the circumstances of actual social life, for example in situations of class domination. (1982, p. 97)

Habermas's tendency to equate the seeking of a cure exclusively with the use of symbolic communication leads into another problematic area in his social theory, which will be taken up below.

Systematically Distorted Communication as Ideology

As I indicated earlier in this chapter Habermas equates ideology with systematically distorted communication. This purely symbolic conception of ideology is problematic, insofar as it excludes a consideration of the degree to which ideology is socially and materially grounded. In addition, Habermas views domination as equivalent to systematically distorted communication, which can be overcome through the self-reflection that is generated in the ideal speech situation. For Habermas, critique is identified with the critique of ideology; that is, with the elaboration of the process of self-reflection and emancipation. In this context, however, interest in emancipation is not linked to any specific material form of domination; emancipation is seen as a universal interest that exists wherever communication is distorted. Given this position,

> it does not make sense to continue to speak of the particular emancipatory interest of the oppressed class [or social group]. Now emancipation can only be predicated on the human race as a whole. The universal interest of human kind replaces the particular interests of the dominated classes. The abstract consideration of distorted communication replaces the concrete analysis of capitalist contradictions. (Larrain, 1983, p.108)

A further problem in equating ideology with distorted communication is that not all distortions are ideological. In psychoanalysis, for example, repression and distortion are seen as a necessary part of the growth of self-identity and the development of personality. Held points out the problem of conflating ideology (neurosis) and distorted communication when he states:

> by seeing both ideology and neurosis through a communication paradigm, Habermas risks deflecting attention form the specificity of each; that is, from the link of neurosis with the dynamic of desire and the necessity of repression in the achievement of self-identity, on the one hand, and on the other, the connection of ideology with the clash of material interests. (1980, p. 394)

A workable theory of ideology must therefore not only demonstrate the way in which ideology is rooted in material practices, but must also be able to distinguish between ideological and nonideological distortions. Habermas appears to do neither of these things, primarily because of his emphasis on ideology as a purely symbolic phenomenon. As such, the notion of systematically distorted communication would possess greater conceptual power if linked to particular social and material practices, and if it was used to critique particular forms of ideological distortion. Figure 1 shows this reconfiguration.

As I indicated in chapter 1 in figure 1, ideology is conceived as consisting of various transformational rules (depending on the ideological meaning system) that mediate between the symbolic structure and the material/power structure of institutions. Systematically distorted communication can therefore be viewed as both the product of the dialectic between ideology and material practices, and as a means by which that relationship is continually maintained and reproduced. The relationship between symbolic structures, ideology, and power will be fully explored in subsequent chapters.

The Ideal Speech Situation and Ideology

Finally, Habermas's conception of the ideal speech situation needs to be examined in the context of its role in ideology-critique. Habermas argues that truth can be generated through a rationally motivated consensus that is achieved through the discursive redemption of claims to validity. This consensus theory of truth is often criticized for being unable to distinguish between genuine, rational consensus and the mere appearance of consensus (McCarthy, 1982, p.304). Habermas's response to this criticism is to characterize a rationally motivated consensus in terms of the formal properties of discourse. A consensus is rational if brought

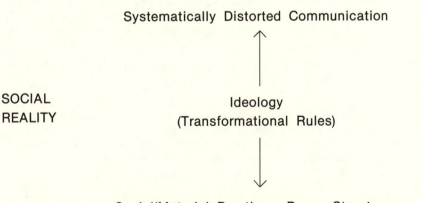

Systematically Distorted Communication

↑

SOCIAL
REALITY

Ideology
(Transformational Rules)

↓

Social/Material Practices, Power Structures

Figure 1   The Relationship Between Systematically Distorted Communication, Ideology, and Power

about purely through the cogency of the arguments adopted. In this sense the ideal speech situation is implicit (if not realized) in every discursive situation: "The very act of participating in a discourse involves the supposition that genuine consensus is possible and that it can be distinguished from false consensus. If we did not suppose this, then the very meaning of discourse would be called into question" (McCarthy, 1982, p.306).

Habermas's argument is adequate if one accepts his equation of ideology with systematically distorted communication. In this context, the ideal speech situation becomes the norm against which truth claims are deemed warranted (consensually true) or unwarranted (distorted or ideological). If, however, ideology is viewed as not merely symbolic but also as grounded in material interests and in the structuring of institutional power, then it becomes difficult to conceptualize how a rational consensus can be judged purely in discursive terms. In other words, there seems to be no guarantee that the ideal speech situation is not itself the product of an ideologically rooted conception of reality. Given that ideology is—at least by Althusser's definition—not recognizable *as* ideology and that, in addition, it is embodied in everyday social practices, how does one distinguish between a consensus that is rational and a consensus that is coercive?

Habermas seems to suggest that because the conditions for the ideal speech situation apply universally across all discursive contexts, then somehow ideal speech itself transcends the distortions of ideological meaning structures; as such, the truth of a rational consensus is juxtaposed against the distortions of a false consensus. What this position does, however, is to suggest that it is possible for meaning formations to exist *outside* of an ideological context—that there is in some sense an ideology-free position from which to critique the suppression of interests that ideology produces. I do not consider this position to be tenable, and I will develop an alternative approach to ideology in a subsequent chapter. Hall, however, articulates a perspective that most closely resembles my own:

> Every social practice is constituted within the interplay of meaning and representation and can itself be represented. In other words, there is no social practice [including discourse] outside of ideology. . . . [However] it does not follow that because all practices are *in* ideology, or inscribed by ideology, all practices are *nothing but* ideology. (1985, p.103)

This position allows us to move beyond a conception of truth that is posited purely in terms of the structure of language, and to focus more on a perspective that deals with the transformation of social practice;

that is, the process of ideology-critique should not attempt to discover the "truth" that ideology distorts, but should rather be concerned with unpacking the ways in which social reality is constructed. Demonstrating the constructed nature of social reality opens up the possibility for new ways of thinking about and acting in the world. This move would not negate the importance of systematically distorted communication as a form of ideology-critique, but would rather deepen its consequences. Instead of fixing the scope of emancipation in terms of an ideal speech situation, discourse can be tied more directly to the lived experience of social practices, demonstrating how systematically distorted communication is produced in the context of the vested, material interests of particular social groups (see Figure 1). As Giddens (1979, p.188) states, "To analyse the ideological aspects of symbolic orders . . . is to examine how structures of signification are mobilised to legitimate the sectional interests of hegemonic groups."

Habermas's theory of knowledge-constituting interests thus offers us a rich and insightful reconstruction of social theory. His development of a model of communicative competence as a means of critiquing ideology and domination has profound implications for the role of communication in the creation of social reality. As I have indicated, however, there are several problematic issues connected with Habermas's project. First, his tendency to treat science and technology *as* ideology obscures the social/class basis of ideology. Second, his definition of interests in terms of rationality needs to be reformulated in order to incorporate fully the materially based interests of social groups. Finally, his notion of ideology-critique is problematic insofar as ideology is viewed as a largely symbolic phenomenon, and thus emancipation from domination is seen as grounded in the universal conditions for rational discourse. Again, this formulation obscures the class basis of domination and its grounding in social practices and institutional structuration. The emancipatory interest must therefore couple self-reflection with the creation of possibilities for transformative practical action.

IMPLICATIONS FOR ORGANIZATIONAL CULTURES

In this final section I want to touch on some of the implications of Habermas's work for the study of organizational cultures, taking into consideration the reformulations discussed above. In particular, I want to examine briefly the relationship between organizational sense-making, ideology, and representation of interests. This will set up the context for the discussion of power and ideology in chapters 3 and 4.

As indicated in chapter 1, organizational sense-making and meaning formation arise out of the system of shared beliefs, rules and practices that constitute organizational culture. This notion of "shared" meaning is generally taken to denote a consensually produced system of sensible, taken-for-granted practices that are expressed through an organization's symbol system. The problem with this position, however, is that "consensus" is often treated as unproblematic; that is, cultures are said to produce and be based upon shared meaning, but there is often little attempt to examine the underlying structural conditions that produce situations of consensus or coercion (or coercively produced consensus).

Forester (1981, 1982) recognizes the problem in talking about "shared" organizational meaning in his analysis of organizational power via Habermas's ideal speech situation. He suggests that the production of social and political relations in organizations can be analyzed using Habermas's four claims to discursive validity, and that power is exercised consensually or coercively depending upon the degree to which these validity claims are satisfied. Analyzing organizational power in terms of ideal speech and systematically distorted communication goes some way to addressing the problematic notion of consensus and shared meaning, but it falls short of adequately characterizing the nature of organizational power. Power is a discursive phenomenon which is located in the context of the material interests that represent different social formations. Power is therefore not *purely* discursive, but must be viewed as an integral part of the structuration process that incorporates both signification and the underlying structure of social relations.

A reformulation of Habermas's notion of interests must therefore overcome the tendency to equate ideology with technology, and focus instead on the degree to which ideology is rooted in the structuring of interests between social groups. Examination of the role of ideology in organizational cultures must focus on the way in which certain meaning formations become detached from the sectional interests that produce them; that is, how does a narrow, particularistic structuring of organizational reality become generalized and perceived as legitimate across social groups?

Several theorists have taken up the question of interests in relation to the structuring of social systems. Dahrendorf (1959), for example, develops a "conflict theory" of society in which social systems are structured in part by the tensions between different interests:

> The occupants of positions of domination and the occupants of positions of subjection hold, by virtue of these positions, certain positions which are contradictory in substance and direction. . . . . Our model of conflict group formation involves the proposition that of the two aggregates of authority

positions to be distinguished in every association, one—that of domination—is characterized by an interest in the maintenance of a social
structure that for them conveys authority, whereas the other—that of
subjection—involves an interest in changing a social condition that de-
prives its incumbents of authority. The two interests are in conflict.
(pp.174–176)

Dahrendorf accepts Weber's notion that the problem of maintaining
or changing particular structures of authority is dependent on the
legitimacy of the authority relations between dominant and subordinate
groups. However, given a conflict theory of society, he suggests that the
legitimacy of such interests is always in question (1959, p.176). For
Dahrendorf, the motivating force behind societal conflict resides in the
tension between the interests of dominant and subordinate groups.
These interests are not individually motivated, but arise out of needs
generated through positioning in the social hierarchy. Thus the managerial class has vested interests in controlling the means of economic
production and increasing capital, while workers have an interest in
obtaining economic rewards, improved working conditions, and so
forth. In a capitalist economy a tension necessarily exists between these
two sets of interests.

While Dahrendorf's quasi-Marxist approach acknowledges only permanent tension between management and labor, more classical Marxist
theories speak of antagonism and contradiction between the respective
groups' interests (Braverman, 1974; Goldman & Van Houten, 1977).
Braverman's study of monopoly capitalism, for example, is an attempt to
describe the dehumanization of the work process that has occurred
through increasing levels of technological innovation. He argues that
while conventional wisdom suggests that increased technical innovation
requires workers with greater skills, the opposite is actually true. By
virtue of being a "dissociated element" in the production process, the
average industrial worker has become no more than an appendage to a
machine. Skill-level requirements *have* increased, however, in the upper
levels of management; here administrative science has developed as one
of the principal means for expanding the unit of capital that the worker
represents to the company. The tendency is therefore toward a polarization of skills at opposite ends of the organizational hierarchy rather
than toward an overall raising of skill levels:

The mass of workers gain nothing from the fact that the decline in their
command over the labor process is more than compensated for by the
increasing command on the part of managers and engineers. On the
contrary, not only does their skill fall in an absolute sense (in that they lose

craft and traditional abilities without gaining new abilities adequate to compensate the loss), but it falls even more in a *relative* sense. The more science is incorporated into the labor process, the less the worker understands the process; the more sophisticated an intellectual product the machine becomes, the less control and comprehension of the machine the worker has (Braverman, 1974, p.428).

Braverman addresses the question of interests in terms of technical control; that is, the relative autonomy/subjugation of the worker in relation to the labor process, versus increasingly sophisticated attempts by management to fine tune the process of capital accumulation. In a sense Braverman's thesis is similar to Habermas's in his emphasis on technical rationality as the cause of domination and exploitation in social systems. At the same time, however, this positing of a direct relationship between monopoly capitalism, technical control, and domination of the working class oversimplifies the complex representation of interests in organizations. That is, the organization is not simply a site of production, but also involves the integration and incorporation of groups with varying and often antithetical interests.

In just this vein Abrahamsson (1977) explores the effect of bureaucracy on the level of participation in organizations. He argues that bureaucracy tends to militate against participation in organizational policy and decision making at all levels, insofar as it detaches organizational administration from the mandators of organizations (those social groups that have a vested interest in shaping organizational goals). The interests of such groups become obscured by the tendency of organizational bureaucracy to take on an autonomous existence. Abrahamsson suggests that a truly participatory organizational environment must dispel the notion that decision making is the prerogative of bureaucrats, and instead view it as involving the representation of all interest groups—workers, managers, entrepreneurs, consumers, shareholders, and so forth.

Such a conception of organizational democracy has generally been resisted because "first, high-level participation cannot as easily be shown to bring economic benefits; and second, that such participation threatens the power positions of the owners with regard to their major goals and utilization of capital resources" (Abrahamsson, 1977, p.188). I would argue also that such a conception of participation does not fit with the structuration of meaning in most organizations. Ideology plays an important role in glossing over the different vested interests of various groups, and articulating an organizational reality that emphasizes uniformity and consistency of organizational values and goals. As such, the power of dominant groups in controlling organizational resources goes hand in hand with the ability of such groups to frame organizational reality in their own terms.[8]

RETHINKING POWER AND IDEOLOGY

Power and ideology, then, are inseparable. Habermas would agree with this claim, but for him power is embodied in systematically distorted communication and the coercive production of a false consensus. The conditions for ideal speech (and hence ideology-free meaning, or truth) and the use of power are thus mutually exclusive for Habermas. In an organizational context, however, the exercising of power must be seen as an intrinsic part of organizational activity. Ideology and power are not critiqued by articulating the conditions for ideology-free discourse and then engaging in discursive testing, but rather by demonstrating how ideology and power limit possibilities for thought and action. Power operates ideologically when it is used to impose a certain form of organizational rationality on members, while simultaneously restricting the articulation of contradictory or competing rationales. But power is also exercised by social actors who maintain a degree of autonomy in the face of ideological meaning formations. In this sense, power is not always in opposition to truth but can also serve to negate the closure that distorted communication (ideology) produces.

Giddens (1979, 1981, 1982) follows this theme through in developing the notion of human agency: "At the heart of both domination and power lies the *transformative capacity* of human action, the origin of all that is liberating and productive in social life as well as all that is repressive and destructive" (1981, p.51). This "dialectic of control," as he calls it, focuses on the ability of the social actor, as agent, to engage in choice, however restrictive the conditions may be. Thus, "The dialectic of control is implied . . . in the logical connection between agency and power. An agent who has no opinions whatsoever is no longer an agent" (1981, p.63). In Giddens's formulation organizations are not simply constraints on action, but also function in an enabling capacity, allowing organization members to reach goals, develop value systems and, potentially, construct alternative versions of organizational reality. Agency and structure are therefore interdependent. The structural nature of organizations is both the medium and product of the practices

---

[8] This should not be taken to mean that dominant interest groups are able to produce an overarching, monolithic organizational reality that goes unchallenged by other groups. Such a position would negate the possibility for the critique of ideology. This issue will be taken up in detail in chapter 4.

that constitute those organizations. This "theory of structuration" explicitly rejects the idea of the social actor as completely subject to the structures of domination embodied in the organization, and suggests instead that organizational practices have a potentially transformative capacity.

By conceiving of organizational structure as both enabling and constraining, then, Giddens provides the necessary link between ideology and domination on the one hand, and transformation and emancipation on the other. The capacity for *both* domination and emancipation is embodied in the everyday practices of organizational life. The ability of these practices to emancipate or dominate is dependent on the structures of signification in which they are acted out. All organizational practices have a symbolic function which signifies their position in a wider system of organizational meaning.

SUMMARY AND CONCLUSION

Jürgen Habermas's philosophical project is an important body of work for communication scholars, insofar as he articulates a theory of truth and a model of society which places communication at its focal point. His theoretical position requires us to scrutinize closely the role of communication, not only in the creation of meaning and understanding, but also in the constitution and maintenance of social contexts characterized by domination and the suppression of human interests. His notion of "systematically distorted communication" is powerfully evocative, bringing into sharp focus the extent to which discourse is vulnerable to manipulation and co-optation by various interest groups. In addition, he clearly demonstrates the extent to which the critique of ideology essentially involves a critique of discourse and the process by which the latter is systematically distorted.

Despite the limitations of Habermas's work that have been discussed in this chapter, one cannot easily dismiss the compelling nature of his argument in favor of an emancipatory knowledge-constituting interest that produces self-reflection, and whose possibility is embodied in the ideal speech situation. It is the possibility of emancipation through self-reflection that impels social actors to examine critically the social conditions that they inhabit. It is the same emancipatory interest in coercion-free discourse that provides the impetus for many social theorists, including myself. The goal of the following chapters is therefore to explicate a theory of organizational cultures that directly incorporates issues of power-as-domination (hegemony) and ideology into understanding how meaning arises in organizations. To this end, chapter 3 takes up the question of power, examining issues surrounding the conceptualization of this social phenomenon, and assessing its most appropriate application in the context of organizational culture and meaning formation.

3

POWER, INTERESTS, AND ORGANIZATIONAL CULTURE

Power is a phenomenon that we confront in almost every aspect of our lives; it is hard to think of a relationship which does not at some point involve issues about the right to influence what another person does or does not do. Thus parents wield power over their children until they "rebel" as teen-agers; bosses direct subordinates and feel aggrieved when orders are not followed; and lovers fight over apparent attempts to "control" the relationship. All of these examples involve questions of influence; that is, getting someone to do something that they might not otherwise do.[1]

The power issues that I am concerned with in this chapter, however, go beyond questions of influence in a purely interpersonal context. Rather, I want to examine power as a structural phenomenon, both as a product of, and the process by which, organization members engage in organizing activity. In particular, the relationship between power and domination will be explored; in other words, situations where power is used in such a way that it militates against the interests of certain organizational groups, and in favor of others. As such, I am not particularly interested in examining the legitimate exercising of power. I am more concerned with those situations in which power functions in a hegemonic fashion to structure the system of interests in an organization.[2] This chapter will therefore lay the groundwork for ensuing discussions of the construction of ideology in organizational

---

[1] This is basically Dahl's model of power, which is presented later in this chapter.

[2] The concept of hegemony is tricky and problematic, and I will more fully explore the implications of this term in the following chapter on ideology. However, it should be recognized that hegemony does not refer simply to the domination of one group by another, but indicates the process by which one group actively supports the goals and aspirations of another, dominant group, even though those goals may not be in the subordinate group's best interests.

55

cultures, which I view as the principal means by which hegemonic organizational structures are produced and reproduced. I will thus examine various theoretical perspectives on power, and then lay out a conception of power that best serves as a way of examining the structuring of organizational reality.

The issues in this chapter will therefore be taken up in the following order. First, a discussion of power as it is used to characterize social relationships will be provided; that is, how is the concept of power best exemplified in terms of its mediatory/regulative role in interactions between individuals or social groups? Second, the role of power in organizations will be outlined to provide a context for the ensuing discussion of the power/ideology relationship. The purpose of this application is to demonstrate that cultures do not arise spontaneously and consensually, but are often the product of certain power distributions which, in turn, are reproduced by particular organizational ideologies. Organizational cultures are not simply the product of a rational, spontaneously derived consensus, but are also "systematically distorted" meaning formations.

THE CONCEPT OF POWER

The development of a rigorous and systematic concept of power has been a major task of the social sciences for the last 25 years. A major polemic has risen around conceptualizing the way in which one person or group can be said to "affect" another in a significant manner. In this context, most theories of power have been largely behavioral; that is, they have been concerned with the degree to which actions by one person or group can be shown to have a discernible effect on the behavior of others.

One of the most widely quoted behavioral theories in the literature on power is that developed by Robert Dahl (1957; 1958; 1961). Dahl (1957) suggests that power is not something that a person possesses, but is rather a relation among people. As such, he defines power in the following way: "A has power over B to the extent that he can get B to do something that B would not otherwise do" (1957, pp.202–203). To this extent, power involves the ability to produce behavioral changes that would not otherwise occur. Dahl uses the following example to demonstrate his position:

> Suppose I stand on a streetcorner and say to myself, "I command all automobile drivers on this street to drive on the right side of the road"; suppose that further all the drivers do as I "command" them to do; still,

most people would regard me as mentally ill if I insist that I have enough power over automobile drivers to compel them to use the right side of the road. On the other hand, suppose a policeman is standing at the middle of an intersection at which most traffic ordinarily moves ahead; he orders all traffic to turn right or left; the traffic moves as he orders it to do. Then it accords with what I perceive to be the bedrock idea of power to say that the policeman acting in this particular role evidently has the power to make automobile drivers turn right or left rather than go ahead. (1957, p.202)

Dahl offers two prerequisites for the exercising of power. First, there must be a time lag between the actions of those designated "powerful" and the responses of those upon whom power is exercised. Second, there must necessarily be a connection between the two parties—there can be no "action at a distance" (1957, p.204). Both these conditions, along with the above example and definition of power, point to a concern with the exercise of power rather than identifying the sources of power. As such, the focus of research lies with the analysis of actual decision-making situations, in which it is established that the outcome would have been different had each party acted independently. Such conclusions can only be reached based on "the careful examination of a series of concrete decisions" (Dahl, 1958, p.466).

Dahl's model of power is developed in response to the ruling elite model, which claims that power is a stable, integral part of any organizational structure, and can be viewed as the possession of a small minority of people (the ruling elite). Dahl contends that such a position in untenable because it focuses on sources of power rather than the actual power. The latter type of power is empirically observable, while the former is not. Dahl explains this point:

There is a type of quasi-metaphysical theory made up of what might be called an infinite regress of explanations. The ruling elite model *can* be interpreted in this way. If the overt leaders of a community do not appear to constitute a ruling elite, then the theory can be saved by arguing that behind the overt leaders there is a set of covert leaders who do. If subsequent evidence shows that this covert group does not make a ruling elite, then the theory can be saved by arguing that behind the first covert group there is another, and so on.

Now whatever else it may be, a theory that cannot even in principle be controverted by empirical evidence is not a scientific theory. (1958, p.463)

Dahl's critique of the ruling elite model is largely accurate. However, his own position has been subject to extensive criticism. Bachrach and

Baratz (1962), for example, suggest that Dahl's concept of power is flawed in two fundamental ways. First, it excludes the possibility that power can be exercised in order to confine the decision-making process to issues that are noncontroversial—only those issues that are "safe" are opened to debate. A notion of power that confines itself to the analysis of "concrete decisions" is therefore inadequate, insofar as

> power is also exercised when A devotes his energies to creating or reinforcing social and political values and institutional practices that limit the scope of the political process to public consideration of only those issues which are comparatively innocuous to A. To the extent that A succeeds in doing this, B is prevented, for all practical purposes, from bringing to the fore any issues that might in their resolution be seriously detrimental to A's set of preferences (Bachrach and Baratz, 1962, p.948).

Bachrach and Baratz's second objection to Dahl's position is that it provides no criteria by which to distinguish between "important" and "unimportant" issues. Such criteria, they argue, are established by analyzing the "mobilization of bias" in a community; that is, "the dominant values and the political myths, rituals and institutions which tend to favor the vested interests of one or more groups, relative to others" (1962, p.950).

Bachrach and Baratz thereby redraw the boundary conditions for power by redefining the question of an "issue," suggesting that an adequate conception of power must incorporate an analysis of both decision making and nondecision making. In this sense, one must identify not only overt issues but also *potential* issues. Against the criticism that such potential issues are not objectively measurable (i.e., you cannot measure what has not occurred), Bachrach and Baratz counter that one should not confuse what is unmeasurable with what is unreal (1962, p.952). Indeed, they charge Dahl with committing the same error with which he charges the elitists: Their assumptions about power (i.e., that it can only be observed in concrete decision-making situations) predetermined their findings and conclusions. Bachrach and Baratz, on the other hand, suggest that questions such as "Who rules?" or "Does anyone have power?" are inappropriate starting points for an analysis of power. Rather, the correct starting point is an investigation of the particular "mobilization of bias" that characterizes a community. It is only in this way that one can examine both nondecisions (dealing with both "safe" issues that essentially affirm the status quo, and deciding *not* to act or make a decision over some issue) and decision making over identifiable and important issues.

Bachrach and Baratz's double-sided theory of power is therefore conceptually less restrictive than Dahl's, moving away from a purely behavioral focus. However, their position is also limiting in certain respects. Lukes (1974) has provided a critique of both the Dahlian model and Bachrach and Baratz's position. He labels the former a one-dimensional theory of power, while the latter he terms two-dimensional. From Lukes's perspective the two-dimensional view is inadequate on three counts. First, it only provides a qualified critique of the behaviorism inherent in the one-dimensional view insofar as it still considers actual cases of decision making or nondecision making to be the central focus. This limits the study of power to situations in which conscious decisions to act or not act are made and, moreover, interprets power in terms of indiv¡dually chosen acts. As Lukes points out, however, this ignores the fact that power is often exercised by individuals without any conscious or intentional decision making on their part. Such unintended consequences of action mean that an individual can exercise power over another simply by virtue of their position in an organization—no conscious decision-making process need take place. One can say therefore that power is not just a relation between individuals, but is sustained by "the *socially structured* and culturally patterned behavior of groups, and practices of institutions, which may indeed be manifested by individuals' inaction" (Lukes, 1974, p.22, emphasis added).

Second, Lukes criticizes Bachrach and Baratz for associating power with actual (either overt or covert) and observable conflict. This ignores the possibility that power may be exercised by shaping the needs of others. Thus A does not simply get B to do what she would not otherwise do, but rather makes B acquire desires and actively pursue ends that are in A's interests (but not necessarily in B's). The existence of a consensus does not therefore eliminate the possibility that power is somehow being exercised. In Habermas's terms, we can say that where a false consensus exists, power is being exercised. The assumption that one needs to identify conflict as a prerequisite for both the exercising and examination of power is therefore erroneous. To do so is to "ignore the crucial point that the most effective and insidious use of power is to prevent . . . conflict from arising in the first place" (Lukes, 1974, p.23).

Lukes's third critique of Bachrach and Baratz is closely linked to the second. Briefly, he argues that they are wrong to insist that nondecision-making power only occurs where grievances are not taken up as debatable issues; that is, they are "denied entry into the political process" (1974, p.24). If such reasoning were followed, it could be argued that the lack of grievances indicates a true consensus. This ignores the possibility that grievances might be prevented by shaping the way in which people perceive situations; social actors are not likely to complain about situations that they consider to be part of the natural order of things. Again, an adequate theory of power must consider the possibility of false or manipulated consensus.

Lukes therefore articulates a theory of power that is conceptually the most radical of the three discussed, particularly in his movement away from a purely behavioral focus toward a consideration of the structural interests that underlie behavior. In addition, his conception of power in terms of structuration transcends purely relational, decision making situations; the process of decision making becomes situated in the wider context of the organizational structure that provides the rules and norms for behavior.

Lukes's integration of power with group interests provides the necessary link between power and ideology. He points the way beyond a relatively crude, behavioral conception of power in order to unpack the question of *latent* conflicts; that is, situations in which the potential for conflict exists but is unrealized due to the lack of recognition of structural contradictions. According to Lukes, a latent conflict "consists in a contradiction between the interests of those exercising power and the *real interests* of those they exclude" (1974, pp.24–25). A fruitful way of analyzing the structure of power therefore is to examine the *ways* in which the system of interests in organizations is produced, maintained, and reproduced. In other words, if a contradiction exists between the interests of the dominant group(s) and the real interests of those dominated, how is this contradiction obscured to maintain the status quo?[3] An examination of the relationship between power and ideology serves to explicate this process.

In the next chapter I will articulate fully the dialectical relationship that exists between organizational power and ideology—a relationship that has already been suggested by the figures in chapters 1 and 2. Basically, ideology invokes transformational rules which provide norms for the interpretation of organizational structure; at the same time ideological meaning systems provide the context in which organizational reality can be formed and transformed. Ideology can thus be viewed as articulating and legitimating certain organizational realities that legitimate particular interests over others, and as simultaneously embodying the potential for transformation and change.

In the next section, however, I want to discuss contemporary treatments of power in organizations. While this has generally been an

---

[3] For the purposes of explanation this issue is somewhat oversimplified here. Most organizations are made up of a complex structure of competing interests, and rarely is it the case that a single set of interests imposes a monolithic organizational structure on other organizational members. Organizations tend to generate multiple realities, each reality being a reflection of a different set of vested interests.

underinvestigated area of research, a number of contemporary theorists (including some in communication) have recognized and explored the intrinsic link between organizational behavior and power. Focus in the next section will therefore be on the treatment of the phenomenon of power at a theoretical level, followed by a conceptual re-articulation in the context of its relationship to ideology. This will provide a framework for the discussion of ideology in chapter 4.

POWER IN ORGANIZATIONS

The issue of power occupies a somewhat tenuous position in organizational theory, due largely to the ambivalent attitude that both organizational scholars and managers hold toward the term. From a theoretical standpoint, the treatment of power has been mostly conservative, due principally to the influence of the structural-functionalist paradigm in the fields of sociology, political science, communication, and so forth. Structural-functionalist approaches to social systems have tended to focus on the ways in which societies maintain order and cohesion through the regulation of structure.[4] In this context, power is usually conceived of as one of the processes through which stability is maintained. As such, the exercising of power becomes the legitimate maintenance of the structure of hierarchy that is an intrinsic part of all reasonably complex societies.

As Burrell and Morgan (1979) have indicated, orthodox social theory has consistently devalued the relationship between power and conflict on the one hand, and social contradiction and radical change on the other. For example, social conflict has usually been treated not as an expression of basic antagonisms between divergent social forces, but rather as a means by which tensions between different groups can be played out and hence defused/diffused; in this sense conflict fulfills an integrationist function, rather than a change function. This orientation toward power and conflict basically enables functionalist social theorists to ignore questions of domination and repression in social structures; all social phenomena can thus be regarded in the context of shared values and a pluralistic social structure. But as Burrell and Morgan state:

> shared values may be regarded not so much as an index of the degree of integration which characterises a society as one which reflects the success

___
[4] As Dahrendorf (1959, p.161) states, "In varying forms, the elements of (1) stability, (2) integration, (3) functional coordination, and (4) consensus occur in all structural-functionalist approaches to the study of social structure."

of the forces of domination in a society prone to disintegration. From one point of view, extant shared ideas, values and norms are something to be preserved; from another, they present a mode of domination from which man [sic] needs to be released. (1979, p.14)

Burrell and Morgan suggest that the order-conflict debate that occupied mainstream sociology in the 1950s and 1960s needs to be revitalized, but in a way that prevents the issue of conflict from being subsumed by the question of social order. This can be achieved, they argue, by focusing on system contradiction rather than system conflict. The former suggests fundamental "incompatibility between different elements of social structure" (1979, p.15) and stands in clear opposition to the functionalist concept of "functional co-ordination." Thus "To argue that the concept of contradiction can be embraced within functional analysis requires either an act of faith or at least a considerable leap of imagination" (1979, p.15).

In the specific context of organizational theory, Weber's (1947) influential study of bureaucracy has been consistently interpreted in ways that promote a conservative view of power. In particular, his notion of *Zweckrational* (purposive-rational action) has permitted organizational structuring to be conceived of as a largely rational process that has little to do with the exercising of power by social actors. This perspective is further emphasized in his distinction between *Macht* (power) and *Herrschaft* (authority). The former is linked to the personality of individuals, while the latter is associated with social roles or positions in formal hierarchies. This permits a view of organizational power as the legitimate exercising of authority by virtue of one's position in the hierarchy. Organizational power-as-domination (*Macht*) is thus a deviation from organizational norms and therefore not viewed as legitimate organizational behavior.

It is clear, then, that the conception of organizational power to be developed in this book (i.e., the playing out of fundamental contradictions in the structuring of diverse group interests) is incommensurate with the conservative interpretation of Weber's work. Clegg (1975), however, has reconceptualized the notions of *Macht* and *Herrschaft* to fit into a more radical view of the relationship between power and organizational structuring. Clegg reinterprets *Herrschaft* as "rule" in order to highlight "the interpretative work that people engage in, when they make sense of the world."[5] All authority, he suggests, is dependent

---

[5] This interpretation of *Herrschaft* is consistent with Weber's notion of *Verstehen* (understanding), which in turn is closely linked to his notion of the "ideal type." Weber conceives of inquiry in the social sciences (*Geisteswissenschaften*) as being directed toward "the understanding of the characteristic uniqueness of the reality in which we move"

on this conception of rule-governed behavior:

> The concept of "rule" links the structural notions explicit in "domination" to the actions of ordinary people. Different types of "rule" provide differing "orders" to which people orient their behaviour. Domination is socially significant as a structural phenomenon because people orient their behaviour towards it. (1975, p.59)

Clegg provides a clear connection between power-as-domination, organizational structure, and interaction: The relationship he articulates is one in which organizational structure acts in a mediatory capacity between interaction and domination. An organization's mode of rationality is embodied in both its structure and in the way in which this structure is manifested in interaction. Domination therefore occurs when the rules of organizational rationality are structured to favor certain vested interests and to militate against others. As Clegg (1975, p.77) states, "Power is about the outcomes of issues enabled by the rule of a substantive rationality which is temporally and institutionally located."

The issue of power in organizations is therefore appropriately conceptualized in the context of the structuration process. That is, power is not simply a part of organizational structure; rather, it is both medium and outcome; it is both enabling and constraining. Power, in essence, is both a product of organizational activity *and* the process by which activity becomes institutionally legitimated. Organizational interaction is therefore not something that takes place *within* the (power) structure of an organization, but is rather the process through which structure is created, reproduced, and changed.

Several authors have explicitly linked organizational structure and power, although by no means all of them escape the limitations imposed by a traditional structural-functionalist approach to the issue. For example, Pfeffer's (1981) work on power in organizations is a systematic attempt to demonstrate the political motivation behind the process of organizing. Pfeffer suggests that power is a systemic property of organizations, and that "politics is the study of power in action" (1981, p.7). Accordingly, three conditions must be present for power to be exercised in organizations. First, a situation of interdependence is necessary, in the sense that the behaviors of organization members

---

(Quoted in Dallmayr & McCarthy, 1977, p. 24). In this context, ideal types serve as mental constructs which, although not existing empirically, provide for the accentuation of the principal elements of the concrete phenomena being studied. Knowledge is therefore directed toward making sense of the social world, rather than toward generating empirically verifiable, universal laws of behavior.

interlock such that the actions of one person can affect others, and vice versa; members therefore develop needs that can only be fulfilled through interaction with others. This condition lays the potential for conflict. Second, heterogeneous, or inconsistent, goals must be present in order that competing interests may arise. Finally, a scarcity of resources produces conditions in which actors with various goals must compete with each other to have their demands met.

Each of these conditions contributes to a situation of potential conflict among organization members. A reliance on the "intrinsic rationality" of organizational structuring is therefore not enough to allow members to achieve their desired goals. Power necessarily implies relations of dependence—those actors with most power are those who are least dependent on the activities of others.[6]

Pfeffer's model of power is predicated largely on the decision-making process in organizations, and thus is similar in many ways to Bachrach and Baratz's theory of power:

> Power is effectively used when it is employed as unobtrusively as possible. The exercise of power and influence is facilitated by the legiti-mation of the decision process, decision outcomes, and the power and influence itself. Most strategies for the exercise of power involve attempts to make the use of power less obtrusive, and attempt to legitimate and rationalize the decision that is to be made as a result of the exercise of the social power of an actor in the organization (Pfeffer, 1981, p.137).

The problems associated with conceptualizing power exclusively in terms of the decision-making process have already been discussed. However, Pfeffer does view decision making in the context of the institutionalization of power in organizations. Thus "Power becomes institutionalized by a process which perpetuates not only the social reality of the distribution of power but also the various structures, procedures, and practices which reinforce the existing power structure" (1981, p.299). Pfeffer shows here that the exercising of power is more than simply making decisions; it involves making decisions within an already framed social structure that provides a sedimented set of practices for organizational behavior. The meaning and outcomes of the decision process are thus partly determined by the ways in which they are structured into an organization's culture.

Despite Pfeffer's treatment of power as a structural phenomenon, I would argue that his perspective is still unnecessarily conservative. To

---

[6] Although as Giddens has shown the dialectic of control suggests that those who are *in* power are also in a situation of dependence in that they are only powerful to the degree that others will recognize and hence legitimate that power.

begin with, he treats power in terms of relationships between individuals who act within a given organizational structure. This dualistic position is essentially a reiteration of the structural-functionalist view of social action. As I have indicated earlier, the relationship between action and structure constitutes a *duality*—a dialectical interplay—through which social actors can both draw upon and reconstitute the organizational structures in which they behave. As such, decision making is not something that takes place *within* organizational power structures; rather, it is *one* of the processes through which those structures are constituted and reconstituted. In effect, the very concept of decision making only takes on significance within the context of a given meaning structure, which itself is a product of the interplay among communication, ideology, and organizational interests. This brings us to the second criticism of Pfeffer's position.

Pfeffer clearly sees the process of decision making as a concrete, behavioral phenomenon that is an expression of organizational power. I would argue that, more importantly, decision making fulfills an essentially symbolic function in organizations; that is, it is not so much *what* is accomplished through decision making, but rather significance lies in the process of decision-making per se. It is therefore the *procedure* that is meaningful rather than the issues that are dealt with through this procedure.[7] However, Pfeffer seems to make a clear split between organizational behavior and organizational symbolism, particularly in relation to the exercise of power:

> It is helpful for social actors with power to use appropriate political language and symbols to legitimate and develop support for the decisions that are reached on the basis of power. However, in this formulation, *language and the ability to use political symbols contribute only marginally to the development of the power of various organizational participants*; rather, power derives from the conditions of resource control and resource interdependence. (1981, p.184, emphasis added)

---

[7] Similarly Weick (1979) demonstrates the fundamentally symbolic function of organizational plans. What is important here is not the fact that an organization lays out and follows a specific plan, but rather that it has a plan at all:

> [Plans] are *symbols* in the sense that when an organization does not know how it is doing or knows that it is failing , it can signal a different message to observers. If the organization does not have a compact car in its line, it can announce plans to have one. On the basis of this announcement the firm may be valued more highly than an organization that makes no such announcement. It is less crucial that the organization is planning to make the car than that all concerned imagine this to be the case. It is in this sense that plans are symbols and that they negotiate a portion of the reality that then comes back and rearranges the organization. (p. 10)

This position inadequately conceptualizes the relationship between symbolic structures and power. I would argue that in a very real sense *all* organizational behavior is symbolic, contributing in some way to the structuring of organizational reality, and hence organizational power. We can therefore make the claim that *organizational power is constituted and reproduced through the structure of organizational symbolism.*[8] This moves beyond a purely representational view of symbolism (in which symbolic forms are seen as expressions of a pre-existing reality), to a perspective which places the symbolic at the locus of the process of reality construction. Language in all its forms is therefore not simply the expression of social practice, but its medium. Therefore when Pfeffer (1981, p.184) says that "those who have emphasized the role of language and political symbols have confused the exercise of power with its foundations," he overlooks the fact that the "foundations" of power are partly produced and reproduced through the symbolic articulation of a particular organizational reality. I will take up this theme in greater detail in a subsequent chapter.

Pfeffer's work is fairly representative of traditional attempts to incorporate the study of power into organizational research. Other authors, such as Bacharach and Lawler (1980) and Astley and Sachdeva (1984), conceptualize power in terms of decision making and then attempt to delineate the structure and sources of power that facilitate the decision making process. While such studies help to focus on the issue of organizational power, they are misleading in their separation of

---

[8] One of the best examples of this symbolic function of power that I have come across appeared recently in a local newspaper. The article was entitled "Washroom Proves the Key."

When an employee receives the key to the executive washroom it means a step up the ladder, but does being asked to give it up mark a step down? In the case of a Passaic County official who refused to relinquish the prized possession, loss is the appropriate word. He will be suspended for three days and docked some $500 in pay. Alex Komar, supervisor of county roads and keeper of the one key to a private washroom next to his office in the Paterson administration building, was asked by Passaic County Administrator Nicola DiDonna to turn in the key [because he was being moved to a different office] . . . Komar resisted, even after he was asked in writing, and responded with a memo to DiDonna requesting that the matter be brought before the Board of Freeholders.

"Anyone who tells me why they won't give up a men's room key is going to get a suspension. It's such a waste of time, I don't want to hear about it," DiDonna said. "There was no way he was going to come before the full board with this."

DiDonna said Komar will be suspended in February after he returns from a vacation. The amount of lost pay will be nearly $500, he said.

"He thought he was the little king down there and he wanted his throne," DiDonna continued. "If he wants to be the lavatory attendant, I can give him those duties."

organizational structure and interaction. Because organizational activity and organizational structure exist dialectically, decision making is not a phenomenon that is independent of the structure within which it occurs. As Brown (1978, p.376) states:

> "making decisions" is not the most important exercise of organizational power. Instead, this power is most strategically deployed in the design and imposition of paradigmatic frameworks within which the very meaning of such actions as "making decisions" is defined. [9]

It is thus apparent that there is an integral connection between organizational behavior and organizational structure, and several authors are beginning to see the importance of this relationship. Ranson, Hinings, and Greenwood (1980), for example, look at the dispersion of organizational power in terms of the process of structuration. Accordingly, "structure [is] a complex medium of control which is continually produced and recreated in interaction and yet shapes that interaction: structures are constituted and constituting" (1980, p.3). This aspect of the organizing process is crucial to the vested interests of groups in organizations. If organizations are conceived as being made up of diverse and competing needs, values, practices, etc., that embody the interests of different groups, then the groups with the most power will be those that are best able to integrate their sectional interests into the very structuring of the organization. A particular group's interests will be best served if those interests become part of the taken-for-granted social reality that structures organizational life. Once these interests become part of the organizational structure, then that structure simultaneously mediates in and reproduces those interests.

It is in this sense that organizational structure is both the medium and outcome of members' social practices, and is thus a defining characteristic of organizational power. As Ranson et al. state, "The structural framework is not an abstract chart but one of the crucial instruments by which groups perpetuate their power and control in organizations: groups struggle to constitute structures in order that they may become constituting" (1980, p.8). This characteristic of the structuration process is perhaps seen most clearly in the concept of organizational hierarchy. The concept of hierarchy is exactly that—a *concept*—which through its instantiation in organizational practice has become reified as a concrete,

---

[9] Here Brown is using the term "paradigm" in the Kuhnian sense, suggesting that organizations articulate a world view that frames the ways in which social actors think about and make sense of organizational activity. Organizational power is thus conceived as embodied in the taken-for-granted rule system that sanctions particular forms of action (see also Imershein, 1977; and Benson, 1977).

tangible aspect of organizational structuring. The symbolic/conceptual constitution of hierarchy leads to a condition in which hierarchy itself dictates the structuring of organizational practice. Managerial interests are thus served by this process in that important issues are deemed to be tied to organizational hierarchy—the more important the issue, the higher up the hierarchy decisions are made.

This symbolic constitution of organizational hierarchy is probably manifested most clearly in the concept of "meeting." Meetings are perceived as a necessary and pervasive characteristic of organizational life—they are events that people are required to engage in if decisions are to be made and goals are to be accomplished. While this is the ostensible rationale for meetings, they also function as one of the most visible and important sites of organizational power. They are examples par excellence of the symbolic structuring of power, and of the reification of organizational hierarchy. As such, meetings can be viewed as important not so much by virtue of what they accomplish, but because they provide a context in which various organizational issues can be played out between those members and interest groups that structure organizational agendas. Meetings are symbolic insofar as those people who occupy positions of power in the organizational hierarchy use this context to signify their power, and thus to reaffirm their status. Duncan discusses the symbolic representation of power in terms of a social drama:

> Superiors must *persuade* inferiors to accept their rule. This is done through the glorification of symbols of majesty and power as symbols of social order in many kinds of social dramas wherein the power and glory of the rules as a "representative" of some transcendent principle of social order is dramatized. (1968, p.53)

Thus meetings provide symbolic contexts in which organization members can dramatize their superiority over others by virtue of their positioning in the organizational hierarchy. It is this hierarchy which is regarded as the "transcendent principle of social order" in organizations, and which is symbolically played out and reaffirmed in meetings. The concept of hierarchy is thereby reified, guaranteeing the reproduction of a certain organizational structure, usually that most suited to maintaining managerial interests.

SUMMARY AND CONCLUSION

Power has been an important topic in social theory for some time, but it has only recently become a focus of interest in organizational communication and related fields. Much of this work, however, adopts a fairly traditional, functionally oriented view of power, focusing on questions relating to the role of power in the decision-making process, in information dissemination, and so on. Some scholars, however, have recognized that the issue of power is more fundamentally a part of the process by which an organization constitutes and reconstitutes its social reality. Power is integrally tied to the structure of interests in an organization, which itself is an intrinsic part of the way organizational practices and hence meaning formations are structured. It is at the level of practice that interests are played out, and the site at which a particular organizational reality is produced and reproduced.

There is still, however, a missing link in the relationship between organizational interests and organizational practice. How is it that certain groups are *able* to secure their vested interests in organizations, at the same time reproducing them at the level of organizational practice? It is apparent that control of the structuration process falls mainly to those groups who wield power—not everyone can have equal access to the resources necessary to produce and reproduce certain relations of power. Indeed, the control of such resources is intrinsic to these power relations. In the next chapter I provide the missing link in this relationship by developing the concept of ideology as the connection between organizational interests and organizational practices. I have already hinted at this relationship, but the following chapter provides a detailed explication of both the concept of ideology per se, and its implications for organizational cultures. In brief, I will argue that an adequate conception of ideology must consider its role both in creating the subjectivity (consciousness) of organization members, and in obscuring the systems of domination that frequently characterize organizational power structures.

4

IDEOLOGY AND
ORGANIZATIONAL CULTURES

Clifford Geertz accurately characterizes the theoretically problematic status of ideology when he states that "It is one of the minor ironies of modern intellectual history that the term "ideology" has itself become thoroughly ideologized" (1973, p.193). McClellan (1986, p.1) adds that "Ideology is the most elusive concept in the whole of social science . . . a concept about the very definition (and therefore application) of which there is acute controversy." The term has passed into common usage laden with connotations that are almost universally negative. When someone is said to be espousing a particular ideology, it is normally taken to indicate that that person is presenting a set of ideas from a particularly prejudiced point of view. Someone who is being "ideological" is emoting rather than engaging in rational, balanced, and constructive forms of argument. In general, ideology has come to be associated with half-truths that emanate from a particularly narrow belief system.

The treatment of "ideology" and "beliefs" as synonymous, however, reduces the conceptual power of the former and masks the degree to which ideology plays a constitutive role in the way people create social reality. This chapter explores the relationship between ideology and social reality, specifically in terms of the way that ideology mediates in the constitution of individual consciousness. It is argued that ideology does not simply provide people with a belief system through which they orient themselves to the world, but that instead it plays a much more fundamental role in the process by which social actors create the reality of the world in which they live. In addition, ideology serves to mask or transmute the contradictions that exist between social reality as experienced by actors, and the competing vested interests of different social groups, such that a collective sense of social reality is created. Thus as Geertz (1973, p.220) states, "Whatever else ideologies may be . . . they are, most distinctively, maps of problematic social reality and matrices for the creation of collective conscience."

The next section therefore takes up the relationship between ideology and consciousness, exploring possible ways to conceive of the connection between the two. The subsequent section will consider more directly the dialectic that necessarily exists between ideology and organizational cultures.

IDEOLOGY AND CONSCIOUSNESS

The production of consciousness, or subjectivity, is a focal issue in most contemporary theories of ideology. Ideology is generally conceived as the means by which social reality is constructed and reproduced, and individual consciousness is seen as intrinsically tied in with this process. The study of ideology is a central concern in examining the process of hegemony in social structures, insofar as it is perceived as the means by which structures of domination are produced and perpetuated. One way of critiquing structures of domination is therefore to examine critically the ideological meaning systems upon which they are built, because structures of domination exist through domination of human consciousness.

Broadly speaking, the study of ideology and domination falls under two separate (but by no means mutually exclusive) theoretical paradigms: *radical humanism* and *radical structuralism* (Burrell & Morgan, 1979) The radical humanist approach focuses on domination of consciousness; it is concerned with critiquing the ways in which the ideological superstructures of capitalism alienate individuals from their conditions of existence. From this perspective, ideology functions principally through the symbolic structuring of reality. Language acts as a "prison-house" that molds individual consciousness. Radical structuralism, on the other hand, focuses more directly on the actual material conditions that produce and reproduce structures of domination. Domination of consciousness is still at issue, but it is contextualized in terms of the socioeconomic conditions of a society. As such, the role of ideology is to reproduce the conditions of capitalist production that are at the root of the structures of domination. The work of Louis Althusser (1970, 1971) is among the most influential in this paradigm.

I adopt a perspective of the relationship between ideology and consciousness that draws on work from both paradigms. On the one hand, I am concerned with the way in which power and domination are symbolically structured; to this extent, I perceive an intrinsic link between ideology, consciousness, and communication. On the other hand, it is important to recognize that this tripartite relationship exists in the context of actual material practices and actual social structures. Language itself is material—it is a social *practice* that regulates the way that social actors interact with one another; at the same time we all function within institutional structures that are tangible—we sit at desks, walk up and down grocery store aisles, and obey traffic signals. To this extent, our behavior and thus our consciousness is structurally constrained.

Broadly speaking, there are three main senses in which the term "ideology" is used: the descriptive sense, the pejorative sense, and the positive sense (Geuss, 1981). In the descriptive sense ideology is used as a neutral concept that does not describe an illusory form of reality, but which reflects the *only* reality that a social group knows by virtue of their positioning in a social structure. Thus every group has an ideology that grounds the way its members think and act toward the world. The pejorative sense perceives ideology as maintaining a distorted and illusory relationship between social actors and the world, thereby obscuring the contradictions that hegemonic systems produce. Finally, the positive sense views ideology as the "driving force" that motivates a particular collectivity to action in order to achieve certain goals. Here, the ideology of a group serves its best interests rather than working against it.

While these three senses of ideology have certain common themes, it is the pejorative conception of ideology that best draws attention to issues relating to domination of consciousness. Within this framework, hegemonic structures are shown to be produced and reproduced through the ideological structuring of the sense-making process. Ideology articulates a view of reality which maintains and supports the interests of dominant groups and suppresses those of subordinate groups. Ideology in this sense reifies dominant meaning formations as the natural, sensible order of things—"just the ways things are"—so that social structures are no longer perceived as *humanly* constructed.

In the context of organizational cultures, we can say that ideology plays a central role in the legitimation and reproduction of organizational meaning structures. Ideology functions to secure certain hegemonic configurations by legitimating those meaning structures that favor the powerful. Thus while most cultural approaches are content to describe the extant meaning formations in organizations, the approach adopted here is concerned with demonstrating *why* certain meaning formations evolve at the expense of others. Culture therefore involves not only meaning formation, but also meaning *deformation*—situations in which ideology structures contradictions and inequities into the very framework of a social system. At the same time these same inequities and contradictions are concealed or naturalized by ideology. As Larrain states:

> by concealing contradictions, ideology serves the interests of the ruling class, which can display the present order of things as natural and in the interests of all sections of society. Ideology serves the interests of the dominant class not because it has been produced by the ideologists of the class—which may or may not be the case—but because the concealment of contradictions objectively works in favour of the dominant class's interests. (1979, p.61)

Ignoring Larrain's rather outmoded use of the phrase "class interests" (I prefer the term "sectional interests"), he does provide the two principal functions of ideology: the concealment of social contradictions, and the serving of dominant interests. The rest of this section explores in greater detail both the functions of ideology and the conceptual parameters of the term. Specifically, I will analyze the concept of ideology by examining its articulation by major social theorists, including Louis Althusser, Goran Therborn, Anthony Giddens, and Stuart Hall. This by no means provides an exhaustive analysis of the concept, but it will give a firm, conceptual basis for the subsequent examination of the symbolic structuring of power.

Louis Althusser: Ideology and the State

Althusser's (1970, 1971) writings on ideology are among the most controversial and yet most widely applied theoretical perspectives of the last two decades (Coward and Ellis, 1977; Silverman and Torode, 1980). Althusser presents a structuralist position that attempts to break free from the notion that ideology is ultimately reducible to a psychological creation of individuals. As such, the widely accepted conception of ideology as false consciousness is considered erroneous by Althusser insofar as it suggests that the subject is the locus of ideology formation.[1] Ideology, for Althusser, arises in material reality itself, and not with the social actor (or subject, as Althusser calls the individual). Ideology is

---

[1] The "decentering of the subject" has been a major task of the structuralist and post-structuralist enterprise. Beginning with Saussure, there has been a consistent attempt to show that meaning resides in structure rather than in individuals. Thus Saussure's assertion that "language is a system of differences" has provided the impetus for a vast amount of research that has attempted to debunk the "homocentrism" present in traditional social theory (see, for example, Culler, 1982; Kurzweil, 1980; Lemert, 1979). Ideology is therefore perceived as residing in "structures of domination" rather than in the consciousness of the individual subject. Foucault (1973, p.387) has thus stated that "Man is an invention of a recent date. And one perhaps nearing its end."

material in two senses: it exists in the apparatuses and practices that structure society, and it constitutes "concrete" individuals as subjects; i.e., ideology provides individuals with a consciousness of the world they live in (Althusser, 1971).

Ideology exists in material practices as part of the societal superstructure, and acts in a dialectical relationship with the economic base. Although there is a "determination in the last instance" of the ideological and political superstructure by the economic base, the former acts in a relatively independent fashion and can act back upon the infrastructure. This allows ideology to perform the role of "the reproduction of the relations of production" (1971, p.127). According to Althusser, the societal superstructure consists of Repressive State Apparatuses (the police, army, prisons, etc.) and Ideological State Apparatuses (the education system, the family, the mass media, religion, etc.), both of which function to reproduce the conditions necessary for the capitalist mode of production to maintain itself. The RSAs are institutions of last resort, functioning only when the very structure of a social system is perceived by the ruling political group to be threatened.[2]

The ISAs, on the other hand, function to produce and reproduce a *willing* labor force and its accompanying skills. Institutions such as the mass media, religion, and so forth, interpellate, or address, social actors so that their relationship to society is "naturalized." ISAs function ideologically to structure the social practices of subjects around the reproduction of the existing economic system. For example, Althusser would argue that in most Western capitalist societies (and particularly in the U.S.A.) the mass media consistently address social actors as consumers, focusing people's lives around need fulfillment and instant gratification.[3] Such a process is a necessary element in the reproduction of the capitalist enterprise.

The two senses in which Althusser views ideology as material are therefore closely related; ideology operates within the specific practices of the plurality of ISAs which, in turn, create the lived-world of social

---

[2] Clear examples of the use of RSAs would be the use of police to suppress civil rights demonstrations in the 1960s, and the mobilization of the national guard against student anti-Vietnam demonstrations in the early 1970s. Both movements were perceived by local and federal government as a threat to established social structure. Today, the apartheid system in South Africa exemplifies a situation in which RSAs must be employed (heavy use of military force, press censorship) in order to maintain the status quo.

[3] Kubey (1986) has even suggested that the pervasiveness of drug abuse in the US is at least partly the product of a collective consciousness that demands instant forms of gratification. This consciousness, he speculates, is the result of the mass-mediated creation of a consumer society in which delayed gratification is seen as more and more intolerable. We not only buy goods to satisfy our material needs, but also our emotional needs. Drug abuse is simply the extension of this process.

actors. Thus ideology constitutes social reality for individuals, but in an imaginary form:

> all ideology represents in its necessarily imaginary distortion not the existing relations of production (and the other relations that derive from them), but above all the (imaginary) relationship of individuals to the relations of production and the relations that derive from them. What is represented in ideology is therefore not the system of real relations which govern the existence of individuals, but the imaginary relation of those individuals to the real relations in which they live. (1971, pp.164–65)

Ideology is not false consciousness because the ideological conditions in which subjects live derive from the objective conditions of existence (the mode of production), and not from the individual. Therefore, insofar as all practices occur within ideological apparatuses, subjectivity (consciousness) exists only to the extent that it is constituted through ideology. "[A]ll ideology has the function (which defines it) of constituting concrete individuals as subjects. . . . all ideology hails or interpellates concrete individuals as concrete subjects, by the functioning of the category of the subject" (1971, pp.171–73). It follows that if there is no subjectivity outside of ideology then social actors must always exist in an imaginary relation to the real relations in which they live—it is never possible for an ideologically constituted consciousness to be aware of the real conditions of existence.

This line of reasoning is problematic for Althusser because it appears to negate the possibility of praxis; that is, theoretically grounded social action that potentially emancipates social actors from repressive socio-economic conditions. Althusser attempts to resolve this problem by placing science in opposition to ideology. The role of science is to overcome the ideological domination of consciousness; ideology is a "pre-scientific" mode of thinking. Scientific thought arises through an "epistemological break" with its ideological "prehistory." In other words, science provides a completely new way of constructing knowledge about the social world—a method that escapes the frame that ideology imposes on consciousness. The "labor of science" therefore "consists of elaborating its own scientific facts through a critique of the ideological 'facts' elaborated by an earlier ideological theoretical practice" (1970, p.184). Science is therefore the means by which the objective conditions of existence are established, and it provides the grounding for praxis.

While this appears to resolve Althusser's problematic conception of the relationship between ideology and consciousness, it also poses another difficulty: his juxtaposition of science and ideology appears to be grounded ultimately in a positivist view of knowledge. His distinction between "real" and "imaginary" conditions of existence certainly supports this view, and he posits science as the only means by which the real conditions of existence can be uncovered. Larrain (1979) criticizes this position as rationalist in that the science-ideology opposition eventually comes down to an abstract confrontation between truth and error. Both concepts are dislocated from their position in the struggle between competing and contradictory sectional interests, expressed through day-to-day social practices. It is this contradiction between interests that is the origin of *both* ideology and praxis, but Althusser denies the possibility of an adequate critique of the former and implementation of the latter through his reification of the ideology/science dichotomy.

Althusser's theory of ideology comes down to "the theory of the necessary domination of ideology" (Larrain, 1979, p.163). Ideology becomes a prerequisite for consciousness, and the individual exists passively in an imaginary relationship to the world, perpetually in a state of *méconnaissance* (misknowing). The subject is "provided with the ideology which suits the role it has to fulfill in class society: the role of the exploited . . . [or] the role of the agent of exploitation" (Althusser, 1971, pp.155–56). True to his structuralist position, Althusser supplants the subject with ideology as a new essence.

Althusser's conception of the relationship between ideology and subjectivity is made even more problematic because he conceives of ideology as a function of the state; that is, as a structural monolith that is always consistent with the will of the state, embodied in the ruling elite. This negates the formation of alternative or oppositional ideologies outside the purview of the state. Althusser gives ideology and subjectivity an abstract isomorphism that does not reflect their actual relationship in everyday social practices. If subjectivity *is* isomorphic with ideology, then there is no possibility of the critique of hegemonic meaning structures. As we will see later, however, such a critique depends upon a disjuncture between the "received meaning" of dominant ideologies and the creation of alternative ways of structuring meaning around institutional practices. The chapter on ideology and organizational symbolism will address this issue directly, concentrating on the way in which ideology is constituted and reproduced through social practices (expressed in various symbolic forms). It follows, therefore, that ideology-critique can take place through examination of institutionally structured symbolic forms, such as organizational narrative.

Althusser's elaboration of a materialist view of ideology is probably his most important contribution to an adequate conception of the term.

This has permitted a transcendence of the notion of ideology as synonymous with beliefs, and has demonstrated its constitutive role in the structuring of human subjectivity. His neglect of the relation between ideology and social practice, however, is an important oversight. Althusser perceives ideology in terms of its *necessary* domination over society and therefore as something imposed *on* social practices. This ignores the necessarily dialectical relationship between ideology and social practices, whereby each is both medium and product of the other, continually producing and reproducing meaning-bound social structures. In Althusser's formulation, ideology transcends social practice, constituting subjectivity but simultaneously remaining beyond reflection and critique. If the subject is constituted solely through the dominant ideology, then exposure of the contradictions and vested interests which the latter hides becomes impossible (Abercrombie & Turner, 1982; Parkin, 1982).

A more appropriate theoretical position, therefore, views ideology as an integral and constitutive element in the practices of social actors. Social reality is produced and reproduced through the interlocking and structured practices of subjects. Ideology is constituted through these social practices and, in turn, articulates the meaning of these practices to the social actor. A critique of ideology must therefore be pursued through the social practices that it structures. The work of Göran Therborn points in this direction.

Göran Therborn: Ideology as Subjection-Qualification

Therborn (1980) presents a conception of ideology that is an explicit critique of Althusser's position. Therborn suggests that the relationship between the social actor-as-subject and ideology is necessarily dialectical. Not only does ideology (as rooted in social practices) constitute subjectivity, but the subject (as social actor) can in turn act to reproduce and transform ideologies. This dialectic is embodied in the ambiguity of the term "subject," which means both subject (subjugated) *to* a particular meaning formation, and "subject" in the sense of the locus of an "I" – an ego that develops social roles in a creative manner. Therborn coins the phrase "subjection-qualification" to capture this ambiguity: As social actors we are qualified in the sense that the social roles we adopt and the practices that we engage in restrict the range of our consciousness; at the same time, however, the roles that we assimilate qualify us to participate fully in (and potentially change) a structured, meaningful social world that incorporates almost infinite behavioral possibilities.

Therborn presents a more differentiated conception of ideological interpellation than Althusser, who sees ideology as addressing the subject in terms of what is "real." Therborn presents three modes of ideological interpellation:

> Ideologies subject and qualify subjects by telling them, relating them to, and making them recognize: 1. *What exists,* and its corollary, what does not exist: that is, who we are, what the world is, what nature, society, men and women are like. In this way we acquire a sense of identity, becoming conscious of what is real and true; the visibility of the world is thereby structured by the distribution of spotlights, shadows, and darkness. 2. *What is good,* right, just, beautiful, attractive, enjoyable, and its opposites. In this way our desires become structured and norm-alized. 3. *What is possible* and impossible; our sense of the mutability of our being-in-the-world and the consequences of change are hereby patterned, and our hopes, ambitions and fears given shape. (1980,p.18)

Ideology therefore functions to articulate the boundary conditions of a subject's social reality. It does not simply produce misrecognition and ignorance, but rather engages the subject in a continuous process of inclusion and exclusion, defining what is, what is good, and what is possible.

Like Althusser, Therborn views ideology as material, determined to a large degree by the matrix of economic and social practices that define the mode of production (the combination of the relations of production and the means of production). In this sense ideology is "determined in the last instance" by the economic base. A particular economic system will therefore qualify subjects through certain means in order to reproduce itself. This is achieved by the operation of affirmations and sanctions that confirm the dominant ideological meaning structures.

For example, the use of time clocks to "punch in and out" is a material reality for many workers in many organizations. Economically it achieves two things: first, it allows "a fair day's work for a fair day's pay"; second, it maintains a two-tiered pay structure in which workers get wages and management receive salaries. Ideologically, time clocks function to structure different senses of organizational reality for workers and management, creating an organizational "class system." Time clocks differentiate between two kinds of labor; labor that is paid by the hour is usually manual, while labor that is compensated by salary is usually considered cerebral and is not constrained by the need to monitor use of time. In addition, time clocks bracket the working day for workers, signaling its beginning and its end. Punching the time card indicates the point at which behavior becomes structured by organizational needs—"punching out" indicates the end of one's organizational responsibilities.[4] Most importantly, the ideological distinction between workers and management is reproduced through an actual material sanction. Ideology does not therefore merely reflect the material conditions of existence, but acts back upon them to fulfill its function of framing what is true, good, and possible within the context of these material social practices. Time clocks are not merely a reflection of a particular socioeconomic structure; they are, in addition, one of the means by which the structure of relations between different interest groups is reproduced ideologically. The relationship between ideology and economic infrastructure is therefore dialectical.[5]

Therborn adopts an essentially descriptive conception of ideology. Unlike Althusser, ideology does not produce misrecogniton or imaginary relations to the world; rather, it denotes "that aspect of the human condition under which human beings live their lives as conscious actors in a world that makes sense to them to varying degrees. Ideology is the medium through which this consciousness and meaningfulness operate" (1980, p.2).

I have already suggested that a pejorative conception of ideology is more powerful in that it directly addresses the issue of hegemony, vested interests, and the concealment of contradictions. Looking at ideology from a pejorative perspective enables us to focus on *ideology-critique*; that is, a deconstruction of the systems of domination that shape social relations. The notion of ideology-critique implies, however, that there is a non-ideological position that one can assume in analyzing hegemonic systems—a position that is unacceptable if one accepts the

---

[4] The importance that management attaches to the constraining function of time cards is borne out by my own experience of working for a crop-spraying contractor during college summer vacations. Official clocking in time was 7:30a.m., and as the workers arrived we would gather in the crew room where the time cards and clock were located. It was common practice to keep watch out of the window for latecomers, and to punch their card for them if it looked like they were going to miss the 7:30 deadline (which would result in loss of pay). This practice was eventually discovered by management (who generally showed up in their company cars somewhat later than the workers) and the offending worker (who punched a coworker's time card) was severely reprimanded. Interestingly enough, several workers retaliated by engaging in an unofficial "go-slow" that morning, taking longer than usual to prepare their tractors for the day's work. Probably more money was lost because of the go-slow than was saved by preventing workers from punching each other's time cards. However, the significance of the role of the time cards in the working day was reaffirmed for both workers and management.

[5] This relationship will be examined in more detail in the chapter on organizational symbolism.

premise that ideology produces and reproduces human subjectivity, i.e., consciousness is possible only within an ideological context.

This problem is obviated if one adopts the position that all social practice takes place within ideology, but at the same time is not isomorphic with ideology. As Hall (1985, p.103) states, "it does not follow that because all practices are *in* ideology, or inscribed by ideology, all practices are *nothing but* ideology." Placed in this context, the issue of ideological versus nonideological social practice becomes moot. The central concern is not what nonideological social practice or discourse might look like, but rather how social practices (or clusters of social practices) function to reproduce or subvert dominant ideological meaning systems. For example, a cluster of organizational stories can be analyzed in terms of the ways that they represent organizational practice, and how these representations either confirm or disconfirm organizational realities articulated by dominant sectional interests. Stories manifest discursive penetration and are potentially transformative when they call into question the received interpretation of organizational reality. In other words, a disjuncture, or rupture, is created between the hegemonic meaning system(s) of the organization and the organizational experience that the stories articulate. In addition, stories that *do* reproduce the dominant ideological structures may be subject to critique in order to deconstruct the nature of organizational reality that they represent.[6]

Ideology can thus be conceptualized as the mode of rationality that mediates between organizational practices (including discourse) and the structure of organizational interests. Interests only become dominant to the extent that ideological meaning structures can be articulated in systems of signification, legitimating those interests over others. Ideology functions to create as close a "fit" as possible between the interpretation of organizational practice and the structure of organizational interests. Discourse, ideology, and interests thus function interdependently in an organization to reproduce continually the structure of organizing. As Ranson et al. (1980, p.7) state, "interested action is typically oriented toward the framework of an organization, with members striving to secure their sectional claims within its very structure, which then operates to mediate or reconstitute those interests."

It is in this context that Giddens's work provides an appropriate framework for analysis. Giddens (1979) presents a theory of ideology as domination, in which one of the main roles of ideology is to reproduce the dominant structure of interests. At the same time, however,

---

[6] This issue will be fully explored in the next chapter.

Giddens incorporates a strong notion of agency into his position, stressing the role of the actor in the relationship between ideology and power interests. It is this role of the social actor as agent that will be explored in the next section.

Anthony Giddens: Ideology and Structuration

The linchpin of Giddens's work is his theory of structuration, which incorporates the concept of duality of structure (1976, 1979). This reflects the recursive nature of social life: "the structural properties of social systems are both the medium and the outcome of the practices that constitute those systems" (1979, p.69). Structure and agency are therefore interdependent. Structure is not imposed upon actors; rather, actors draw upon the rules and resources that make up structure in the process of interaction. At the same time this structure is reproduced and reconstituted through interaction. In this sense, "structure is both enabling and constraining . . . [and] thus is not to be conceptualized as a barrier to action, but as essentially involved in its reproduction" (1979, p.69–70).

Similarly, power and ideology are contextualized in terms of the duality of structure, in that power is seen as a routine aspect of social practices. Power is not a dependent variable of structure, but is produced through relations of autonomy and dependence that are negotiated in interaction. Power is gained through the utilization of the implicit rules and resources that constitute organizational structure; power is exercised when the use of such resources can structure the meaning of interaction in ways that supports certain group interests over others. Hegemonic groups are thus able to control the negotiation of meaning in organizations. This negotiation of meaning takes place symbolically at the level of social practice.

As Giddens indicates, however, simply to be a human agent necessarily involves the exercise of power. Just by virtue of our positioning in a matrix of interlocked social practices we "carve out spaces of control" (1982, p.197) that allow us to exercise influence over even the most powerful. At the most basic level, simply being in someone's presence requires that person in some way to alter their behavior in order to recognize one. This "dialectic of control" recognizes that a reciprocal relationship exists between agency and power, and that power relations are an ongoing product of the structuration process.

Giddens conceives of ideology as the means by which structures of domination are legitimated, and as the medium through which power is exercised to both secure and obscure sectional interests. In other words, ideology provides a meaning context that favors certain groups over others, while simultaneously disguising the hegemonic nature of this meaning system. These ideological meaning structures are produced and reproduced through systems of signification which, in most organizations, take the form of stories, jokes, rituals, memoranda, meetings, and so forth. All of these organizational practices are symbolic forms that either reproduce or reconstitute ideological meaning systems in organizations. As Giddens states:

> To analyze the ideological aspects of symbolic orders . . . is to examine how structures of signification are mobilized to legitimate the sectional interests of hegemonic groups (1979, p.188). . . . To examine ideology institutionally is to show how symbolic orders sustain forms of domination in the everyday context of "lived experience" . . . To study ideology from this aspect is to seek to identify the most basic structural elements which connect signification and legitimation in such a way as to favor dominant interests (1979, pp.191–192).

This position is very different from a representational view of language, in which organizational symbolism is viewed as simply the expression of already established relations of power.[7] In contrast, Giddens explicitly links symbol systems and the interests of dominant groups. Power cannot be conceived as a static, a priori quality of an organization's structure; rather, it is produced through the co-optation of an organization's system of signification by sectional interests, who symbolically construct an organizational reality that works in their favor. Again, a duality is in operation: Dominant interests are best able to mobilize symbolic structures in their favor, and in turn these symbol systems produce and reproduce the dominance of certain group interests.

Given that ideology and power are produced and reproduced through structures of signification, then the structuring of an organization member's consciousness, or subjectivity will be largely dependent upon his or her level of discursive socialization. In this context, Giddens distinguishes between "practical consciousness" and "discursive consciousness," both of which are premised on the idea that "social actors are knowledgeable about the conditions of social reproduction in which their day-to-day activities are enmeshed" (1982, p.29). Practical consciousness denotes the taken-for-granted knowledge that social actors draw upon while engaging in meaningful organizing behavior; discursive consciousness speaks to the social actor's ability to *account for* particular kinds of behavior; that is, to articulate their knowledge of how

---

[7] See the position expressed by Pfeffer (1981) in the previous chapter.

and why social structures operate the way they do. According to Giddens, what an actor can say about his or her actions in a given context is by no means all that he or she knows about them. Discursive consciousness can never exhaust the relationship between knowledge and action (1982, p.31).

The distinction between practical and discursive consciousness bears directly on the relationship between ideology and organizational culture. Practical consciousness represents a form of human subjectivity in which social actors are largely unaware of the degree to which culture is structured ideologically. Because meaning is largely taken for granted there is little reflection upon the extent to which an organization's reality is framed by the configuration of power interests in the organization. In Habermas's terms there is little in the way of an emancipatory knowledge-constituting interest. Discursive consciousness, on the other hand, reflects a form of subjectivity in which there is a greater awareness of the relationship between ideology and culture. It is recognized that organizational meaning systems are not "natural," but are produced by vested interests that frame "reality" in ways that reproduce those interests. A particular definition of organizational reality can therefore be questioned to the degree that a social actor possesses discursive penetration into the mode of rationality that mediates between organizational practice and organizational power.

Practical and discursive consciousness, however, do not exist in an either/or relationship, but are rather at opposite poles of the same continuum. That is, implicit in every social situation is the ability to reflect upon the taken-for-granted knowledge that frames our understanding and behavior. Social actors possess *degrees* of practical consciousness and discursive consciousness. The extent to which a social actor can deconstruct discourse (and therefore meaning) is the degree to which he or she recognizes the ideological structuring of culture. In both Althusser's and Hall's terms, a person possesses discursive consciousness when he or she has insight into the process by which systems of signification "hail" or interpellate him or her as a conscious subject.

Hall (1985) provides an interesting example of both the ideological interpellation of subjectivity through discourse, and the simultaneous discursive penetration of the system of signification that this discourse articulates. He presents a "reading" of the "particular complex of discourses that implicates the ideologies of identity, place, ethnicity and social formation generated around the term 'black'" (1985, p.108). Hall speaks with considerable eloquence of the systems of signification that are articulated around the term "black" and its many variants, and of the role that these systems play in the constitution of his own subjectivity. It is a marvelously erudite reading that is worth quoting extensively:

At different times in my thirty years in England, I have been "hailed" or interpellated as "coloured," "West-Indian," "Negro," "black," "immigrant." Sometimes in the street; sometimes at street corners; sometimes abusively; sometimes in a friendly manner; sometimes ambiguously. (A black friend of mine was disciplined by his political organization for "racism" because, in order to scandalize the white neighborhood in which we both lived as students, he would ride up to my window late at night and, from the middle of the street, shout "Negro!" very loudly to attract my attention!) All of them inscribe me "in place" in a signifying chain which constructs identity through the categories of color, ethnicity, race. . . . As a concrete lived individual, am I indeed any of these interpellations? Does any of them exhaust me? In fact, I "am" not one or another of these ways of representing me, though I have been all of them at different times and still am some of them to some degree. But, there is no essential, unitary "I" — only the fragmentary, contradictory subject I become. . . . I was also on many occasions "spoken" by that other, absent, unspoken term, the one that is never there, the "American" one, undignified even by a capital "N." The "silence" around this term was probably the most eloquent of them all. Positively marked terms "signify" because of their position in relation to what is absent, unmarked, the unspoken, the unsayable. Meaning is relational within an ideological system of presences and absences. "Fort, da." (1985, pp.108–109)

Hall's analysis directly addresses a central concern in examining the relationship between culture and ideology; that is, how does a particular "ideological chain" operate to constitute a certain "semantic field," or cultural meaning system, within which social actors are situated? According to Hall, a particular ideological chain (such as "Black" and its variants) becomes a site of ideological struggle, a contested terrain, when there is an attempt to transform or rearticulate the system of meanings that are associated with a particular body of discourse (1985, p.112). Thus the term "Black" has been transformed by the civil rights movement from a term with largely pejorative connotations to one that signifies a positive social identity. "'Black,' then, exists ideologically only in relation to the contestation around those chains of meaning, and the social forces involved in that contestation" (1985, p.113).

Similarly ideology exists at the locus of Giddens's dialectic of control in that it contextualizes the struggle between dominant and dominated groups. Ideology does not, as Althusser maintains, simply reproduce the relations of production; rather, it is the site at which this reproduction is contested. As such, ideology "*sets limits* to the degree to which a society-in-dominance can easily, smoothly and functionally reproduce itself" (Hall, 1985, p.113). The ideological control of meaning formations is based upon the ability to articulate particular kinds of relationships between discourse and meaning; in other words, to manufacture a "fit" between human subjectivity and the discourse that interpellates that subjectivity. However, as both Hall and Giddens show, such a fit is always imperfect, fomenting a struggle to rearticulate the way in which a social group perceives its "fit" in a cultural meaning system. In such cases a rupture appears in the ideological meaning system, transforming the relationship between a particular body of discourse and the semantic field that it signifies.

One of the ways to explicate this struggle between various articulations of meaning formations is to examine more closely the functions of ideology in privileging certain articulations over others. There are various ways to frame the functions that ideology performs (e.g., Therborn, 1980), but I have chosen Giddens's (1979) formulation as the most appropriate for purposes of analyzing the articulation of subjectivity in ideology.

Giddens (1979, pp.193–196) presents three principal functions of ideology: (1) The representation of sectional interests as universal; (2) The denial or transmutation of contradictions; and (3) The naturalization of the present through reification. The first function points to the process through which ideology defines interests that are specific to a particular group in such a way that these interests are perceived as universally valid. This function of ideology is perhaps best expressed through Gramsci's (1971) concept of hegemony. Hegemony is frequently misconstrued as the ideological domination by one class (or grouping of class fractions) of another. Instead, hegemony involves "the ability of one class to articulate the interests of other social groups to its own" (Mouffe, 1979, p.183). In this sense hegemony is a question of leadership rather than of domination and control. It is achieved via "the colonization of popular consciousness or common sense through the articulation of specific social practices and positions within ideological codes" (Grossberg, 1984, p.412). As such, a "collective will" is produced through "intellectual and moral reform" (Gramsci, 1971, pp.12, 60–61). It is here that Gramsci clearly indicates the link between ideological hegemony and culture:

> From this one can deduce the importance of the "cultural aspect," even in practical (collective) activity. An historical act can only be performed by "collective man," and this presupposes the attainment of a "cultural-social" unity through which a multiplicity of dispersed wills, with heterogenous aims, are welded together with a single aim, on the basis of an equal and common conception of the world. (1971, p.349)

Far from being based upon coercion and domination, therefore, ideology functions through active consent rather than through the

passive acceptance of already articulated social forms. Ideological hegemony involves "effective *self-identification* with the hegemonic forms"
(Williams, 1977, p.18).

The second function of ideology—the denial or transmutation of
contradictions—refers to the way in which fundamental system contradictions are reformulated as more superficial issues of social conflict.

The primary contradiction in capitalist society—that between
privatized appropriation (capital) and socialized production (labor)—is
obscured through the ideological bifurcation of the political and economic spheres. Workers are not recognized as having the same political
rights in the workplace as they do in other social contexts. Thus
management often feels quite justified in excluding large sections of the
workforce from participation in organizational decision making on the
ground that such workers are not qualified, or else that such a
participatory process would hurt efficiency and hence productivity.[8] The
legitimate political sphere is conceived simply in terms of the relationship between the individual and the state (Mason, 1982; Pateman, 1970).
This strict separation of the economic and political spheres allows
management to conceptualize organizational behavior largely in terms
of technical rationality and to relegate human concerns to a secondary
status. The result is often a preoccupation with issues of control,
producing a deskilling of the labor process and profound alienation of
workers from the organizational environment that they occupy
(Braverman, 1974).

The third function of ideology, reification (Lukacs, 1971), concerns
the way in which humanly constructed social relations and meaning
formations come to be perceived and experienced as "objective" and
independent of the people who created them. In this way what is "real"
becomes fixed and immutable; common sense tells us that this is "the
way things are." In organizations the reification of day-to-day experience limits the possibility of conceiving of alternative social realities or,
if such alternatives are articulated in some way, they are usually derided
as unworkable, too radical, or against the best interests of the organization. Again, the principle of participatory decision making is a good
case in point.

This concept has been maligned from the perspective of technical
rationality as "inefficient" and "unproductive," but the issue also centers

---

[8] Many companies are beginning to recognize the value of more participatory forms of
decision making. This has not arisen out of any altruistic desire to improve the quality of
life of workers, but because more and more studies have indicated that more participatory
organizational structures can actually raise productivity levels (See Harrison, 1986; Mason,
1982; Pateman, 1970).

around the fundamentally hierarchical structure of organizations. The concept of hierarchy has been reified to the point where the structuring of organizations is perceived as "naturally" occurring from the top down. As such, decision making has been traditionally conceived as the natural prerogative of upper-level management. The diffusion of decision making power to all levels of an organization challenges the fundamental and "inviolable" nature of organizational hierarchy. Management will therefore not easily share decision making power because this presents an alternative conception of organizing that threatens their position as the corporate elite. It is no accident, therefore, that high-level managers surround themselves with the trappings of power such as large, well-furnished offices, numerous secretaries, thick carpets, and so on. All of these artifacts serve further to reify and objectify the concept of hierarchy, making it a more tangible and explicit aspect of organizational experience.[9]

I have argued, then, that ideology is materially grounded in the organized practices of social actors. Ideology constitutes subjectivity through its ordering of these practices into a coherent lived-world for the individual. Ideology and power are inextricably tied together insofar as ideology articulates social reality in terms of the interests of the dominant social group(s). In organizations, power is most successfully exercised by those who can structure their interests into the very framework of the organization. Ideology therefore acts to support these interests by continuously reproducing the structure of social practices which best serves them. In this sense, power and ideology are not purely structural phenomena, separate from the interaction of social actors; rather, they are both the medium and the product of that interaction.

In the final section of this chapter the role of power and ideology in the structuring of organizational cultures will be considered more directly. In brief, we need to examine the relationship between "interested action" and the form of organizational cultures. This can be achieved by understanding organizations in terms of ideological constructs, i.e., the orientation of sense-making toward the interests of dominant groups. This will lay the foundation for the following chapter, which closely examines the role of organizational narrative in the construction of ideological meaning formations.

---

[9] Many organizations have extremely rigid pecking orders that are maintained to the point where rules exist that determine what managers at different levels are allowed to have in their offices. For example, in a certain multinational corporation with its headquarters in New Jersey, one must reach a certain level before being allowed to have photographs of family members adorning desks and walls. In other companies, carpets are routinely torn up and replaced when offices change hands and the new occupant is of a different status than the old one.

ORGANIZATIONAL CULTURE AND IDEOLOGY

Power and ideology in organizations are practical, rather than ideational, social phenomena. It is inadequate, therefore, to characterize a ruling ideology in terms of the dominance of a certain set of ideas over the way that people think about themselves and their organization. The power relations that structure an organization are instantiated in the everyday, taken-for-granted social practices of that organization. As Giddens (1979, p.192) states, "The . . . 'order' and 'discipline' of daily life, including but not limited to the routines of industrial labour, might be regarded as the most profoundly embedded ideological features of contemporary society."

Organizations are task-oriented structures, and the degree to which social actors are embedded in that structure is characterized by the degree to which organizational practices are taken for granted and treated as routine. In this section, therefore, we consider the way in which power and ideology act as the organizing principle in the production and reproduction of organizational behavior. In essence, the main issue is centered around the way in which "culture" can function ideologically to structure the interests of organizational stakeholders in certain ways. In this section and in the following chapter, it will be suggested that culture plays a fundamental role in privileging certain interests over others and that—in most cases—these interests are managerial in nature. Thus power and ideology serve as a fundamental, organizing principle that consistently reproduces organizational conditions that favor managerial interests over and above others.

Clegg (1975, 1981; Clegg & Dunkerley, 1980) has dealt extensively with the issues of power and control in organizations. Clegg and Dunkerley (1980, p.481) argue that:

> individual power relations are only the visible tip of a structure of control, hegemony, rule and domination which continues to appear to be *the* natural convention. It is only when control slips, taken-for-grantedness fails, routines lapse and problems appear that the overt exercise of power is necessary. . . . Thus, although everything occurs so as to make it appear that power is either an individual property or relationship between individuals, it is in fact a social relationship determined by the mediation of the organization with the environment of the world economy that this mediation constitutes and the critical issues that the organization's functioning engenders.

Clegg and Dunkerley's position illuminates the relationship between ideology and power by articulating organizational structure in terms of a set of selection rules that provide the basis for an organization's mode of rationality. "Rules" refers to the historical structure that underlies social practices that are manifested at the surface of organizational life. These rules are sedimented, not necessarily cognizant to individual organization members, and largely dictate what is perceived as "natural" organizational practice. This organizational practice is therefore a reflection of the organization's particular rule-bound mode of rationality.

Clegg's development of the notion of selection rules and "mode of rationality" is quite compatible with my own earlier development of the role of ideology in organizations. The sedimentation of a particular set of rules makes for the reproduction of a certain organizational structure, with attendant meaning formations, social practices, and so on. This structure is also the means by which such rules are themselves reproduced. The relationship is necessarily dialectical in nature.

The notion that organizational practices are both grounded in and are a reproduction of an organization's underlying rule system fits neatly with Giddens's explication of the structuration process. Giddens's (1979, 1981, 1984) theory of structuration, with its assertion that structure is both the medium and outcome of social practice, provides a model for the analysis of organizational interaction that explicates the way in which certain practices become an intrinsic part of an organization's meaning system. In the case of both Giddens and Clegg, the exercise of power involves the reproduction of the structure that best serves the interests of the dominant group(s) in the organization.

In examining organizational culture from such a perspective, the task is one of unpacking the process by which sense-making and meaning formation get structured into an organization. My argument is that shared meaning structures do not arise spontaneously and consensually, but are produced through the system of vested interests that characterize all organizations. Such interests provide a grounding for ideological meaning formations which, in turn, are the medium and product of organizational practices. It is this system which tells a member what is good, true, and possible (and their opposites) in an organization. Hegemony operates in such a context when the social reality that is produced is framed by the dominant interests; furthermore, this social reality is often taken for granted and actively supported by organization members. Most importantly, the reproduction of a particular organizational structure is contingent on the perceived rationality of that structure. Ideology functions to preserve this perceived rationality by reifying it and by obscuring contradictions in the organizational structure that might challenge its pervasiveness.

A strong case can be made, for example, that bureaucracy functions ideologically in many organizations. Bureaucracy is perceived as an integral part of most organizations of any size, although people often use the term pejoratively to refer to the "faceless" aspect of organizational life; that is, bureaucracy is that part of organizational structuring where social actors are confronted by an ineffable, ineluctable process that discriminates against no one in terms of the way it "screws" people.[10] But this "faceless" image that bureaucracy presents constitutes an ideological function in that it helps to obscure the structure of an organization by hiding the nature and origin of power within that organization. The ideological effect is to produce and reproduce an ostensibly decentralized, pluralistic structure which serves the interests of no one in particular, presenting sectional interests as universal. As Abrahamsson (1977, p.11) points out, however, "Organizations are *deliberately designed social structures* which have been established by a certain person, group or class, in order to implement certain goals. These persons, groups or classes are . . . the *mandators* of organizations."

Abrahamsson develops the notion of "mandator" to explicate the nonpluralistic nature of power relations in organizations, and thus deconstructs the mystification process that bureaucracy performs. Because bureaucracy "represents a tendency within an organization's administration to disengage itself from those very interests which it is supposed to work for" (1977, p.21), location of power sources becomes problematic. By exposing the ideological function of bureaucracy, however, we can come to recognize the contradiction inherent in the relationship between the dominant interests that bureaucracy serves, and the plurality of interests that an organization purports to accommodate. Bureaucracy therefore functions both as an organizational feature which reproduces the structure in which it is embedded, and as a means by which organization members are distanced from the power interests that help control the meaning of organizational practices. In the last analysis, bureaucracy is also an element of organizational culture that allows people to make sense out of their powerlessness; it is easy to be

---

[10] At Rutgers University, for example, students actually talk about the "RU Screw" in referring to any administrative action which renders them "victims" of the system (e.g., de-registration for no apparent reason, bad dormitory food, lack of availability of classes needed for graduation, and so on). This phrase is not only succint and convenient, but also functions symbolically to differentiate between Rutgers and other institutions of higher learning in the treatment of their students. Interestingly enough, I recently talked to a student who transferred from the University of Tennessee, and who told me that the students there spoke of the "Big Orange Screw" to refer to the same phenomenon. This "uniqueness paradox" is discussed extensively by Martin et al. (1983).

a victim of a system that one apparently has no control over and, from a managerial perspective, bureaucracy provides a convenient means of deflecting responsibility for organizational problems.

An analysis of the hegemonic structures that arise out of the organizing process must therefore focus on how this sense-making occurs. The fundamental question is: How are organization members predisposed to make sense out of their organization in certain, nonarbitrary ways? What are the mechanisms that lie behind the privileging of certain readings of organizational reality? I have already argued that it is through the structuring of power and ideology that sense-making is constrained in certain ways, but I have yet to provide an explicit analysis of the role of organizational symbolism in this process.

As indicated in chapter 1, organizational structuring can be conceived in terms of a tripartite relationship between organizational symbolism/behavior, ideology, and deep structure power interests. In this relationship, ideology mediates between vested organizational interests and symbolic structures, providing a mode of rationality through which organizational events can be interpreted. Thus on the one hand, deep structure interests are produced and reproduced through the ideological framing of organizational events and symbolic practices; on the other hand, ideology is itself instantiated in the actual social-symbolic practices of organizations. As such, the vested interests in an organization are reproduced through their articulation in social-symbolic practices, which are in turn framed by the ideologically mediated deep structure of the organization. According to Giddens, structure is simultaneously enabling and constraining, but it is the role of ideology in this duality that grounds the relationship between enablement and constraint.

The following chapter therefore develops the role of organizational symbolism in the production and reproduction of organizational power and ideology. Focusing principally on organizational discourse (and stories in particular) I want to show how organizational communication functions not simply as a means of information transmission, but rather as a material social practice that creates and re-creates an ideologically structured organizational reality. Austin (1962) and his followers (Searle, 1969) recognized speech as action, but they neglected the degree to which the process of communication can operate in the service of power and domination. The dissemination of ideological meaning structures is intrinsically related to communication, and in an organizational context communication can be mobilized to legitimate a particular form of social reality that serves the interests of certain social groups. Organizational discourse functions to articulate contexts of meaning through which members are able to perceive and make sense out of their organization. This process of articulation and sense-making is ideological when certain meaning formations are legitimated to the exclusion of others for no other reason than that it serves the vested interests of a particular group to frame organizational reality in this way. Discourse that instantiates such meaning structures is therefore systematically distorted, excluding the recognition and consideration of alternative frames of reference.

SUMMARY AND CONCLUSION

Despite its slipperiness and intractability ideology proves itself to be a useful and powerful concept in exploring the relationship between communication, social reality, and power. It is essential to our understanding of the communication process that we recognize the degree to which symbolic structures are bound up with the creation of social reality. Such a process is by no means neutral and consensually derived; human discourse is frequently the site of ideological struggle, in which various groups attempt to frame understanding in terms of their particular view of what constitutes appropriate social structure. This struggle to co-opt the process of communication is generally uneven insofar as certain vested interests are better situated economically and politically than others.

It is no accident, for example, that in organizations the managerial interest most frequently characterizes the framing of organizational reality. This is not to say that other forms of organizational reality are impossible, but rather that the managerial interest is powerful enough to control the ways in which other interests perceive what is good, possible, and so forth. Alternative views of reality generally emerge and are perceived as legitimate only when a certain group can structure the communication process in a way that articulates a compelling view of society, the organization, et cetera. Hall's (1985) deconstruction of the term "Black" is just one example of the importance that signification plays in structuring social actors' perception of reality.

In this chapter we have examined various conceptions of the notion of ideology. To summarize, it can best be conceived as the process through which social actors develop a sense of their own subjectivity and place in society; it interpellates individuals materially through its embodiment in the social practices—including communication—that people engage in as a consequence of their positioning institutionally. It is through the meaning inherent in such social practices that people understand and make sense of their social world. Ideology plays an integral part in this sense-making process in that it systematically functions to reify dominant meaning systems, universalize sectional interests, and to obscure inherent contradictions in the structure of social systems. This process can be deconstructed by examining organizational communication specifically from an ideological perspective. This issue is taken up below.

5

IDEOLOGY AND
ORGANIZATIONAL SYMBOLISM

For several years now, organizational theorists and researchers who align themselves with the interpretive paradigm have regarded organizational symbolism as the focal point of their analyses. Unlike the functionalist approach, with its tendency to treat organizational communication in terms of information transmission, interpretivists have concentrated on explaining the role that symbolic structures play in sharing meaning systems among organization members. Organizational discourse has been conceived as intrinsic to the process by which organizational reality emerges over time; symbolic structures not only *disseminate* beliefs, norms, and values among organization members, they are also seen as integral to the constitution of those beliefs, norms, and values. From this perspective, therefore, it could even be argued that the process of communication and the process of organizing are one and the same.

This view of organizational symbolism rejects positivist views of language in which discourse is viewed in representational terms; that is, as simply re-presenting an already existing, empirically objective world. For the interpretivist, on the other hand, language becomes the principal medium through which social reality is produced, maintained, and reproduced. This perspective is derived largely from work in the areas of phenomenology and hermeneutics (Berger & Luckmann, 1971; Deetz, 1973; Gadamer, 1975; Merleau-Ponty, 1962). Gadamer (1975, pp.345ff), for example, sees language as the primary medium of experience. The intrinsic relationship that he posits between language and understanding reflects the notion that experience only comes fully to fruition as it emerges dialogically. In this sense, language does not interpret an already-experienced, understood reality; rather, language is constitutive of understanding.

While Gadamer demonstrates the linguistic nature of understanding, Berger and Luckmann (1971), following Schutz (1967), emphasize the way in which language creates a shared and objectified body of knowledge for a linguistic community:

> Language objectivates . . . shared experiences and makes them available to all within the linguistic community, thus becoming both the basis and the instrument of the collective stock of knowledge. Furthermore, language provides the means for objectifying new experiences, allowing their incorporation into the already existing stock of knowledge, and it is the important means by which the objectivated and objectified sedimentations are transmitted in the tradition of the sedimentation in question. (1971, pp.85–86)

This conception of language—with the close connection between language and social reality—is the one most frequently adopted by those researchers who examine organizations from a cultural perspective. Indeed, Evered (1983, p.26) neatly encapsulates this view when he states:

> The organization has no objective reality (in a positivistic sense), but rather is created daily by the linguistic enactments of its members in the course of their everyday communications between each other; that is, by the way in which members talk, hold discourse, share meanings.

The notion of a daily, linguistic enactment and continuous recreation of organizational reality is a theme that I want to develop extensively in this chapter. I want to make it clear, however, that this symbolic creation of meaning in organizations is not merely subjective or ideational; rather, it is a product of the interaction that emerges between organization members and the symbolic *texts* that they encounter in their day-to-day activities. Simon's (quoted in Weick, 1979, p.1) story of the baseball umpires serves well in reiterating this issue:

> The story goes that three umpires disagreed about the task of calling balls and strikes. The first one said, "I calls them as they is." The second one said, "I calls them as I sees them." The third and cleverest umpire said, "They ain't nothin' till I calls them."

Weick (1979, p.5) is right to point out that the third umpire's assertion encapsulates the way in which people play a key role in creating the organizational environments that they inhabit. However, the issue is actually deeper than even this assertion and, at base (pun intended) is a linguistic, symbolic issue. The third umpire is the cleverest, not only because he recognizes the intersubjective nature of social reality, but also because he realizes that this reality is fundamentally linguistic in nature. Social phenomena are called into being through their "naming" in language—they only reach fruition as meaningful human events when they are interpellated (addressed) by social actors. Thus by calling a "strike" the umpire is not simply labeling an already defined event; he is realizing (making real) the whole system of institutional meanings that are inscribed in the culture of baseball. The umpire's call is the act of linguistically connecting the concept of a "strike" to the wider systems of meaning in which the throwing of a ball and indeed, the whole game of baseball are located.

The same can be said for the nature of discourse in organizations. As Deetz (1982, p.135) states, "The conceptual distinctions in an organization are inscribed in the systems of speaking and writing. Speaking and writing are thus epistemic. They provide the possibility for having a perception in each and every report of one." In this sense organizations can be viewed as made up of an interconnected system of language communities that exist within other, larger language communities. Organization members frequently operate simultaneously within several such communities, whether at a cultural, societal, or organizational level. In each instance the interpretive frame through which the social actor makes sense of the world is delimited in a different way. Each language community draws upon the natural language of the wider culture in different ways to articulate a different sense of social reality.

In organizations, for example, it is not enough merely to suggest that a particular organizational group utilizes a certain lexicon that is more specialized than that of the wider community. Rather, the discourse (written or verbal) of a certain organizational group is the medium through which members' behavior is framed for themselves and others as peculiarly "organizational." The language of organizations thus creates epistemically both the possibilities for, and the boundary conditions of, organizational practice. Organization members therefore create their own sense of reality through the structuring of their discourse.

The main purpose of this chapter is therefore to examine the ways in which organizational discourse shapes reality. I want to adopt the perspective outlined above. But as a further theoretical development it is necessary to explicate the relationship among discourse, ideology, and power. For while the hermeneutic tradition has done much to highlight the symbolic constitution of our sociohistorical world, it has rather neglected "the ways in which the social-historical world is *also* a field of force, a realm of conflict and coercion in which 'meaning' may be a mask for repression" (Thompson, 1984b, p.10). It will therefore be argued that discourse is a product of (and reproduces) the dominant power interests in organizations; it is the principal means by which the dominant ideological meaning structures in an organization perpetuate themselves (Deetz & Mumby, 1985; Mumby, 1987). Organizational discourse operates ideologically insofar as it serves sectional organizational interests by articulating and reifying certain perceptions of organizational reality over and above other possible ways of perceiving the organization. This is possible partly because organization members are both natural language users, and competent users of organizational discourse. The latter, however, often discourages critical thought by virtue of its positional and partial nature. In other words, organizations often selectively appropriate natural language in order to privilege an organizational reality that best serves certain vested interests. Thus when Pateman (1980) speaks of "impossible discourse," he is referring to the way in which language is often structured such that it disenfranchises many people, excluding them from active participation in political discourse. Words such as "democracy," "anarchy," "society," and so forth, are stripped of their conceptual content and become purely referential expressions, existing outside of critical reflection. In Habermas's terms we might say that the political use of such terms is excluded from validity testing and hence is systematically distorted.

In the two previous chapters I have tried to lay out a theory of power and ideology which looks at the way in which meaning formations might be perpetuated that best serve the interests of certain organizational groups. This chapter will address the role of organizational symbolism in this process; that is, how does organizational symbolism get articulated as systematically distorted "impossible discourse?" The relationship between various symbolic forms—stories, myths, metaphors, rituals, etc.—and ideology and power is manifest in the way that behavior becomes inscribed in the day-to-day process of organizing. Symbolic forms can instantiate ideological meaning formations, producing and reproducing individual and collective organizational consciousness. Discourse thus positions the social actor to perceive and respond to the world in a particular way. Such positioning involves more than simply holding sets of beliefs and attitudes; it constitutes the individual's very existence as a *social* actor.

Following social theorists such as Giddens (1979, 1981, 1984), Thompson (1983a, b, 1984a, b), and Habermas (1975, 1979, 1984), I conceive of communication as the principal medium through which relations of domination are produced and reproduced. Language is ideological to the extent that it is systematically distorted (Habermas, 1975, 1979). In organizations this systematic distortion of communication involves the legitimation and maintenance of one form of organizational reality at the expense of other forms of reality. As Thompson (1984b, p.132) states, "different groups have differing capacities to make a meaning stick." In order to make a particular meaning system "stick," a certain organizational group (or coalition of groups) must not only control the material and economic resources of an organization. Perhaps even more importantly, they must control the systems of signification in the organization; that is, the process by which meaning becomes "attached" to organizational practices.

Examining organizational communication as ideological provides insight into the ways in which symbolic structures shape organizational reality in nonarbitrary ways. Dominant power interests are served when a structured, coherent, acceptable vision of organizational reality is articulated, and oppositional views are systematically excluded. Organizational reality often *appears* to be derived consensually by virtue of the ideological masking of contradictions and oppositional voices. This does not mean that alternative views of reality cannot be articulated, but rather that oppositional groups usually have less of an ability to make meanings "stick." It is through the process of structuration that discourse becomes constitutive of organizational reality, and because managerial interests usually control the structuration process they thereby control what is regarded as acceptable and meaningful organizational practice.

To date, only a handful of organizational theorists have even begun to study the relationship among language, ideology, and power in organizations. Martin and Powers (1983, p.97), for example, recognize that "organizational stories legitimate power relations within the organization," but they characterize this legitimation process in terms of the way that stories disseminate *information* to organization members. As I discussed in chapter 1, such a conception of organizational symbolism/communication does not go far enough in focusing on the *constitutive* power of organizational communication. Martin and Powers's conception of language is largely representational, and thus neglects the degree to which organizational language *constitutes* organizational consciousness.

Other theorists, however, have begun to recognize the necessity of studying the intrinsic link between organizational symbolism and the power-based creation of forms of social reality. Conrad (1983), for example, shows how organizational conflict can be analyzed in terms of the relationship between deep structure power and surface structure symbolic forms. Symbols such as rituals, rites, and metaphors both manifest and embody the underlying deep structure power relations, the latter being "preconscious, deeply held assumptions about what are and what are not appropriate actions in a particular organization" (Conrad, 1983, p.186). Despite this important connection, Conrad does not provide any explanation of the *ways* in which symbols such as myth and metaphor help to structure and restructure continuously the underlying power relations in an organization.

In an excellent article, however, Rosen (1985) does just this. Adopting an ethnographic approach, Rosen takes "social drama" as his unit of analysis in explicating the way in which a specific organizational ritual—an annual company breakfast—serves to reaffirm the underlying and asymmetrical power relations of the organization. He is able to show that specific symbols and rhetorical techniques are manipulated to reproduce the existing social order.

> Though the manifestations of contradiction—conflict through dissent and struggle—are not foreign to the bureaucratic terrain, recreation of the power order inherent to the form is nevertheless primary. Recreation is largely accomplished through manipulation of the symbolic order, reimpregnating the bureaucratic consciousness with meaning sufficient to largely recreate the lived order. In the economic realm this is one of asymetrical [sic] social group control and domination. (Rosen, 1985, p.32)

The strength of Rosen's analysis lies in his recognition that culture is not simply a configuration of consensually produced meanings, but rather that it is at least partly created by those vested interests that are able to make certain meanings "stick" to organizational practices and processes. Thus Rosen views culture as "communicated through symbols, each standing ambiguously for a multiplicity of meanings. It is this ambiguity which enables a system of symbols to maintain the facade of order, the perception of rational process" (1985, pp.32–33). Ambiguity is an essential element in the symbolic construction of systems of power, because it is through this ambiguity that dominant interests can strategically manipulate the way in which meaning systems are structured (Eisenberg, 1984).

This point is similar to one made by Thompson (1984b) in his discussion of the relationship between language and ideology. Thompson claims that to interpret discourse as ideology one must "*construct* a meaning which unfolds the referential dimension of discourse, which specifies the multiple referents and shows how their entanglement serves to sustain relations of domination" (1984b, p.138). Thompson adapts Ricoeur's notion of the "split reference" to illustrate how discourse can explicitly refer to one thing while simultaneously referring implicitly to something else. It can be argued that the use of such multiple referents creates a complex signification system within which the received interpretation becomes "up for grabs." In fact, the "legitimate" interpretation of these tangled systems of referents is usually the one created by the dominant interest group(s).

Perhaps an example will help to illustrate this point. Recall the organizational success story related in chapter 1, telling the tale of the rapid rise to fame and fortune of the Proctor and Gamble executive. At an explicit level this story recounts the success of a specific individual, providing a quasi-historical narrative of events. Implicitly, the story has several referents. For example, one prominent theme is "the ordinary guy who makes good." That is, the story not only recounts the success of a single individual, but also implies that such success is possible for anyone who is prepared to work hard. In essence, the story embodies the American-Protestant work ethic, in which success is based purely on the ability of the individual to work hard and overcome obstacles. Dupree is thus singled out as the personification of all that is good and positive about the U.S. capitalist system of free enterprise, which allows those with talent and resourcefulness to rise to the top of the pile.

But how does the story operate ideologically; that is, how does it reproduce meaning systems that sustain asymmetrical relations of domination? I would argue that stories such as this (and there are many that are very similar in structure and content) function ideologically by presenting a view of the world that supports dominant, corporate interests and simultaneously obscures contradictions in the capitalist system. For example, the Dupree story implicitly glorifies the capitalist enterprise as the system which best supports individual motivation and success. However, for every Dupree there are countless people who are victimized by a system in which a tiny minority of the population owns the vast majority of the wealth. The story clearly articulates a managerial perspective in that it presents a *managerial* definition of what is, what is good, and what is possible; what it *hides* is a vision of the extent to which many people are systematically denied access to the opportunities that the capitalist enterprise offers. The story thus helps to produce a reified organizational reality that sustains managerial interests and simultaneously socializes other organization members into this meaning system. Economic relations of domination are thus maintained symbolically.

The above analysis is not intended to be an exhaustive interpretation (no construction of a story's meaning *can* be exhaustive); rather, it is used to indicate the importance of examining "the ways in which ideology is actually manifested in the conceptions and expressions of everyday life" (Thompson, 1983b, p.212). The study of ideology cannot be separated from the study of the various forms in which discourse manifests itself in institutions. When discourse is institutionalized it becomes infused with forms of power; it is this infusion of power which maintains relations of domination between different interest groups.

The rest of this chapter will therefore examine the relationship between discourse and ideology. This does not involve a study of the intrinsically ideological nature of language, but rather demands an examination of the ways in which meaning can be utilized to create a social reality that privileges the interests of certain groups over others. Representational views of language are unable to make this critical turn because of their concern for a demonstrating a correspondence between language and some objective reality. This position negates the possibility that language *evokes* a particular reality rather than being a simple expression of it. Language does not simply inform; it creates the very possibility for the creation of meaning environments. While the referential aspect of language is clearly important, an adequate theory of language and meaning must explicitly consider the relationship among language, meaning, and power. Language is an instrument of power as well as an instrument of knowledge and communication.

As the organizational culture literature has clearly shown, organizational symbolism takes many varied forms, including stories, myths, metaphors, rituals, logos, and so forth. Each symbolic form has the potential to function ideologically to sustain certain meaning systems and power structures, and thus to reproduce relations of domination. However, I am particularly interested in the role of organizational narratives in this process (Mumby, 1987). Narratives deserve attention, both because of the pervasive and continuing influence of storytelling on our culture, and because narrative is an especially powerful vehicle for the dissemination of ideological meaning formations. As Thompson (1984b, p.11) states:

> ideology, in so far as it seeks to sustain relations of domination by representing them as "legitimate," tends to assume a narrative form. Stories are told which justify the exercise of power by those who possess it, situating these individuals within a tissue of tales that recapitulate the past and anticipate the future.

The next section will therefore directly examine narrative in its role as an organizational symbolic form. Organizational stories are a prominent feature of research from the cultural perspective. The section therefore begins by examining and critiquing the dominant approach to storytelling, and then presents an alternative perspective, based on the theory of language and ideology presented above.

THE IDEOLOGICAL FUNCTION OF ORGANIZATIONAL NARRATIVES

Adopting a largely managerial orientation, Wilkins (1983b) defines organizational stories as an important area of study insofar as they are

"important indicators of the values participants share, the social pre-
scriptions concerning how things are to be done, and the consequences
of compliance or deviance . . . " (p. 82). In this context, stories are
viewed as an important source of information for workers and management alike, showing the former how to participate successfully in
organizational life, and providing the latter with important indicators of
organizational climate. Stories act as "cognitive shortcuts" for organization members, allowing them to internalize rapidly the implicit rule
system that guides organizational behavior; stories function to exemplify and encapsulate the organization's tacit value system.

Organizational theorists have therefore traditionally emphasized the
role of organizational stories as overt expressions of underlying codes of
conduct. As such, stories are frequently explicated in terms of their
organizational *functions*, such as description, energy control, and system
maintenance (Dandridge et al., 1980), and facilitation of recall, generation of belief, and encouragement of commitment (Martin et al., 1983;
Martin & Powers, 1983; Wilkins, 1983b). For example, recall of important organizational information is more complete when such information has been related to members in story form rather than as a set of
statistics. Stories are regarded as more salient sources of information,
and are thus considered more effective in the process of socializing
organization members.

There are two main problems with this perspective on organizational
narrative. First, as I have already indicated, storytelling does more than
act as an information source that fulfills several different organizational
functions. Discourse in general, and storytelling in particular, provides
a medium for understanding which plays a constitutive role in the
creation of organizational reality. Second, stories are generally conceived as a form of organizational enrichment, enabling members to
become more fully encultured into the complex meaning structures of
the organization. In this context, stories are seen as "equivocality
reducing mechanisms" (Kreps, 1986; Weick, 1979) which enable organization members to make sense more easily out of initially ambiguous
patterns of behavior, and to provide a collective sense of organizational
culture. Organizations are viewed as functioning optimally when there
is a shared sense of values and goals, and stories help to expedite this
process. Smircich (1983a) exemplifies this approach when she states:

> the set of meanings that evolves gives a group its own ethos, or distinctive
> character, which is expressed in terms of belief (ideology), activity (norms
> and rituals), language and other symbolic forms through which organiza-
> tion members both create and sustain their view of the world and image of
> themselves in the world.

I would argue that this is only part of the role of organizational symbolism; equally important is its role in the process of cultural *de*formation. Cultural deformation refers to the process whereby an organization's culture is systematically distorted such that symbolic practices maintain and reproduce certain relations of dependence and domination. Organization members come to accept uncritically the process of sense-making and meaning formation as articulated by dominant interests. The notion of cultural deformation encapsulates the relationship between ideology and organizational symbolism: Organizational symbols not only create a sheared reality, they can also act to reify and make "natural" the extant political conditions in the organization, serving to promote the social reality that favors dominant interests, and limiting the conceptions of alternative meaning systems. Symbolic structures, such as narratives, can serve the dominant ideology by interpellating subjects and qualifying them for certain kinds of participation in organizational life. Such participation may involve the acceptance of and commitment to interests that serve only a small number of organization members—those in positions of power.

An excellent example of the way in which symbolic action can produce cultural deformation appeared in a recent issue of the *Chronicle of Higher Education*. A university secretary complains about the way that higher education is built on a type of caste system which sharply differentiates faculty members and non-teaching staff:

> A key feature of any caste system is that those above behave as if those below were non-people. In academe, secretaries are thought not to share the same level of humanity as faculty members. For example, for a time my desk was in a foyer leading to the faculty offices. The faculty members would discuss private details of their students' performances and qualifications, or say what they thought of their colleagues, within my hearing. It was as though they assumed I could not comprehend their conversation, or perhaps they thought of me as a piece of furniture. Whatever the case, I was treated as a non-person, forced to feign deafness to protect their indiscretions. (Gillett, 1987)

What is most extraordinary about this example is the way that a particular interest group in an organization—the secretarial staff—is interpellated (addressed) by *not* being addressed. Their sense of organizational subjectivity is produced and reproduced through their systematic exclusion from participation at certain levels in the symbolic culture of the organization. In this context, the structure and pattern of organizational discourse serves to reaffirm and reproduce existing relations of domination by symbolically constituting legitimate and nonlegitimate organizational practices. One can argue, therefore, that such patterning of discourse does not merely reflect an already existing ideological and socioeconomic structure, but rather serves to produce and reproduce continuously this structure. Organizational discourse is thus both the medium and product of organizational structure.[1]

It is in this context that we need to examine the role of organizational narrative. Riley (1983), for example, examines the political functioning of organizational stories by analyzing Dandridge et al.'s classification in terms of Giddens's theory of structuration. Symbol systems are viewed as both the product of the rules and resources that individuals draw upon to engage in meaningful interaction, as well as the medium through which such rules and resources are reproduced. Organizational symbolism is thus seen as the instantiation of organizational structure, as well as the vehicle of its reproduction or transformation. To paraphrase Giddens (1979), an analysis of organizational narrative requires an explication of the ways in which signification and legitimation are connected in order to favor the interests of dominant groups. Better than any other symbolic structure, narrative is able to provide the crucial connection between signification and legitimation. It is the special quality of narrative *structure* (and its relationship to ideology and domination) that will be examined next.

Narrative Politics

Traditionally, storytelling has been regarded as an apolitical activity unless the story being told is explicitly political in content. Several theorists, however, have argued that stories are narrative devices which cannot be viewed independently of the ideological meaning formations and relations of domination within which they are communicated (Culler, 1982; Jameson, 1981; Mumby, 1987; Nakagawa, 1983, 1987). Stories are produced by and reproduce these relations, helping to position subjects within the historical and institutional context of the material conditions of existence. An interpretation of organizational stories that focuses on their ideological functions must explicitly address this positioning process.

Such is the task of what has become known as deconstruction; that is, the attempt to provide a political reading of narrative that uncovers its

---

[1] This example is particularly germane to my own academic institution, which recently experienced a strike by clerical and maintenance staff. An especially interesting feature of this strike was that it was viewed by the strikers as not simply an attempt to gain better economic benefits, but more importantly as a struggle for greater recognition and respect in the university community. The symbolic value of the strike action could therefore be viewed as just as important as its economic value.

"strategies of containment" (Jameson, 1981, p.53). Deconstruction examines the way that forms of discourse such as narrative produce ideological closure; discourse is examined in terms of its relationship to institutional relations of domination. Jameson's "strategies of containment" refers to the process by which narratives impose a sense of closure on the realities which they construct, bringing to the fore certain experiences of the world and hiding others. Narrative can place a sense of determinacy on the social actor's world, simultaneously obscuring ways in which reality is *over*determined; that is, structured by the underlying relations of power that place *material* limitations on how social reality is framed.

For example, if we return to the case cited above of the secretary who felt excluded from the collegial system in which she worked, we can see that the reality that she experiences is a product not simply of the symbolic environment in which she works, but also of the structural and economic system that she inhabits. First, secretaries usually work in situations where everyone has access to the space that they inhabit; they frequently do not have their own offices, and if they do, people feel free to enter and leave as they please. This is not a trivial issue in terms of relations of power and domination, because it places the secretary *structurally* in a certain relationship to other classes of office personnel. The type of symbolic environment that the secretary inhabits is at least partly determined by this structuring process. All groups have access to the secretary, but she (few men occupy secretarial positions)[2] is limited in her access to other groups. As such, the kind of discourse that takes place around her is overdetermined by the structure of her work environment. Second, the secretary's symbolic environment is partly a product of her socioeconomic status. Most secretaries can be classified as "pink collar" labor; that is, low-paid females who are employed in clerical and service positions. Such positions may not be treated contemptuously in any conscious way by academics (the great majority of whom are men, despite affirmative action programs), but the difference in socioeconomic rank between professors and secretaries is such that certain discursive practices inevitably reaffirm and reproduce this status difference. Academia defines secretarial workers as less valuable (both economically and socially) than their scholar-colleagues, and this socioeconomic relationship is continually reproduced at a discursive

---

[2] A local corporation has a female vice-president who employs a male personal secretary. The secretary frequently accompanies her when she interviews job candidates, although the candidate is not initially aware who is the vice-president and who is the secretary. Any candidate who automatically assumes that the male is the vice-president is excluded from consideration for the position.

level. Again, Gillett (1987) provides an excellent example of this discursive structuration process:

> Last winter the chancellor inadvertently provided a telling commentary on
> the status of staff members. During a particularly severe snowstorm he
> announced that students and faculty members should not attempt to get
> to the university but that staff members should report as usual. His voice
> echoed all day on the radio, saying in effect that, unlike us, the faculty
> members were too valuable to risk their lives. To show their upper-caste
> status, faculty members exhibit a child-like naivete about the bureaucracy
> in which they work. "Order this form for me," one of them will say to me.
> "You understand the purchasing system better than I do." Or, "Fill out
> this travel request, and I'll sign it." Ignorance of the administrative
> structure of the university, especially personnel policies, is an unfortunate
> characteristic of many academics. They expect a secretary, who may be
> classified as a clerk or typist, to function also as an administrative assistant
> or travel agent, yet they seldom try (much less fight) to get her position
> upgraded to reflect her real duties.

Once the power relations in an organization are structured in a
particular way, discursive practices enable the continued reproduction
of this structure. In the above example, discourse is both
overdetermined by, and reproduces, the material conditions of existence, in this case involving issues of sex, socioeconomic status, and
organizational structure.

The production and reproduction of women's domination in organizations is thus achieved through a process of incorporation and omission. Women in organizations are interpellated in a way which simultaneously identifies them and makes them invisible. They are thus
identified as secretaries, clerks, housewives, sex objects, and so on,
while at the same time made invisible as decision makers, rational
thinkers, managers, etc. As Meissner (1986, p.53) points out, it is this
continual omission which reproduces the domination of men over
women in organizations, insofar as visibility is a condition for influence.
In a real sense, the primary form of visibility attributed to women in
organizations is as sex objects, while the issue of competence is
relegated to a secondary concern.

Significantly, apparent ruptures or anomalies in these relations of
domination are frequently repaired through their reinterpretation and
reincorporation into the dominant meaning system. For example, Finder
(1987) relates how he once took a job as a secretary in a large bank so that
he could earn a steady income while trying to "make it" as a writer. His
story clearly documents how his fellow workers were unable to accept
that *he* was "just a secretary:"

An executive from another floor came up to my desk and said, "The girl's on leave?" He thought I was a management trainee helping out the beleaguered clerical staff. I told him that, no, I was the new secretary, but he just laughed, certain I was kidding.

The other secretaries on the floor were plainly disbelieving. "So what do you do?" asked one of the older women, after coffee break one day. "What do you mean?" I said. "I'm a secretary." She laughed. "Are you a student?" "No, actually I've graduated."

"Come on," she said, "this stuff is too boring for you." She paused, then added, "Honey, I've got to do this. You don't have to. You'll be moving into management. Guys aren't secretaries."

This story is an excellent example of the degree to which dominant ideologies are produced and reproduced, even in the face of apparent challenges to the accepted structure of social reality. In this case, both those in power (the executive) *and* those who are relatively powerless (the other secretaries) do their best to fit anomalous behavior into the dominant ideological framework. Of course, it is in the best interests of the executive to refuse to recognize the legitimacy of a male secretary, insofar as it undermines the male domination of the corporate world, but the fact that the other secretaries react similarly indicates the degree to which subordinate groups can accept and actively support the dominant power structure. One can imagine how the story of "the male secretary" might be told and retold throughout this organization long after Finder had left, serving to reaffirm and reproduce continually the ideological meaning system and material structure that maintains male-female differences in the corporate setting.[3]

Narratives are therefore not generated in a socioeconomic vacuum, but are both produced by and reproduce the material conditions generated by the political and economic structure of a social system. Narrative aids in the reproduction of these material conditions by articulating an internally coherent sense of itself and the world that it describes. Stories punctuate and sequence events in such a way as to privilege a certain interpretation of the world. They impose an order on reality that obscures the extent to which this reality is motivated by underlying group interests. Thus it is in the vested interests of the male-dominated managerial elite that the idea of a male secretary is

---

[3] This seems particularly true in the banking profession, which is well known for its conservative employment practices that discriminate against the placement of women in executive positions.

perceived as outside of the realm of acceptable "reality" for most organization members. In this way the status quo is maintained.

The task of a deconstructive analysis of the ideological structure of narrative is thus to challenge the perceptual closure that narrative often presents; the task is to show that narrative and the politics of experience are inextricably linked. The goal of such an analysis, however, is not the privileging of a *different* set of interests, but rather "the progressive liberation of life experience from systems and forms of domination" (Deetz, 1984, p.62). Deconstruction provides an explicitly political reading of narrative which attempts to overcome a naive acceptance of stories as politically neutral and independent from the socioeconomic structure in which they are articulated. As such, the locus of investigation for deconstruction is not simply the narrative-text as human artifact, but also "the interpretations through which we attempt to confront and appropriate it" (Jameson, 1981: 9–10). Any narrative is thus always pre-interpreted to the extent that it is located within a certain political and socioeconomic structure, and thus is subject to appropriation by the vested interests that make up that structure. As Thompson (1984b, p.133) states, "To undertake an analysis of discourse is to produce an interpretation of an interpretation, to re-interpret a pre-interpreted domain."

The relationship between the structure of narrative and the process of interpretation is important insofar as it is at this interface that meaning emerges. Stories interpellate the reader-listener, articulating a "fit" between the narrative and the subject's world-as-experienced. This fit is not perfect, however, otherwise the interpellated subject would be completely subjugated to the meaning constructed by the narrative. As Nakagawa (1983) points out, this margin of difference between story and reader-listener translates into a tension between what is highlighted (present) and what is hidden (absent). It is this difference that a political reading of narrative exploits, seeking to create a disjuncture between the privileged (ideological) interpretation and that constructed by the reader-listener. For example, Gillett's chronicling of the injustices that she experiences as a secretary is in itself testament to the extent to which she is able to reinterpret the structure of discourse within which she is enmeshed. She is able to recognize it for what it is; not simply a politically neutral set of discursive practices, but rather a signification system that privileges certain meaning formations and hence interests over others.

All discourse does not, therefore, simply reproduce the dominant ideological meaning system in which it is situated. Although there is no discursive practice outside of ideology "it does not follow that because all practices are *in* ideology, or inscribed by ideology, all practices are *nothing but* ideology" (Hall, 1985, p.103). Discourse is also potentially transformative and constructive in the sense that it can create a disjuncture between its interpretation and the world-as-experienced. Discourse can thus function simultaneously as a form of ideological domination and as a means of enablement, as a vehicle through which social actors can transform the way in which they conceive of the social structure that they inhabit.

This process of interpretation and appropriation of meaning of narrative by the subject can be closely linked to the actual structure of narrative. White (1980, p.10) goes so far as to claim that we have developed "a notion of reality in which 'the true' is identified with 'the real' only insofar as it can be shown to possess the character of narrativity." A story's claim to represent reality, White argues, is tied up with the ability of the narrative structure to display a coherence, fullness and sense of closure "that is and can only be imaginary" (1980, p.27). Narrative speaks to us out of a particular morality that seeks to legitimate the authority of the social system out of which it arises.

Narrative, then, can be distinguished from other forms of discourse by virtue of the moral imperative that it incorporates. By their very structure, stories lead us to particular conclusions about the nature of the world; in a very basic sense, they provide us with a beginning, a middle and an end (i.e., a plot), and hence provide a sense of a complete and fully articulated reality. White states this issue in the following manner:

> The historical narrative . . . reveals to us a world that is putatively "finished," done with, over, and yet not dissolved, not falling apart. . . . Insofar as historical stories can be completed, can be given narrative closure, can be shown to have had a *plot* all along, they give to reality the odor of the *ideal*. . . . The demand for closure in the historical story is a demand, I suggest, for moral meaning, a demand that sequences of real events be assessed as to their significance as elements of a *moral* drama.(1980,p.24)

Although White's concern is with the role of narrative in the historical representation of reality, his position can be applied equally well to stories recounted in an organizational context. Most organizational stories do, after all, recount events that have occurred in the organization's history, and such narratives help to establish an organization's culture by legitimating and giving authority to a particular sociopolitical structure and its attendant mores and values. Thus "Where, in any account of reality, narrativity is present, we can be sure that morality or a moralizing impulse is present too" (White, 1980, p.24).

The connection between narrative and morality can be explained in terms of a reciprocal relationship between the narrative force of a story and its moral function. On the one hand, the "moralizing impulse" of a story is sharply focused by its narrative structure. For example, many organizational stories focus on rule violations by members, expressed in terms of a confrontation between two protagonists, usually of different corporate status. The sequencing of events—identification of protagonists, rule violation, admonition, repair behavior—serves to punctuate the story in such a way that the reader-listener is predisposed toward a certain interpretation of the story's moral, i.e., that organizational rules must be obeyed. At the same time, the moral of the story acts as a unifying principle that gives impetus to the flow of the narrative. Tellers of the story relate it and people listen to the telling, not simply because of the information that is provided. Rather, the main appeal of the story lies in its ability to produce a cathartic effect in both speaker and audience. Narrative structure produces a sense of anticipation of a particular denouement, or resolution, the disclosure of which elicits an affective response by the audience.

That information transmission is not the raison d'étre of storytelling is evidenced by the fact that stories are not only related over and over, but also that they can be told more than once to the same audience. In this context stories function as transmitters of culture, creating a sense of community and setting a particular group, organization, or sub-culture apart from the rest of the social system. In this sense, the continual reproduction of stories serves to strengthen the identity that members feel with their organization, even in a situation where a particular story has been heard many times before. Slaughter (1985, p.117), following Walter Benjamin, describes the paradigm of storytelling in the oral tradition in terms of "the teller who is often imagined as someone who has come from afar, and the listener, who is the villager, often the tiller of the soil." The teller's role is one of relating experience that he or she has gained, and which contributes to the lore and traditions of the listener's culture:

> What legitimizes and validates this experience is the authority of the living teller, or the one who told him, or the one who told him. Tales told face-to-face or mouth-to-mouth are tales told person-to-person or man-to-man. We accept them as we accept (the word of) the man himself. We share the company of the storyteller and we establish with him the emotional bond given in face-to-face encounters. (Slaughter, 1985, p.117)

Much of the process of relating group experience and intelligence takes place in the form of ritual. The ritualistic quality of narrative is important not so much for its information value, but rather for the role that it plays in instantiating and legitimating a particular set of morals and values. The force of an organizational story thus depends, at least in part, on its ability to evoke and encapsulate simultaneously the value system that implicitly underlies organizational practices. While *what* the story might say is plainly important, the way in which it is structured is more central for its role in the socialization of organization members. The following story, for example, has an archetypical narrative structure that makes it suitable for telling in many organizational contexts:

> everyone was required to sign in in the morning. Everyone. Even Charles signed in. One day, when Revlon was in the process of moving from 666 Fifth Avenue up to the General Motors Building, in 1969, Charles sauntered in and began to look over the sign-in sheet. The receptionist, who was new, says "I'm sorry, sir, you can't do that." Charles says, "Yes I can." "No sir," she says, "I have strict orders that no one is to remove the list; you'll have to put it back." This goes back and forth for a while with the receptionist being very courteous, as all Revlon receptionists are, and finally Charles says, "Do you know who I am?" And she says, "No, sir, I don't." "Well, when you pick up your final paycheck this afternoon, ask 'em to tell ya." (Martin et al., 1983, p.441)

This story follows a well-established formula, involving a confrontation between two protagonists who come from different ends of the corporate hierarchy. In this variation, the low-status employee is a neophyte who is unaware of the status of the person that she is confronting. The impetus of the narrative is derived from the anticipation that it creates regarding the story's outcome: How will the boss react? Will the secretary be reprimanded, fired, or complimented for doing her job? Whatever the resolution, the story addresses listeners in a powerful way, providing them with a strong sense of appropriate and inappropriate organizational practice. The story is significant and meaningful insofar as members identify it as exemplifying typical organizational practice. For members who are already socialized it provides an affirmation and reminder of "how things are done"; for new members it serves the function of implicitly providing rules of conduct.

Whether such a story has any basis in truth is really irrelevant: The confrontation between Revson and a "green" secretary may well have occurred as described, but even if the story is apocryphal it has little effect on its discursive power. Such power is derived in part from the fact that stories have the ability to evoke simultaneously important themes and issues, while closing themselves off from validity testing (Witten, 1986).

In Habermas's terms, it might be said that the implicit claims to truth made by each discursive act are not readily redeemable in the case of narrative. As Slaughter indicates above, the teller of a story and the story itself generate a certain authority and legitimacy by virtue of the bond that is established between teller and listener. The telling of a story demands suspension of disbelief; it demands that we, as listeners, are drawn into it and become psychologically and emotionally involved, just as we would if watching a play or reading a novel. In such a context we do not distance ourselves to reflect upon the veracity of the story, but allow ourselves to become involved in its narrative structure and development. The only evaluations of the story that we are likely to make relate to the quality of its telling, and its internal consistency. As Witten (1986) further points out, the rules of storytelling are different from those of ordinary conversation in that there is no turn-taking, and therefore little chance to engage in the normal dialectic of claim and counterclaim. When someone tells a story we are unlikely to challenge the truth of specific points, even if we recognize them to be false. We convey an authorial status on storytellers which makes them exempt from the usual conversational rigor for adherence to truth. In Goffman's (1959) terms, one could say that teller and listener engage in "defensive" and "protective" practices respectively. In other words, both speaker and listener work to maintain the form of self-presentation that the speaker projects. Exposure of a speaker's form of self-presentation as false (for example, suggesting that a story told is untrue) causes social embarrassment for all involved in the interaction. We thus presume truth in a story, not simply because we don't believe that the teller would lie to us, but because it is in our own best interests to do so. After all, given the nature of narrative, it is very likely that we will tell the same story to someone else, complete with our own personal embellishments, and we expect the same protection for our own storytelling as we would give to others.

Attempts to view organizational narratives as reflections of organizational practice—as ways of disseminating organizational information—thus oversimplify the relationship between narrative and organizational reality. The relationship between organizational stories and the reality that they depict cannot be formulated in purely representational terms. Narrative does not function mimetically, mirroring organizational behavior, but rather is tropical in nature:

> Tropic is the shadow from which all realistic discourse tries to flee. This flight, however, is futile; for tropics is the process by which all discourse *constitutes* the objects which it pretends only to describe realistically and to analyze objectively. . . . Discourse, in a word, is quintessentially a

mediative enterprise. As such, it is both interpretive and preinterpretive; it is always as much *about* the nature of interpretation itself as it is *about* the subject matter which is the manifest occasion of its own elaboration. (White, 1978, pp.2–4)

Organization members therefore do not experience organizational reality directly, but as mediated through its discursive practices, particularly through the articulation of narrative discourse. Fisher (1984, 1985) has even argued that narration is not simply one mode of discourse, but rather provides a paradigm for conceptualizing the communication process; humans, in effect, can be regarded as *homo narrans*. People interact with one another largely by relating events and experiences, whether this be in an organizational, familial, or peer group context. The meanings that people share are produced and reproduced largely through narration.

In the case of organizational narrative, my principal concern is with examining the way in which stories told in organizations function ideologically to maintain and reproduce the existing relations of domination. White's statement above that discourse "pretends only to describe realistically" provides a starting point for the interpretation of ideology as mediated discursively. Organizational stories can function ideologically by mediating "realistically" between organization members and their perception of the organization, constructing a reality that serves the interests of only a handful of organization members. Stories thus function by making truth claims that are difficult to challenge, and which claim to represent an objectively existing reality.

The interpretation of narrative-as-ideology must therefore explicate the role of this particular discursive practice as a "strategy of containment" (Jameson, 1981). That is, one must examine the way in which narrative positions social actors in a certain fashion in relation to the social structures that they inhabit. In organizational cultures, such strategies of containment involve the articulation of prescribed and proscribed organizational practices, and the interpellation of members such that they develop an organizational consciousness that "fits" with the existing power relations within the organization. These power relations are reproduced discursively insofar as narrative strives for closure by portraying events as essentially moral dramas—dramas in which a particular set of values are given legitimacy and authority. Stories, in this sense, embody the *ideal* of the political reality that they portray.

In the next section I provide an interpretation of the ideological functioning of a specific organizational story. This analysis is not in any way intended to be exhaustive, but rather demonstrates one way in which one might apply the theoretical model that has been laid out above.

Organizational Narrative as Ideology: An Application

The main problem that one faces in providing an interpretation of a body of discourse—whether written or oral, poetry or prose—is the question of validity. That is, to what extent can one claim that a particular interpretation is more "accurate," "correct," or "appropriate" than any other interpretation? I do not want to engage in an extensive treatise on interpretation theory at this point (that is not the purpose of this analysis); however, I do want to distance myself from positions that might argue for an "objective" or "verifiable" process of interpretation. As Ricoeur (1976) among others has shown us, the process of interpretation involves recognizing the "surplus of meaning" that discourse embodies. No single interpretation can exhaust the multiplicity of meanings that a text might yield. Neither appeals to authorial intent, nor exploration of the social conditions in which a text was produced allows us privileged insight into a text's "ultimate" meaning. The process of interpretation is, finally, a creative act in which the interpreter constructs and projects a possible meaning for a text.

The multiplicity of meanings that one might potentially construct from a text does not mean, however, that the interpretive process is completely relativistic and subjective. Interpreting a text is not an entirely pluralistic enterprise in which every interpretation, however idiosyncratic or superficial, is considered to be equally worthy of consideration. Such a position ignores the need for a careful, theory-based construction of a means of analysis. Just as we would not readily accept as legitimate a layperson's judgment of another's psychological condition, so should we be equally wary of textual analyses that are not firmly grounded conceptually and theoretically.

The critique of ideology is especially tricky in that, by definition, the articulation of an ideological meaning system in discourse is not articulated *as* ideology. Ideology, by its very nature, is that which enables relations of domination to be maintained, not only by those who dominate, but also by those who are dominated. As we have seen already, however, the ideological domination of one group by another is never complete. All groups, however repressed, are able to engage in some degree of discursive penetration and hence critique the structures of domination in which they live. Narrative, as such, does not necessarily just reproduce the dominant ideological meaning system within which it is located. Hall (1985, p.103) indicates that although there is no social practice outside of ideology, this does not mean that all practices—

whether discursive or otherwise—are completely subjugated to the ideological meaning structures within which they are located. Discourse may be reinterpreted such that it critiques the relations of domination within which it is inscribed.

The interpretation of the ideological structure of narrative thus involves explicating the connection between the relations of domination in which the narrative takes place, and the structure of meaning that the narrative articulates. Such an interpretation does not involve adopting a position outside of ideology, but rather of distancing oneself from the structures of meaning such that a critical perspective can be adopted. This does not mean that one presents a nonideological reading of a narrative structure, but rather that the interpretation presented is emancipatory in Habermas's sense, allowing for critical self-reflection on the part of those interpellated by the system of signification analyzed. Such an analysis, of course, is fraught with difficulties. Thompson points out:

> by the objectification obtained through distanciation, it is limited by the relation of belonging which is the counterpart of distanciation. The critique of ideology is necessarily partial, fragmentary, incomplete. It can never be conducted from a position outside of the history and the society to which we belong. The critique of ideology is only a moment—albeit an important moment—in the endless hermeneutical task of renewing and appraising our social-historical heritage. (1984b, p.188)

No privileged reading of discourse (in the sense of laying claim to Truth) is therefore possible, or even desirable. However, analyzing discourse in terms of its ideological function serves to expand the process of interpretation by explicating the relationship between discourse and the relations of domination which it helps to maintain. The critique of discourse in the service of ideology necessarily involves the critique of domination.

Pragmatically speaking, therefore, what form might the interpretation of ideology take? Thompson (1984b) suggests that the analysis of ideology involves three stages. The first stage involves *social analysis*, in which one examines the social-historical conditions under which forms of domination are created. Such an analysis can be conducted at the level of: (a) action, in which specific interaction situations are examined; (b) institutions, in which certain definable social structures (ATT, IBM, etc.) are examined in terms of the way they both generate and constrain action; and (c) structural elements that structurate institutions; for example, in most U.S. corporations it is the relationship between wage-labor and capital that specifies the conditions under which specific institutions are maintained and reproduced. The second stage requires that one moves to the level of *discursive analysis*. Thompson (1984b, p.136) maintains that "The forms of discourse which express ideology must be viewed . . . as *linguistic constructions which display an articulated structure*." As such, discourse must be analyzed in terms of the role that it plays in articulating ideology. Thompson suggests that the articulated structure of discourse can be examined at the levels of narrative, argumentative structure, and syntactic structure. The third stage in the analysis of ideology is *interpretation*. This stage allows for "a creative construction of meaning" (1984b, p.137), and recognizes that, however formal and systematic one's method of analysis might be, it is finally up to the researcher to propose "a possible meaning which is always risky and open to dispute" (1984b, p.137). It is at this point that one explores the potential of discourse to "say something about something," to configure a multiplicity of meanings together in a single image, phrase, or story. It is this ability of discourse to invoke multiple referents, and to tangle them together in a complex web of meaning that enables discursive practices to operate ideologically and hence to sustain relations of domination.

Thompson suggests that the above analytic model not be seen as involving discrete and distinct methodological stages, but rather that each stage be seen as a different theme of analysis in the overall process of interpretation. In the remainder of this chapter I want to examine a specific organizational story, examining it in terms of the role that it might play in the discursive reproduction of relations of domination. In providing the analysis, I will utilize both the functions of ideology as laid out by Giddens (1979) and the analytic stages suggested by Thompson.

Martin et al. (1983, pp.439–440) document a story in which a female supervisor at IBM challenges Thomas Watson, Jr., the chairman of the board. The story is related as follows:

> The supervisor was a twenty-two-year-old bride weighing ninety pounds whose husband had been sent overseas and who, in consequence, had been given a job until his return. . . . The young woman, Lucille Burger, was obliged to make certain that people entering security areas wore the correct clear identification.

> Surrounded by his usual entourage of white-shirted men, Watson approached the doorway to an area where she was on guard, wearing an orange badge acceptable elsewhere in the plant, but not a green badge, which alone permitted entrance at her door. "I was trembling in my uniform, which was far too big," she recalled. "It hid my shakes but not my voice. 'I'm sorry,' I said to him. I knew who he was alright. 'You cannot

enter. Your admittance is not recognized.' That's what we were supposed
to say.

The men accompanying Watson were stricken; the moment held unpre-
dictable possibilities. "Don't you know who he is?" someone hissed.
Watson raised his hand for silence, while one of the party strode off and
returned with the appropriate badge.

Martin et al. interpret the moral behind this story by suggesting that
for higher status organization members the message is "Even Watson
obeys the rules, so you certainly should," while lower status employees
should "uphold the rules no matter who is disobeying" (p. 440). The
implication is that while other corporate heads may flout regulations,
Watson sets an example to all of his employees. Martin et al. use this
and other stories to illustrate ways in which organizations display
qualities that are unique, differentiating them from other organizations.
Interestingly enough, Martin et al. demonstrate that stories similar in
form and content are common to many organizations.

While Martin et al. provide useful insight into the way in which the
above story functions organizationally, they do little to suggest how the
story might operate in the context of the power relations that partially
structure this organization. The story can be more adequately analyzed
by conducting a critical interpretation of its role in the production and
reproduction of ideological meaning formations. In other words, the
analysis that follows makes explicit the link between organizational
narrative on the one hand, and legitimation and ideological domination
on the other.

First, therefore, the story needs to be examined in terms of the social,
economic, and political conditions that provide a context for the events
that unfold in the course of the narrative. The story does not occur in a
vacuum, but is intimately tied to the institutional and societal features
that structurate IBM as a company. At the level of action, the protagonists are engaged in an interaction which is characterized by an extreme
disparity in terms of status, but which is structured by the organizational roles that the two people are required to play out. In this sense,
the action that occurs is situation-specific. Thus on the one hand the
significance and impetus of the story is created by the status difference,
while on the other hand the action that each individual engages in is a
product of the aims that each pursues in playing out their organizational
roles—Burger as the security guard and Watson as the organizational
patriarch.

At the institutional level, IBM offers a stable framework within which
action is conducted. Members of the organization have fairly clear

guidelines regarding prescribed and proscribed practices. IBM is generally recognized as an institution which places a strong emphasis on the clear delineation of the structure of authority, and structures authority relations in a traditional, hierarchical fashion. This hierarchy does not *determine* organizational action as such, but rather establishes an interpretive frame through which organizational behavior emerges. Such authority relations therefore produce the conditions under which the situation related in the story might take place. Thompson (1984b, p.135) states that "Institutions are the *loci* of power and the crystallization of relations of domination." In this context, the narrated confrontation between Burger and Watson can be seen as an exemplification of these "crystallized" relations. The story articulates a specific spatiotemporal "moment" in the history of IBM which encapsulates the underlying structure of authority relations. As with the example of the secretary cited earlier, one might say that the confrontation and its significance is overdetermined by the structural relations of domination which characterize IBM as an institution.

At the third level of social analysis, one needs to examine IBM in terms of its situatedness within the wider context of the U.S. corporate/capitalist enterprise. The confrontation between Burger and Watson is not simply an interaction between two people at a purely interpersonal level. Rather, the two protagonists are personifications of the primary relationship in capitalism—that between wage-labor (Burger) and capital (Watson). The whole structure of capitalism is built upon the premise that labor sells its skills to the owners of capital at a price less than what it is worth, thus allowing the accumulation of surplus value, enabling the expansion of capital and therefore the ongoing reproduction of the system. At a structural level, then, it is clear that the Burger-Watson interaction is structured and constrained by this most fundamental relationship. The confrontation is both an expression and a reconstitution of the most basic structural elements that undergird both IBM and the wider capitalist system.

Unpacking the ideological function of the story at the level of discursive analysis requires that we show the connection between the narrative form and the relations of domination. In large part this has been accomplished in the earlier discussion of the structure of narrative. Let me briefly recapitulate by indicating, first, that narrative provides a sense of closure to discourse by delineating some kind of moral drama which is resolved in some fashion. In this specific case we have a clearly defined narrative structure—high-status person attempts to break a rule, intervention by lower status person, high-status person complies with rule—which leads listeners to draw certain conclusions about the importance of rules in this particular organization. Second, such stories are not open to the same level of validity testing as other forms of discourse, and thus take on a considerable level of legitimacy and authority in their depiction of organizational events. Thus the IBM story, whether true or not, may be disseminated widely throughout the culture without anyone challenging its veracity. The very fact that it is a story that lends itself to infinite retellings is partly the basis for its symbolic power.

The final level in analyzing the ideological role of the story is interpretation. At this point I want to construct a meaning for the story by utilizing Giddens's three functions of ideology outlined in the previous chapter. Such an analysis is partial rather than exhaustive, but allows for a way to make explicit the connection between meaning and the relations of domination indicated in the two levels of analysis above.

The first function of ideology—the representation of sectional interests as universal—is clearly present in the story. Recall that this function enables social practices that further the interests of a particular group to be perceived as the interests of *all* groups. In the context of this story, the issue of sectional-versus-universal interests manifests itself in the question of adherence to rules. In terms of universal interests, the story tacitly suggests that the corporation's rules are laid down for the benefit of all employees. The fact that Watson is required to take orders from a low-status employee has the effect of temporarily suspending the corporate hierarchy, in which sectional interests are grounded. Rules, as such, appear to transcend sectional interests; all employees, of whatever rank, are required to follow the rules.

What the story obscures, however, is the fact that the formal system of rules is created *by* the corporate elite (of which Watson is the head) to protect their own interests. IBM is a profit-making organization, one goal of which is to maintain as large a share of its market as possible. Part of this involves employment of strict security to protect corporate secrets. Staying ahead of its competition in the area of technology ensures the competitiveness of IBM products. The corporate rules that the story deals with, then, are in place for the benefit of people like Watson, and not for people like Lucille Burger.

The issue of rule breaking becomes clearer in looking at the role of the story in denying or transmuting contradictions. In a sense, the story as a whole is a contradiction. The moral it conveys demonstrates that no one at IBM is "above the law." However, the mere fact that the story has become part of organization lore indicates that it is exceptional in some way. If Watson *was* subject to corporate rules in the same way as other employees, then this story would have little significance. The story is further contradictory in the sense that it depicts Watson simultaneously as "ordinary human being" who can be spoken to by any employee, and as a larger-than-life figure about whom fables are told. Thus the story comments on itself: On one level it is a straightforward narrative that tells the listener/reader something about the way IBM operates; on a second, meta-level, the story operates reflexively, building a particular image of Watson by saying "This is a story about the (in)famous chairman of IBM." The contradiction between Watson the individual and Watson the powerful corporate executive is obscured by the story focusing on his interaction with an employee, to whom he ultimately defers.

The material reality of Watson's corporate position is effectively obscured by placing the narrative in an interpersonal context, and yet it only has impact because of the huge divide that separates the protagonists on the corporate hierarchy. In this sense, the effectiveness of the story depends on a tension between disparate elements: The story tells us that position on the corporate ladder means little when it comes to following rules (rules are for the good of everyone), but at the same time the listener/reader must appreciate Watson as a highly charismatic figure who commands the respect of everyone.

The story perhaps best serves an ideological function through the process of reification. Simply by virtue of its narrative structure, the story form lends itself to an infinite number of recountings. As Martin and Powers (1983) point out, an organizational story is easier to recall than a set of statistics containing the same information. Stories, of course, occur in all cultural settings, and one of their aims is to present the listener with a "slice of life" that exemplifies and animates some aspect of the culture in which the story is set. Through the ongoing process of retelling, events in a story become taken-for-granted by members of the culture. Even in the case of apocryphal tales, the division between fiction and reality is blurred to the point where a narrative event becomes "real" if it is retold enough times.

Of course, the effectiveness of a story depends at least partly on the quality of its telling. In the case of the example used here, there is no way of knowing how this story might be related in the organizational context. No doubt the basic structure remains fairly constant, while the embellishments will differ with each recounting. However, there is enough detail in the example given to demonstrate the process of reification in operation. First, there is a sharp contrast in the way that the two principal characters are described in the story. In fact, little or nothing is said about Watson himself, except that he was "surrounded by his usual entourage of white-shirted men." The description of Burger, on the other hand, is detailed by comparison. She is "a twenty-two-year-old bride weighing ninety pounds whose husband has been sent overseas." We are told that she is wearing a uniform that is "far too big" for her, and that she is very nervous at the prospect of her confrontation with Watson.

This relatively detailed description of Burger serves to accentuate the status difference between her and Watson. In this context, the story draws heavily on traditional sex role stereotypes. For example, Burger is not simply a woman, but a "bride," suggesting both the traditional role of homemaker, and a strong sense of näivete; she has suddenly found herself, through circumstances beyond her control, in a position to which she is ill-suited. This is confirmed and accentuated by the ill-fitting uniform, which suggests an incongruence between her and the role she is required to perform. The term "bride" thus suggests an innocence and dependence which contrasts sharply to the cynicism of the "real" corporate world. Furthermore, her weight implies lack of physical stature which, in most Western cultures at least, is associated with lack of authority. Again this serves to throw into sharp relief the status difference between the two protagonists.

The lack of detail provided for Watson serves to enhance his status as an almost mythical character. The term "entourage," used to describe the men accompanying him, is a word normally applied to those who attend royal figures. In addition, Watson at no time speaks during the course of the story. At one point someone even speaks for him ("Don't you know who he is?"). Even at a moment where he might have spoken, he simply raises his hand to gain the attention of those around him. All of these details, although not central to the ostensible theme of the story, serve to contrast Watson sharply to Burger. What the listener/reader gets is not a picture of an ordinary organization member, but a figure of heroic proportions. The story thus serves to reify Watson-as-hero by demonstrating his effect on the day-to-day life of the organization.

In addition, and perhaps most importantly, the story serves to reify ideologically the organizational rule system itself. Organizational rules are humanly constructed systems of norms which provide members with an organizational grammar through which action is framed and contextualized. Rules provide direction for organizational structuration, both enabling and constraining the behavior of organization members. In contrast, the IBM story negates the human element inherent in organizational rules by stripping them of their enabling/constraining grammatical function. Lucille Burger's single-minded adherence to the rules reflects not so much a heightened sense of corporate loyalty, but rather an enforcing of rules *because they exist*.

In a sense, the story demonstrates rules as having an importance all of their own, independent of the function that they perform within the organization. Placed in this context, the rule system and the process of organizing are bifurcated, existing in an almost antithetical relationship. Such an antithesis is often experienced by people who work in large, bureaucratic institutions. Frequently the overwhelming feeling is that the bureaucratic structure quite happily perpetuates itself via an elaborate and impenetrable system of rules (exemplified by the ubiquitous triplicate forms), and continuously works against the accomplishment of the organization's ostensible goals. As a result of this reification process organizational activity "takes on the character of a thing and thus acquires a 'phantom objectivity,' an autonomy that seems so strictly rational and all-embracing as to conceal every trace of its fundamental nature: the relation between people" (Lukács, 1971, p.83).

Finally, the narrative performs the ideological function of control by providing an example of "intellectual and moral leadership" for organization members. As Gramsci (1971) has indicated, the process of hegemony works most effectively when the world view articulated by the ruling elite is actively taken up and pursued by subordinate groups. In the case of the IBM story, we have a striking example of a situation in which organization rules are rigorously reinforced by subordinate members. The story has all the more impact, insofar as those rules are enforced from the bottom up, rather than from the top down. In this context, the story conveys the legitimacy and appropriateness of IBM's organizational structure. It suggests that employees are prepared to go to extreme lengths to protect that structure, even to the point of incurring the wrath of superiors. Commitment to the system is therefore identified and equated with its legitimacy.

The above analysis thus provides an interpretation of the ideological function of the IBM story, demonstrating ways in which it is possible for narrative, as a social practice, to reproduce the dominant meaning formations of a particular social structure. The interpretation provides attempts to make explicit the link between narration and meaning on the one hand, and relations of domination on the other.

There are, of course, severe limitations associated with the analysis of a single story, not the least of which is the fact that this particular story has been analyzed independently of the social context in which it was related. As such, we have no way of being able to position it in the context of other stories and other forms of discourse which occur simultaneously or concurrently. In addition, one cannot in any sense justify claims that a single story is representative of the totality of meaning formations and relations of domination that exist within a particular organization. Any cultural formation produces a system of practices which is far more complex than can be explained in terms of a straightforward opposition between two opposing ideologies. The relationship between discursive practices and ideology is much more tangled and messy than can be explicated by the analysis—however sophisticated or erudite—of a single organizational story. Hall presents the relationship between discourse and ideology in the following manner:

> Ideologies do not operate through single ideas; they operate, in discursive chains, in clusters, in semantic fields, in discursive formations. As you enter an ideological field and pick out any one nodal representation or idea, you immediately trigger off a whole chain of connotative associations. Ideological representations connote—summon—one another. So a variety of ideological systems or logics are available in any social formation. The notion of *the* dominant ideology and *the* subordinated ideology is an inadequate way of representing the complex interplay of different ideological discourses and formations in any developed society. (1985, p. 104)

Any fully adequate analysis of the ideological system of meaning in an organization must therefore examine the discursive practices of various interest groups, each of which represents a different system of logic or mode of rationality. These discourses do not exist in a mutually exclusive relationship to one another, but rather interlock and overlap in a way that creates a complex and often inconsistent organizational meaning structure. For example, it is quite possible for organization members to belong to more than one interest group simultaneously. A female corporate executive may be considered a member of upper management, but at the same time she might experience the discrimination associated with male-dominated areas of the corporate structure. In terms of discursive practices, then, she might be interpellated as both a "female" (with all the connotations associated with this term in a male-dominated system) and as an "executive" who is a member of the corporate elite. This interpellation process situates her in a complex and ambiguous "web" of meaning in which she experiences and makes sense of the process of organizing in various ways. Such ambiguity is an essential quality of ideological meaning formations in that it allows those groups with the most power to interpret this ambiguity in a way that best suits their own interests.

SUMMARY AND CONCLUSION

This chapter has explored at some length the relationship between ideology and discourse. It has been suggested that organizational discursive practices, in their various forms, play a central role in the production and reproduction of organizational meaning. Discourse is not politically neutral, however, but functions as a means by which certain power structures in an organization are produced, maintained, and reproduced. In this context, ideology is discursive in character. Discourse both manifests and instantiates the ideology of organizations, providing the means by which people situate themselves in the organization.

The study of ideology thus involves the examination of the link between structures of discourse and relations of domination. Specifically, narrative was examined as one signifying system by means of which this relationship is established. The articulation of ideology takes a largely narrative form. Stories are an exceptionally powerful means of constructing and maintaining an organization's underlying mode of rationality, providing a vision of the organization which is relatively complete, stable, and removed from scrutiny. In this sense, narrative has a legitimacy beyond other forms of discourse, attaining a level of authority that excludes it from the normal rigors of discursive validity testing. By means of narrative, organization members engage in the ongoing structuration of organizations, creating the conditions under which certain relations of domination are reproduced.

The analysis provided in this chapter is largely conceptual in nature, and does little to examine the relationship between specific existing discursive practices and relations of domination. The single analysis of the IBM story is thus intended to provide theoretical guidelines for research rather than to present exhaustive analyses of a particular corpus of data. The careful application of this theoretical model to a specific corpus of organizational stories must await another study.[4] My main intention here has been rather to explicate the conceptual richness that can be developed by undergirding extant perspectives of organizational symbolism with neo-Marxist conceptions of the relationship between meaning and systems of domination. The result is, I believe, a much more powerful mode of theorizing about the symbolic construction of reality in organizations.

The next chapter explores some of the epistemological issues that arise around the theoretical model that has been developed in the preceding chapters. It is argued that the traditional conception of knowledge-as-Truth provides an inadequate means of framing and evaluating social theory and research. What is required is an extensive reorientation towards questions of "appropriateness" and "validity" in organizational studies.

---

[4] I am currently in the preliminary stages of conducting a study examining the symbolic aspects of an industrial dispute. The study intends to explore competing symbolic constructions of the nature of the strike, and to explicate the degree to which this symbolic structuring affected the nature of the conflict between management and workers.

6

IDEOLOGY, EPISTEMOLOGY, AND TRUTH

The previous five chapters have developed a theory of organizational cultures that reconceptualizes extant notions of culture and organizing. This chapter develops the implications of this approach for the status of knowledge in social theory. Issues of ideology and domination raise fundamental epistemological questions about what we can consider to be appropriate and fruitful conceptions of truth. I therefore want to examine epistemological issues raised by the conception of organizational cultures as ideologically based meaning formations. In this context, I will draw on some contemporary theories of knowledge, and examine their role in reformulating the relationship between knowledge generation and research. What, for example, are the reasons for engaging in social science research? What are the researcher's responsibilities to the social actors whom he or she studies? In addition, specific methodological considerations will be taken up in relation to such questions.

Traditional positivist philosophies of social science have treated knowledge as largely unproblematic; from this perspective truth, although not fully realized, is merely contingent on the development of an adequate observation language. In this context, philosophy serves as the "tribunal of pure reason" which judges the adequacy of knowledge claims in terms of their correspondence to reality. The provision of this epistemological foundation not only allows theories of knowledge to be subject to rigorous verification, but also provides the means by which competing theories can be tested for their commensurability; that is, the degree to which they make similar claims about the world. In this way, theory building becomes a continuous, uninterrupted process in which universally valid truth claims lay the ground for new, as yet more equivocal, theories of human behavior.

Although this attempt to make the human sciences as "rigorous" and "objectively valid" as the natural sciences has been subject to considerable critique in recent years, its influence still holds sway in most social science disciplines, the study of communication included. The search for generalizability, replication, and prediction and control reflects the prevalence of a perspective which views the establishment of human "essences" as the end goal of science (Rorty, 1979). Such an approach is conceived as essentially value-free in that researchers claim to make purely ontological statements about the world, arrived at through rigorously tested methods which minimize researcher influence on the object of study.

Interpretive or hermeneutic approaches to the human sciences prefer to talk about "understanding" rather than "explanation," and they criticize positivist approaches for their insistence on the possibility of an objective, empirically verifiable world. Furthermore, postfoundationalist theories of knowledge generally express a concern for the social actor as a central element in saying anything meaningful about the social world.

From an interpretive perspective, then, positivist approaches err in two principal ways in their conception of the relationships among the researcher, social actors, and knowledge formation. First, social actors are considered to have nothing interesting or worthwhile to say about the world they inhabit. Knowledge about this world is constituted behind their backs, and mainly from the perspective of the researcher. Second, an overconcern with method (procedural sublimation) has led to a situation in which the researcher is often no more than an appendage to a particular scientific technique. In this case, both the researcher's own insight and the ontology of the object of study itself are largely determined by the a priori concepts and methods employed. Knowledge claims are therefore verified via a consensus achieved prior to the actual research (using the "correct" methods and applying the "appropriate" concepts). This contrasts with a more hermeneutic approach in which concept formation arises during the process of investigation in the dialectic that develops between the researcher and the object of study.

While somewhat brief and oversimplified, the above represents the basic dichotomy that characterizes research in the social sciences. Interpretivists, on the one hand, accuse their positivist counterparts of being too "objectivist" and insensitive to their objects of study. Positivists, on the other hand, argue that interpretivists risk falling into relativism and solipsism through their lack of interest in empirically verifiable, generalizable truth claims. Of course, to suggest that this dichotomy is absolute would be wrong; indeed, it is extremely hard to identify any theoretical perspective that would fit neatly into one of Burrell and Morgan's (1979) four sociological paradigms.

It is against the background of this debate, however, that one must assess the epistemological implications of the theory of organizational cultures developed here. While I have suggested that organizational reality is socially constructed, I have also indicated that the construction of this reality cannot be separated from the deep structure power relations that constitute the material conditions of an organization. As Jameson (1981) indicates, the material infrastructure of institutional practices mediates in the way that the "texts" of such institutions (stories, myths, etc.) are interpreted or given meaning by organization members. An acceptable theoretical framework must therefore consider not simply the adequacy of the "fit" between propositions and observed reality, or merely the ability of social actors to construct their own reality. Rather, one must frame such considerations within the context of questions of power and ideology. The incorporation of these issues into the process of knowledge generation makes theory formation more compatible with the complexities of an institutionally oriented social world.

THEORIES OF KNOWLEDGE

The debate over what constitutes knowledge is centuries old, but recent works (Bernstein, 1983; Gadamer, 1975; Kuhn, 1970; Rorty, 1979, 1982; Winch, 1958) have rejuvenated issues that had been neglected following the rise to hegemony of positivism in the late nineteenth century.

Kuhn's (1970) treatise on the nature of scientific paradigms, for example, explores the notion that paradigm shifts have little to do with appeals to deduction, verification, confirmation, and so forth. As such, "There is no neutral algorithm for theory-choice, no systematic decision procedure which, properly applied, must lead each individual in the group to the same decision" (1970, p.200). For Kuhn, certain scientific theories do not become dominant because they correspond more closely with an objective reality than other theories. Rather, a sort of nonviolent academic "coup d'état" occurs, in which a particular scientific community with a particular set of shared values frames the way that theory construction takes place. Scientific revolutions are not precipitated by individuals (as textbook histories of science would have us believe), but are the product of particular values being more persuasive than others — values which lie outside the domain of normal science as defined by positivism. What is considered "real," therefore, is dependent not simply on what "exists," but on the political climate of the scientific community at a given time.

Kuhn's critique of scientific rationality is significant in its rejection of pure notions of objectivity. Its strength lies in its ability to cast doubt on the whole issue of commensurability as a foundational principle of scientific investigation. Here, commensurability refers to *both* the compatibility of knowledge claims across theories, and the accuracy of representations vis-à-vis the empirical world within the framework of a given theory. Both notions are fundamental to a foundational conception of epistemology insofar as they presuppose a view of truth as incorrigible, i.e., as the reflection of agreed-upon and stable criteria for coherence. Rationality in normal science thus consists of the accurate reflection of an objective world via a universally acceptable set of precepts.

Writing from a hermeneutic perspective, Rorty (1979) commends Kuhn for his debunking of realist conceptions of normal science, but criticizes him for putting an idealist epistemology in its place. According to Rorty

> Kuhn's claim that no algorithm was possible . . . was, however, obscured by [his] own "idealistic"-sounding addenda. It is one thing to say that the "neutral observation language" in which proponents of different theories can offer their evidence is of little help in deciding between the theories. It is another thing to say that there can be no such language because the proponents "see different things" or "live in different worlds." (1979, p. 324)

Kuhn's conception of a paradigm change as something akin to a gestalt switch leads him open to charges of subjectivism and relativism, in which he substitutes an accurate "mirroring" of the world for "an idealistic account of the malleability of the mirrored world" (Rorty, 1979, p.325). Rorty suggests, however, that this polarization of idealism and realism can be overcome by abandoning epistemology as a way to truth. In its place he offers a hermeneutic alternative, in which different discourses (as opposed to theories) about the world are assessed not in terms of their truth, i.e., accuracy of representation, but rather as different ways of talking about the world, which may prove useful in helping us to cope with life in a pragmatic manner. Thus "Hermeneutics does not need a new epistemological paradigm, any more than liberal thought requires a new paradigm of sovereignty. Hermeneutics, rather, is what we get when we are no longer epistemological" (1979, p.325).

Rorty thus conceives of a philosophy of "edification," in which agreed-upon criteria for verifying the truth of statements are rejected in favor of "finding new, better, more interesting, more fruitful ways of speaking" (1979, p.60). Rorty does not distinguish between disciplines as such—there are no disciplines which are edifying and some which are not—but rather separates "normal" from "abnormal" discourses. In the former, statements about the world are judged according to agreed-upon conventions, while the latter occur "when someone joins in the discourse who is ignorant of these conventions, or who sets them aside" (1979, p.320). This abnormal discourse has a therapeutic goal in that it aims at opening up possibilities for the ways in which the world can be conceptualized. This view of philosophy, embodied in the phrase, "continuing the conversation" (1979, pp.373 et passim), rejects universal commensuration because of the closure of discourse that occurs through the privileging of foundational knowledge.

The overcoming of the antagonism between objectivism and relativism is therefore achieved by denying the traditional oppositions that are presumed to characterize the two camps—explanation/understanding; value-free/value-laden; objective/subjective; quantitative/qualitative, and so forth. Instead, Rorty suggests that the real issue concerns the preferred ways we wish to talk about humans and the world we live in. Theories which advocate prediction and control should not be opposed to theories which seek understanding, nor should any theory of human behavior be seen as grounded in any way. Equally erroneous are assertions by interpretive social scientists that natural phenomena and people are intrinsically different and, therefore, require different modes of inquiry.

In his debate with Dreyfus (1980) and Taylor (1980), for example, Rorty (1980) rejects the split between natural and social science. Those who argue for the separation do so because of a perceived difference between people and things. According to Rorty, however, this is simply a confusion of ontology and morals. An identification of human essences reverts to a foundational, correspondence theory of truth. Theories which aim at prediction and control of human behavior are not less suited to humans than to things because of any intrinsic difference between the two. Rather, it is the case that we have more interesting things to say about humans than whether their behavior is controllable. Rorty thus replaces the ontological privileging of foundational knowledge and commensurability with the *moral* privileging of human description:

If the line I am taking is correct, we need to think of our distinctive moral status as just *that*, rather than as "grounded" on our possession of mind, language, culture, feeling, intentionality, textuality, or anything else. All these numinous notions are just expressions of our awareness that we are members of a moral community, phrased in one or another pseudo-explanatory jargon. This awareness is something that cannot be further "grounded"—it is simply taking a certain point of view on our fellow-humans. The question of whether it is an "objective" point of view is not to any point. (1982, p.202)

The privileging of any kind of methodological or ontological issue is therefore superseded by the "appropriateness of a vocabulary for a purpose" (1980, p.48), in which the equation of knowledge and representation of reality is displaced by the equation of knowledge and coping. Thus "being 'interpretive' or 'hermeneutical' is not having a special method but simply casting about for a vocabulary which might help" (1982, p.199).

The accusations of relativism and subjectivism which are leveled at Kuhn would thus appear to be equally valid when applied to Rorty. Once knowledge is separated from notions of foundationalism and accurate representation then questions of validity become a problem. Rorty (1979, p.320) himself acknowledges that abnormal discourse can range from "nonsense to intellectual revolution." On the other hand, the importance of normal discourse is not denied:

the possibility of hermeneutics is always parasitic upon the possibility (and perhaps upon the actuality) of epistemology, and . . . edification always employs materials provided by the culture of the day. To attempt abnormal discourse *de novo*, without being able to recognize our own abnormality, is madness in the most literal and terrible sense. To insist on being hermeneutic where epistemology would do—to make ourselves unable to view normal discourse in terms of its own motives, and able to view it only from within our own abnormal discourse—is not mad, but it does show a lack of education. (1979, p.366)

Rorty thus assigns abnormal discourse to a reactive role, to challenge the normal discourse of the day. This task, and the discourse itself, loses its point when it is appropriated by the mainstream of social science or philosophy.

What, then, is the significance of Rorty's "moral imperative" in relation to questions of knowledge formation? His appeal to "continue the conversation" is a direct attack on the closing off of discourse produced by universal commensuration, and signals an attempt to overcome the repressive tendencies of theories of representation. The main purpose of edifying philosophy is to destroy the illusion that a particular vocabulary—a way of characterizing the world—is a description of "the way things are." As Rorty (1979, p.377) states, "The resulting freezing-over of culture would be, in the eyes of edifying philosophers, the dehumanization of human beings." The appeal to open and ongoing discourse is a call for a particular ethics of communication in which no single voice is privileged over others, and no perspective is denied expression (Deetz, 1983).

Rorty's use of rhetorical devices such as "conversation" and "discourse" in place of "theories" is indicative of his deconstruction of traditional epistemology. It would be mistaken, however, to conclude from this that Rorty views theory construction as meaningless. A particular theory is meaningful insofar as it contributes to the "conversation of mankind"—it is one voice in the ongoing flow of that conversation, rather than a way of thinking which has "discovering truth" as its end goal. While the notion of conversation aids in seeing "human beings as generators of new descriptions rather than as beings one hopes to describe accurately" (1979, p.378), it is problematic when placed in the context of the theory of culture developed in this work. Dallmayr (1984, pp.176–177) points out that the very notion of conversation contains implicit ambiguities concerning its form and content. How, for example, does one prevent the open-endedness which characterizes Rorty's dialogue from degenerating into empty rhetoric or idle chatter? Furthermore,

> what is left somewhat unclear . . . is the character of the "voices" or participants and also the status of language itself. To the extent that the voices are treated as individual speakers or speaking "subjects," conversation readily shades over into a clash of idiosyncratic "expressions" if not into attempts at reciprocal manipulation . . . if subjectivism is avoided, the result may be conceptual uniformity (patterned on the idiom of "science"). In either case, language functions basically as a means or instrument in the pursuit of ulterior motives (such as gain or information). (Dallmayr, 1984, p.177)

Dallmayr's questioning of the form of participation in conversation is particularly apposite when framed in the wider context of institutionalized social structures. I have argued in the previous chapter that discourse generated within organizational cultures is produced by (and reproduces) the ideological meaning formations and power structures that give sense to the organization as a meaning-centered construction. The same is true of social science research in organizations. Rorty's notion of conversation, however, does not seem able to account for the fact that discourse is situated within a particular sociopolitical milieu. While he does talk of concepts such as repression and closure, these are contextualized in terms of *theoretical* closure; for example, the way in which foundational epistemology closes off the possibility for "new, better, more interesting, more fruitful ways of speaking." As such, there is no discussion of the way in which certain power relations articulate ideological forms of conversation in which the illusion of continuity and open-endedness is created.

This is not to say that Rorty completely abstracts his notion of conversation from the community in which it is produced. On the contrary, a major aspect of his deconstruction of "objectivity" and "scientific method" is to show that the social sciences can be conceived as coextensive with literature: "as interpreting other people to us, and thus enlarging and deepening our sense of community" (1982, p.203). But as seen in the previous chapter, the use of the poetic and metaphorical is double-edged; it can broaden our sense of the world we inhabit, or it can reify it, closing off the possibility of alternative, enriching world views. Literature is thus subject to the same historically located material conditions as any other form of discourse (Jameson, 1981).

Ultimately, it seems that the question with which Rorty is grappling is whether an ostensibly simple notion, such as "conversation," can take the place of rationality (conceptualized in terms of seeking "objective truth") as the goal of philosophy and social science. Rorty (1982, p.165) states that "there are no constraints on inquiry save conversational ones." In other words, the success of philosophical inquiry is equated with simply viewing conversation as its own end—as being continuous rather than having a particular end goal. Unfortunately, Rorty does little to clarify what the conditions for "continuing the conversation" are. That is, how should social science research be appropriately conducted, given the institutional constraints frequently placed on it? I am not suggesting that he should specify normative foundations upon which such "conversation" can be evaluated, but if my thesis is correct, discourse is potentially antirational under the appropriate social conditions. Such irrationality has little to do with "lack of correspondence to reality," but refers to the deformation of meaning which distorts the ability of the social actor to reflect on his or her socially constructed, lived-world.

Rorty (1982, pp.191–210) attempts to address this issue in a comparison of Dewey and Foucault. Both, he maintains, are equally critical of foundational notions of objectivity, truth, etc., but each has a different conception of the role of social science as a particular discourse in the "conversation of mankind." While Dewey emphasizes its role in deepening and enlarging our sense of community, stressing the connection between knowledge and solidarity, Foucault views social science as an instrument of domination, and focuses on the relationship between knowledge and power. Rorty opts for Dewey because "his vocabulary allows room for unjustifiable hope, and an ungroundable but vital sense of human solidarity" (1982, p.208). Foucault's conception of power, when deconstructed, is nothing more than Deweyan notions in a new vocabulary:

> Once "power" is freed from its connotation of "repression," then Foucault's "structures of power" will not seem much different from Dewey's "structures of culture." "Power" and "culture" are equipollent indications of the social forces which make us more than animals—and which, when the bad guys take over, can turn us into something worse and more miserable than animals. (1982, p.208)

The problem with Rorty's equation of power and culture is that it sets up power as a neutral entity which is problematic only when appropriated by the "bad guys." If power and culture and synonymous, then I would argue that any kind of tension between what I have called "cultural formation" and "cultural deformation" disappears. In a sense, the structuring of meaning formations centers around the struggle between competing interests—at different times different interpretations of social reality prevail, but there are always alternative realities present, if only in a latent fashion (Hall, 1985). By conflating the distinction between power and culture, Rorty appears to close off the possibility of a critical turn in looking at the way that institution members make sense of the world.

Rorty would argue, of course, that notions such as power, ideology, subjectivity, and so forth, are simply one more set of jargon words that attempt to offer principles by which rationality can be distinguished from irrationality. In other words, it is another misguided attempt at privileging a particular set of assumption over others. I would argue in return that Rorty's insistence on the notions of conversation and edification as central to social science is essentially correct, but nevertheless betrays a certain political naïvete. The process of edification occurs within the context of certain power relations. As such, different "conversations" do not compete with each other on an equal basis, but are subject to the prevailing ideological closure of discourses that reflect those power relations.

Rorty provides us with a view of philosophy as edification that deconstructs the traditional foundational view of knowledge and truth. The question one might pose in response to Rorty, however, is "Edifying to whom?" Rorty suggests that all discourses about the world should be viewed as ways of coping, but what might be fruitful and edifying to one group may well be repressive to another. Edification cannot take place under conditions of domination, and it seems that Rorty's moral imperative founders without the ability to expose and critique the systems of domination that produce conversational closure. As such, Rorty's position is simultaneously radical and conservative: It is radical in its deconstruction of accepted epistemology, but conservative in its description of the way in which a reconstructed view of knowledge ties in with the critique of domination.

I would therefore argue that a more radical conception of Rorty's notion of conversation is desirable. While at a purely metatheoretical level it might be appropriate to view different theories as so many voices in an ongoing conversation, this metaphor does not work as well when it is applied to actual social contexts. Here, certain voices in the conversation become privileged, not because they better mirror the objective world, but because they are able to frame perceptions of the world in their own terms, hence excluding other perspectives. In advocating the reconception of social inquiry as conversation, Morgan (1983b, p.376) states:

> One of the fine, flexible things about conversation is that it can begin anywhere and explore many different themes according to the way it becomes structured by those involved. A conversation usually only needs a starting point. Once this is provided, those whose interest is engaged can usually be relied upon to do the rest. Such conversation will prove edifying so long as the participants feel a genuine involvement in the issues being explored and use the course of conversation to confront and reflect on the views they hold and to act on any significant conclusions that emerge.

Here, Morgan extols the virtues of conversation as a means of generating insight, but at the same time fails to reflect on the conditions necessary for such conversation to occur. For example, he rightly points out that conversation "needs a starting point." However, such starting points are frequently predetermined and do not just begin anywhere. As I have indicated previously, ideology can function to qualify social actors in a particular way so that what is possible is already fixed and reified and largely taken-for-granted by subjects. Ideology imposes its own form of certainty on discourse by predisposing the interlocutors toward certain interpretations of events. At the same time, the illusion of open-endedness can be maintained by ostensibly allowing a wide range of interests to be represented. Such open-endedness is frequently no more than the dialogical ideal of "letting everyone have their say," after which the interests of the dominant group are implemented.

Organizational researchers, however, have tended to treat organizational discourse as if it is interest-free. Their goal is mainly to demonstrate ways in which the process of sense-making allows organizations to function coherently. Little attention is given to the positional and political nature of the way in which organizational practices come to make sense. Such acritical, "conversational" approaches to both research and organizational discourse itself are exemplified in Pacanowsky's (1983) quasifictional accounts of police work, where day-to-day practices are romanticized in novelistic form. Although a move is made to go beyond pure description, the research serves not as the provider of critical insight, but as the embellisher of received definitions of organizational structuring.

So far, then, my argument suggests that Rorty is essentially right in arguing for the abandonment of a foundational epistemology. Theory building should not be conceived as the search for essences, but as a way of contributing to the continual flow of interesting and useful things that can be said about the world. Where I take issue with Rorty is in his conception of conversation as the principal marker of philosophy and social science. The idea of theories conceived as discourses is largely unproblematic at a metatheoretical level, but the issues become more complex once such "conversations" are contextualized in terms of systems of domination and ideological meaning formations. Social science can be edifying (and moral) only to the extent that such systems of domination can be exposed and critiqued. Closure and coercion at an institutional level is more difficult to detect than at an individual level, insofar as the former is "naturally" structured into institutions and communities. As such, the notion of conversation is misleading in its evocation of an ongoing dialectic between participants who are all equally placed to contribute to the flow of discourse.

In the previous chapters I have developed a theory of organizational cultures that emphasizes the means by which social closure occurs through the systematic distortion of the sense-making process. A critique of this closure is possible only through examining the conditions under which particular meaning formations are produced and reproduced; that is, by looking at the system of power relations and discursively generated ideological forms. Beyond critique, a means for overcoming and reconstructing institutional domination needs to be formulated. As such, the remainder of this chapter will be concerned with articulating a more radical version of Rorty's notion of "keeping the conversation going"—or, at least, a version which is more directly situated in the social context of organizational life. Both metatheoretical and methodological concerns will be taken up as a means of developing a unified and critical model.

RADICAL CONVERSATION

Both Gadamer and Habermas are criticized by Rorty for making claims to truth that have foundational overtones, but each provides beginning points for a conception of knowledge that enriches and complements the theory of organizational cultures developed here. While representing a move beyond the privileging of scientific method, Gadamer's (1975) development of a universal hermeneutics which lays out anontology of understanding is viewed by Rorty as simply one more attempt to provide universal conditions for the production of truth. Similarly, Habermas's ideal speech situation and theory of knowledge-constituting interests is an attempt to provide a normative grounding for communication. Rorty thus claims that Habermas "goes transcendental and offers principles" (1982, p.173).

For my purposes, Gadamer is useful and insightful because of his conception of the conditions for understanding, through which he explicitly critiques the search for methodological canons by which to find truth. For Gadamer, understanding arises through the dialectic of questioning that emerges in the course of genuine conversation. Whether it be a written text, a work of art, or another person, the object of interpretation is not a static entity whose meaning needs to be discovered and reproduced. Rather, both parties in the dialectic are always already situated within a humanly constituted world, and are only meaningful in this context. Understanding is therefore achieved not by some psychologistic appropriation of the other's consciousness, but through "the conscious assimilation of one's own fore-meanings and prejudices" (1975, p.238). In other words, a dialectic of understanding occurs only because both subject and object are rooted in tradition, and therefore possess their own particular historical horizons. The fusion of horizons that occurs in the hermeneutic situation results in the production of new understanding that is irreducible to the prejudices of either of the interactants.

In the context of the social sciences, research can never be value neutral, insofar as it involves an explicit recognition and bringing to bear of one's own prejudices. The challenging of these prejudices in the interpretive situation makes possible the production of new understanding, in the sense that the object of study "may present itself in all its newness and thus be able to assert its own truth against one's own fore-meanings" (1975, p.238). Here, truth is not conceived as a mirroring of objective reality, but refers to that which is revealed, i.e., experienced-as-new, in the dialectical situation. Truth thus resides in the uncovering of that which was previously unseen.

Language is the principal medium of the hermeneutic experience for

Gadamer. The intrinsic relationship between language and understanding signifies that experience only comes fully to fruition as it is articulated in language. Gadamer thus views language and being human as inseparable—all discursive acts presume preunderstandings that are grounded in the whole of the sociocultural tradition of a community. To speak is to evoke that tradition. Understanding emerges in those situations where tradition is most effectively engaged, and new experiences come to fruition through the universal medium of language. The most authoritative truth claims are therefore made by those individuals who are most thoroughly encultured within a community's tradition, i.e., those who best embody the community as a whole. The truth of their statements resides in their ability to articulate the tradition anew, in ways that are strange, questioning, and enlightening to the community members. For Gadamer, all thought—including critical reflection—is possible only on the condition of participation within a cultural tradition.

Habermas's work has already been dealt with extensively in chapter 2, but it is worth briefly describing the similarities and differences between his philosophical project and Gadamer's. Both are concerned with the fundamental question of how understanding is possible, and both ground the process of understanding in a theory of language. Indeed, their mutual intent in privileging the role of language in understanding is to articulate the sense of community which all understanding presupposes. Bernstein indicates:

> Each of these thinkers points, in different ways, to the conclusion that the shared understandings and experience, intersubjective practices, sense of affinity, solidarity, and those tacit affective ties that bind individuals together in a community must already exist. A community or a *polis* is not something that can be made or engineered by some form of *techne* or by the administration of society. There is something of a circle here, comparable to the hermeneutical circle. The coming into being of a type of public life that can strengthen solidarity, public freedom, a willingness to talk and to listen, mutual debate, and a commitment to rational persuasion presupposes the incipient forms of such communal life.(1983, p. 266)

Of course, Gadamer and Habermas ground this sense of community in different ways—Gadamer through his universal hermeneutics, and Habermas via a universal pragmatics that presupposes the will to reason and self-reflection (embodied in the ideal speech situation). Both, however, offer theories with a practical-moral intent, in which primacy is placed on mutual understanding and truth generated through consensus. In this sense, each makes an equally strong appeal for the privileging of the ethical dimension of communication, i.e., an attempt to establish the conditions for constraint-free dialogue in everyday practice.

The principal difference between Gadamer and Habermas resides in their respective treatments of the issue of authority and tradition. Gadamer views our embeddedness in tradition as essential to the process of understanding, and equates authority with the ability to articulate that tradition. Habermas, on the other hand, is concerned with critiquing the way in which tradition, as embodied in institutions, can systematically distort the communication process. Habermas argues, against Gadamer, that one cannot take the legitimacy of tradition as given, because it is through such lack of critique that "ideologically frozen relations of dependence" emerge. Gadamer, in response, suggests that the very possibility of reflection (including critical reflection) is dependent on our being encultured within a tradition. As such, Habermas overvalues reflection, which is always inevitably limited by taken-for-granted preconceptions and prejudices.

Further, Gadamer claims that the critique of ideology is not beyond hermeneutic understanding—in his terms, it involves the rejection of unjustifiable prejudices. Habermas is thus accused of setting up a false dichotomy between understanding (as the affirmation of traditional prejudices) and critical reflection (as the breaking down of traditional prejudices). Habermas's rejoinder is to suggest that an ontology of understanding based solely on the natural language competence of native speakers is overly restrictive. Such a perspective devalues the construction of social theories which attempt to go beyond the intuitive nature of ordinary language competence.

McCarthy nicely sums up the principal difference between Gadamer and Habermas:

> Gadamer's universalization of hermeneutics rests on a logical argument against the possibility of methodologically transcending the hermeneutic point of view: any attempt to do so is inconsistent with the very conditions of possibility of understanding: the linguisticality and historicity of human existence. Habermas's counterposition is an attempt to mitigate the radically situational character of understanding through the introduction of theoretical elements; the theories of communication and social evolution are meant to reduce the context dependency of the basic categories and assumptions of critical theory. (1982, p. 193)

As mentioned above, however, it would be wrong to view Gadamer and Habermas as holding mutually exclusive positions: Hermeneutics can be pursued critically, while critical theory necessarily entails drawing upon the tradition that grounds each communication community.

In terms of my project, the development of a radical theory of organizational cultures requires, on the one hand, a recognition of the inevitability of institutional constraint and, on the other hand, the ability to expose and critique circumstances in which constraint becomes coercion and domination. The solution that I have constructed in previous chapters involves developing a theory of ideology and power, in which sense-making is subject to distortion and deformation through the appropriation of natural language by dominant groups. Like Gadamer, then, I view language as the primary medium of experience but, following Habermas, recognize the need to develop a theoretical standpoint that accounts for the effect of socio-political conditions on natural language.

The problem with Habermas, however, is that his notion of the ideal speech situation evokes the possibility of a transcendence of the domination of power and ideology. That is, truth emerges when discourse takes place under conditions that are constraint-free—a situation that is unrealizable in practical situations. Given the notion of ideology as constituting subjectivity, what is to prevent the ideal speech situation itself from being subject to ideological distortion? The answer to this apparent contradiction lies, I think, in negating the separation that Habermas makes between truth and power (relations of hegemony). Power and truth need only be regarded as irreconcilable if it is presumed that one is somehow able to maintain a position outside of ideology in critiquing the power relations that sustain it. A more appropriate and fruitful conception of this relationship is to argue that it is not possible to stand outside of ideology, but it is possible to penetrate discursively the institutionally formed constraints and distortions that influence sense-making (Giddens, 1979, p.5; Hall, 1985). This recognition is dependent largely on the fact that ideological language is derivative of and appropriated from natural language. In Habermas's terms, for example, one might say that the dominant organizational ideology is predicated on the ability of dominant groups to articulate technical interests—through natural language—to the exclusion of practical and emancipatory interests.

In this context, Giddens's (1979, 1981, 1982) development of the notion of human agency and the concomitant concept of "dialectic of control" is essential to the reunification of power and truth. As shown in earlier chapters, Giddens views institutional structure as both enabling and constraining. Human agents are not merely subject to the constraints and domination of an imposed organizational structure, but are also able to draw on the rules and resources of an organization to act in a transformative capacity. While members can never escape the constraints of organizational structure, they can draw upon their natural language to penetrate discursively institutional meaning formations, and hence articulate emancipatory interests. Although Habermas would not disagree with this view, it is difficult to see how his ideal speech situation (and the self-reflection it evokes) can be anticipated in the context of organizational structures.

Giddens therefore offers the possibility for preserving the notion of ideology as domination, but allows for a critique of that ideologywithout having to adopt a perspective which is external to it. In a sense, Giddens's notion of discursive penetration—the fact that "every social actor knows a great deal about the conditions of reproduction of the society of which he or she is a member" (1979, p.5)—situates Rorty's notion of coping within an institutional framework. That is, it provides a way of articulating modes of discourse that circumvent the received, doctrinaire version of "what exists." Bernstein sums up the possibilities inherent in this concept in the following manner:

> what is characteristic of our contemporary situation is not just the playing out of powerful forces that are always beyond our control, or the spread of disciplinary techniques that always elude our grasp, but a paradoxical situation where power creates counter-power (resistance) and reveals the vulnerability of power, where the very forces that undermine and inhibit communal life also create new, and frequently unpredictable, forms of solidarity. (1983, p.228)

Without wishing to stretch Giddens's theoretical position too far, it seems that he does offer a way out of some of the problems that beset Gadamer and Habermas. His statement that "We should not cede tradition to the conservatives!" (1979, p.7) suggests his recognition of the degree to which social knowledge is sedimented in institutional forms and practices. But, unlike Gadamer, Giddens is more concerned with the way in which tradition serves in the production and reproduction of social relations. As such, tradition can be perceived as an instrument of domination (the reproduction of power relations) rather than as simply the grounding for the fusion of horizons through which truth emerges.

Similarly, Giddens recognizes the importance of Habermas's notion of systematically distorted communication, insofar as he relates ideology to the distortion and restriction of discursive penetration. The notion of discursive penetration can also be tied closely to Habermas's concept of self-reflection (by means of which the emancipatory interest is realized). In contrast to Habermas, however, Giddens does not contextualize the reflective process in terms of a set of ideal conditions. Self-reflection (discursive penetration) involves the ability to reframe the system of rules and resources of an organization in terms of interests other than those of the dominant group. In other words, members develop a level of discursive consciousness which allows them to deconstruct the dominant organizational ideology. This is not achieved from a perspective external to the ideology, but involves the utilization and transformation of the rules and discursive practices which ground and articulate that ideology.

As demonstrated in chapter 5, organizational symbolism can be appropriated by the dominant interests to produce and reproduce a particular organizational ideology. This means that one cannot talk about a particular symbol system as being intrinsically ideological (e.g., the language of ideology versus scientific language); rather, symbol systems become ideological when they sustain and reproduce relations of domination in the interests of a certain group. In the context of discursive penetration, organization members can be emancipated from the repression of dominant interests by appropriating alternative forms of organizational discourse; for example, moving away from organizational language which emphasizes the technical interest, and adopting ways of talking about organizational life that focus on practical-moral, quality-of-life issues.

An important question that needs to be answered here, however, involves the role of the researcher in the generation of knowledge (i.e., insight into organizational structure). For researchers influenced by the functionalist paradigm, this issue has been largely unproblematic because, following positivist philosophy, a strict bifurcation exists between subject and object. That is, the role of the researcher is to find the most effective means by which to represent accurately the phenomena being described and, ultimately, to be able to make law-like generalizations about the way a certain object-of-study will behave, given the effects of certain variables. Ideally, the researcher plays the role of passive observer, serving only to manipulate the appropriate variables, and to describe the effects of such manipulations as dispassionately as possible, using a neutral observation language. If the researcher is deemed to have influenced his or her object of study in any way other than via the research instrument used, then any data collected are considered to be contaminated.

In the final section of this chapter, however, I want to explicate some of the methodological implications that arise out of the epistemological questions discussed above. Clearly, the role of researcher-as-neutral-observer is inappropriate. In contrast, I wish to suggest a methodological approach that is explicitly value-laden rather than value-free.

RADICAL METHODOLOGY

Clifford Geertz incisively characterizes the move from functionalist to interpretive approaches in the social sciences when he states:

> To turn away from trying to explain social phenomena by weaving them into grand textures of cause and effect to trying to explain them by placing them in local frames of awareness is to exchange a set of well-charted difficulties for a set of largely uncharted ones. Dispassion, generality, and empirical grounding are earmarks of any science worth the name, as is logical force. Those who take the determinative approach seek those elusive virtues by positing a radical distinction between description and evaluation and then confining themselves to the descriptive side of it; but those who take the hermeneutic, denying the distinction is radical or finding themselves somehow astride it, are barred from so brisk a strategy. (1983, p.6)

It would be wrong to argue that functionalist and interpretive forms of social science employ mutually exclusive modes of inquiry; indeed, in terms of specific research methods, many techniques are common to both paradigms—open-ended interviews, survey questionnaires, and so forth. As Geertz points out, however, it is the goals of the respective paradigms which differ greatly. Hermeneutically grounded researchers are more interested in developing a picture of the social world "from the actor's point of view" than their functionalist counterparts. They engage in what Geertz (1973) calls "thick description," i.e., the in situ description of a particular social context which attempts to generate insight into the way that human agents go about making sense of their world. This contrasts with the "thin description" of functionalist research, the goal of which is to make generalizable and predictive claims about human behavior. In a sense, the actor's *reasons* for particular behavior are much less important than the fact that such behavior occurred under certain measurable conditions.

The individual as such is considered to have little of significance to say about the reasons for his or her actions—it is the researcher's job to provide the rationale for such actions. Giddens (1979, p.71) has called this methodological stance "a derogation of the lay actor," and suggests that it has wider political implications:

> If actors are regarded as cultural dopes or mere "bearers of a mode of production," with no worthwhile understanding of their surroundings or the circumstances of their action, the way is immediately laid open for the supposition that their own views can be disregarded in any political programmes that might be inaugurated. This is not just a question of

"whose side are we on?"—although there is no doubt that social incompetence is commonly attributed to people in lower socio-economic groupings by those in power positions, or by their associated experts. (1979, pp.71–72)

The political impact of a more radical, participatory concept of the social actor in the context of research will be taken up below. First, however, it is important to note that "gaining access to the conceptual world" of the individual, as Geertz puts it, should not be equated with the attempt to "walk in the shoes" of those studied. Such a view of interpretive research perpetuates "The myth of the chameleon fieldworker, perfectly self-tuned to his exotic surroundings, a walking miracle of empathy, tact, patience, and cosmopolitanism" (Geertz, 1983, p.56). As Gadamer (1975) puts it, the role of the researcher is not to reproduce the mental constructs of individuals, but to engage with them in such a way as to articulate a fresh way of viewing their world. The problem for the interpretive researcher, then, is one of avoiding the objectifying proclivities of functionalist research while at the same time avoiding the pitfalls of relativism that open up when one starts to talk about seeing things "from the social actor's standpoint." While such issues are normally confined to anthropology, the problem applies equally well in any context in which the researcher is an "outsider," such as is often the case in organizational studies. The temptation to be avoided is to suggest that the only adequate description of the way that a social actor makes sense of his or her sociocultural context is through utilizing the language and concepts naturally employed in that context (e.g., Winch, 1958).

Geertz (1983, pp.57–70) suggests that the problem is one of maintaining an appropriate balance between "experience-near" and "experience-distant" concepts. Experience-near concepts are those naturally employed by an informant to describe his or her environment. Experience-distant concepts are those that a researcher employs to describe his or her informants' descriptions. The problem that the researcher faces is thus one of

how, in each case one ought to deploy [the two types of concepts] so as to produce an interpretation of the way a people lives which is neither imprisoned within their mental horizons, an ethnography of witchcraft as written by a witch, nor systematically deaf to the distinctive tonalities of their existence, an ethnography of witchcraft as written by a geometer. (Geertz, 1983, p.57)

As an anthropologist, the task Geertz faces is one of providing descriptions of alien cultures that do justice to both his own and their sense of "what they do." As he puts it, "The trick is to figure out what the devil they think they are up to" (1983, p.58). From the perspective adopted throughout this book, however, the researcher's role is more problematic. I have argued that organizations can be viewed as the site of both cultural formation and cultural deformation. In the former, members engage in organizational practices with a communally derived sense of "organizing;" meaning formations are produced through a consensually realized sense-making process and reflect a plurality of interests. With cultural deformation, sense-making is distorted through the hegemony of a particular organizational ideology which shapes the way that members view organizational reality. This ideology reflects the world view of the most powerful vested interests within the organization.

Viewed in this context, the role of the organizational researcher is to expose and critique the process by which a particular organizational ideology produces and reproduces the corresponding structure of power within the organization. Ideally speaking, one of the products of such research would be the articulation of an alternative organizational reality that opposes or reconstructs the dominant ideology. This alternative reality would not be produced and imposed on organization members by the researcher, but would rather be generated via the dialectic between researcher and organization members.

If one puts the notion of organizational ideology in Geertz's terminology, one could say that "experience-near" concepts refer to those discursive practices which organization members "naturally" draw on in making sense of their environment. That is, they frame organization members' subjectivity from within the dominant ideology. As Geertz points out, such "concepts" are not really recognized *as* concepts by their users, but are rather used spontaneously and unself-consciously—they are inextricably bound up with the reality they describe.

In contrast, experience-distant concepts can be seen as falling largely outside the lived world of the organization member. They articulate organizational reality in a way that provides a different interpretive frame through which members make sense of their organization. Unlike Geertz, therefore, I conceive of experience-distant concepts not simply as a kind of second-order description, but rather as a way of deconstructing the uncritically received reality that the dominant ideology produces and reproduces. In the previous chapter, for example, I showed how the narrative structure of organizational language can predispose members to make sense of their organization in a certain way (experience-near concepts). Alternative narrative structures, however, while still drawing on the natural language of organization members, can provide counterintuitive ways of construing organization structure and practices (experience-distant concepts), or may function to make explicit aspects of the organizing process that had previously been experienced at a less conscious level. The experience of the department secretary documented in the previous chapter is a good example of the latter, where the experience of interpellation as a non-person is made explicit through narrative. Ideally, such stories can be incorporated by other organization members into their own experience of the day-to-day organizing process, hence making those in both dominant and subordinate positions more sensitized to the potentially repressive nature of certain social practices.[1]

It is therefore possible to distinguish two distinct sets of methodological issues in nonfunctionalist approaches to research. The first, broadly defined by the interpretive paradigm, is concerned with providing adequate descriptions of the social actor's process of sense-making. As such, primacy is given to the individual's own account of the world in which he or she lives. The alternative perspective—and the one I wish to develop more fully—adopts a more critical stance. Here, the focus is not simply on providing insight into an individual's sense-making practices, but also on uncovering the deeper structure power relations which partly determine these practices. Further, a more critically oriented method provides social actors themselves with the means by which to both critique and change the extant meaning structures of an organization.

One way of characterizing the distinction between these two modes of research is to say that interpretive approaches seek to provide insight into organization *practice*, while more critical approaches seek to generate organization *praxis*. Heydebrand makes the following distinction between practice and praxis:

> When . . . goal-directed problem-solving activities are institutionalized and become habitual, one may speak of organizational practices. By

---

[1] The story of the secretary and her experience of the university caste system was copied and widely disseminated among the faculty and support staff in my own department. Although the secretaries indicated that the department was relatively free from such discrimination, they were readily able to identify with the discriminatory practices cited in the story. Interestingly enough, the article provoked a considerable response in the "Letters" section of a subsequent edition of *The Chronicle* (3/11/87, p. 44), with reactions ranging from strong identification to sarcasm. For example, a faculty member wrote "In [the article] the author laments how she, a secretary, is not treated as a peer by other faculty members. Perhaps she would be if she acted like one. Doing so would mean signing her own name to the Point of View piece. Otherwise, how could she list it on her vita?" One cannot help but be struck by the level of defensiveness in this response, indicative perhaps of the kind of reassertion of position a dominant group feels impelled to make when their perceived superiority is challenged in some way.

contrast, organizational praxis refers not only to the technical transformation of the environment and to the solution of practical problems, but also to the conscious self-transformation of collective actors. This requires a high level of understanding and insight into the motivational and causal links among actors, social structures and history. Thus organizing activity, cooperation, undistorted communication, and domination-free interaction are central in the concept of organizational praxis. (1983, p.306)

Heydebrand's incorporation of technical, practical, and transformatory (emancipatory) elements into the concept of praxis obviously owes a great deal to Habermas's theory of interests. However, the notion of praxis provides a useful anchor point for assessing research methods that operate in a transformative capacity.

Two Modes of Inquiry

Action research and participatory research are two modes of inquiry which explicitly cite social change as their primary goal. Both incorporate the social actor as an active participant in the planning and implementation of such change. Each differs, however, in terms of the way "social change" is defined; or, put another way, each has a different conception of the relationship between the individual and his or her social context. Both methods will be examined below.

The most oft-quoted definition of action research is provided by Rapoport (1970, p.499) when he states that "Action research aims to contribute both to the practical concerns of people in an immediate problematic situation and to the goals of social science by joint collaboration within a mutually acceptable ethical framework." Generally action research takes place within an organization in which a specific structural or task-related problem has been identified. The aim of action researchers is to provide organization members themselves with the necessary competencies to engage in problem-solving behavior. In a review of action research, Susman and Evered (1978) are at pains to contrast it to the epistemological shortcomings of positivist science. While traditional research methods aim at producing law-like generalizations, making predictions, and detaching the researcher from what he or she is observing, action research

is directed toward the development of action competencies of members of organizations, and can be described as an "enabling" science. Typically, the kinds of skills which action research develops are interpersonal and problem-defining. Competence is developed in interpretation and judgment, in establishing problem-solving procedures, acting in contingent and uncertain situations, learning from one's errors, generating workable new constructs from one's experiences. Such skills are needed by persons in organizations, and positivist science has generally made negligible contributions to providing such skills. (1978, p.599)

The knowledge generated by action research methods is thus very much contingent on the context of study. Each situation is unique in terms of the problems it generates, and the possible solutions to such problems. Pasmore and Friedlander (1982), for example, employed an action research program to solve the problem of recurring and steadily increasing employee injuries in an organization. While traditional methods for establishing the cause of the problem had failed, implementation of techniques such as group problem solving involving employees, interviews, feedback sessions, and so forth, produced a sharp decline in the incidence of the problem. The actual solution of the problem was perhaps not as significant as the fact that it was achieved by relying heavily on the employees' own knowledge of their organization. Not only were data collected by employees, but recommendations for change in the organization were made by employees as well. Pasmore and Friedlander (1982, p.361) thus conclude that "given responsibility, employees are capable of (1) acting in the best interests of the organization, (2) helping to guide the course of scientific investigations, and (3) recommending effective courses of action for solving serious organizational problems."

Action research thus criticizes the conservatism of traditional social science rigor, and emphasizes instead the importance of "useful knowledge," i.e., knowledge that will have an immediate impact on social systems (Gustavsen, 1979). However, the notion of "change" used here is defined in the context of an already specified frame of reference. In Pasmore and Friedlander's study, for example, the organizational problem was already predefined by the management as a "sore arm" problem. As such, the researchers were invited by management to develop possible solutions within this context. The successful conclusion of such a study is therefore heavily dependent on acceptance of the legitimacy of existing power relations within an organization. Action researchers tend to emphasize consensus and cooperation in their studies because suggestions that conflicts of interests may exist within an organization could jeopardize the completion of research. In Pasmore and Friedlander's case, a suggestion that management style might have been partly responsible for the "sore arm" problem was met with hostility by the management group (1982, p.350).

Brown and Tandon (1983, p.290) indicate, therefore, that action research methods are most likely to be successful when "distributions of resources and authority are accepted as legitimate, when the relevant parties accept researchers as credible, and when rewards are available for integrating problem solving and research." In other words, action research tends to support the structure of the status quo, concentrating on problem solving at an individual, interpersonal, and group level. Consideration of organizing at the structural level (i.e., power relations and their concomitant ideologies) is thus not a feature of action research. Evidence that a particular system of power relations is deemed legitimate by members of an organization does not necessarily mean that structures of domination do not operate. It will be recalled that one of the principal functions of ideology is to articulate sectional interests in a universal manner. Action research is unable to cope with situations where this occurs insofar as it accepts the definition of the situation provided by the group representing the dominant interests in the organization.

An alternative to action research, therefore, is participatory research (Brown & Kaplan, 1981; Gaventa and Horton, 1981; Hall, 1981; Vio Grossi, 1981). As mentioned above, this type of research is highly dependent on active participation by social actors for its implementation, and views radical social change as its primary function. Unlike action research, participatory research rejects the status quo and seeks to transform the existing power relations. In this sense, participatory research is emancipatory. Brown and Tandon (1983, p.291) indicate that participatory research strategies can be adopted when "the legitimacy of power and resource distribution is questioned, when client groups are aware and mobilized to influence their situation, and when researchers are ideologically committed to social transformation." Participatory researchers are not interested in solving problems within a predefined context; rather, they are more concerned with redefining the context itself, providing the means by which previously oppressed interests can be voiced and considered in the structuring of social environments.

Hall (1981, p.7) defines participatory research as "an integrated activity that combines social investigation, educational work and action." He summarizes its characteristics as follows:

• The problem originates in the community or workplace itself.

• The ultimate goal . . . is fundamental structural transformation and the improvements of the lives of those involved. The beneficiaries are the workers or people concerned.

• Participatory research involves the people in the workplace or community in the control of the entire process of the research.

• Focus . . . is on work with a wide range of exploited or oppressed groups; immigrants, labour; indigenous people; women.

• Central . . . is its role of strengthening the awareness in people of their own abilities and resources and its support to mobilizing or organizing.

• The term 'researcher' can refer to both the community or workplace persons involved as well as those with specialized training.

• [Outside researchers] are committed participants and learners in a process that leads to militancy rather than detachment. (1981, pp.7–8)

Again, participatory research is used as an antidote to the positivist orientation of traditional social science, with its tendency to affirm the status quo. As such, the central role of power in participatory research must be further developed.

It is a mistake to imagine that because participatory research relies heavily on the active role of the individual that community/organization members possess the "real" knowledge of a certain social structure. This "spontaneous naive" approach "[denies] the very existence and efficiency of the whole ideological apparatus of domination set up by the hegemonic sectors" (Vio Grossi, 1981, p.46). In Giddens' (1979) terms, to idolize such popular knowledge is to confuse practical consciousness with discursive consciousness. The researcher's role is to transform practical consciousness into discursive penetration by exposing the ideology of the dominant power structure—a process that Vio Grossi (1981, p.46) refers to as "disindoctrination."

Another potential problem in the use of participatory research methods is to equate popular power with social change. The fact that a change has occurred within a particular social system does not necessarily mean that a fundamental structural shift in power has also occurred. Indeed, it is a basic characteristic of many social systems that they are able to appropriate and incorporate ostensibly radical, fringe groups into their structure. The use of "punk" jingles to advertise Pepsi, scooters, and designer jeans is only one example of the degree to which subcultures are very quickly appropriated and exploited by corporate elites as a way of maintaining a consumer-oriented society. In this instance, punk has come to represent the very antithesis of what it originally stood for—such is the power of the dominant, corporate ideology.

The problem of the relationship between power and change is equally applicable in the case of organizational cultures. Changes may be implemented within an organization—use of quality circles, reduced working hours, suggestion boxes, etc. —but this in no way guarantees that any real shift has taken place in terms of representation of interests. Ultimately, most organizational changes have their roots in the need for greater efficiency and productivity, while quality-of-life issues are a secondary concern.

The goal of participatory research is thus one of introducing fundamental structural change through exposing the myths that a dominant power structure imposes on people. *Genuine* change can only be sustained, however, if knowledge can be reframed in terms of the interests of the subordinate groups, i.e., as "popular" knowledge:

> The creation of popular knowledge is a form of "anti-hegemonic" activity, an instrument in the struggle to control what the social agenda is. . . . popular knowledge can be seen as preventing those in power from maintaining the monopoly of determining the wants of others, thus, in effect, transferring power to those groups engaged in the production of popular knowledge. (Hall, 1981, p.14)

This popular knowledge becomes the basis for alternative forms of organizing. Participatory research holds praxis as a specific goal in that the insight provided by popular knowledge leads to structural social change that alters the status quo (Vio Grossi, 1981). Social actors develop a transformative capacity that arises out of the dialectic between their situatedness as members of a particular community, and the guidance and insight provided by the researchers.

As might be expected, however, participatory research is not without its problems, primarily because of its status as a radical mode of social inquiry. Epistemologically speaking, the principal argument against participatory research is that it is unscientific. That is, rather than adopting a value-free stance, the researcher deliberately supports the values of a particular group in society. This argument is usually presented by those social scientists who believe that the human sciences should emulate the methods of the natural sciences. The problem with this form of foundationalism has been discussed earlier in the chapter. A participatory researcher would also point out that the attempt to claim value neutrality allows the social scientist to ignore the power relations and mechanisms of domination that inevitably co-opt any "value-free" perspective. Farganis states:

> even the most apparently neutral methodology, the methodology of the natural sciences, when it is applied to the social world, becomes political in its findings and implications. It would follow, then, that there can be no objective knowledge in the social sciences, but that all such knowledge is

infused with politically relevant values. Even if one self-consciously becomes scientific and attempts to articulate and control the impact of values on social research, the very methodology employed entails evaluative presuppositions about man and the social world which are embedded in its concepts and categories and procedures; and, these presuppositions make the goal of an objective social science an impossible and futile undertaking. (1975, pp. 483–484)

Participatory research makes no claim to value neutrality and objectivity; rather, it is a deliberate attempt to offer a radical alternative to mainstream social science. In Rorty's terms, its goal is to provide social actors with a way of coping, not just in the sense of being able to "get along," but in the sense of being able to transform the social context in which they live and work. This move requires a synthesis of theory and practice (praxis) in which the researcher provides individuals with the research skills necessary to take action against the dominant groups in an emancipatory fashion.

A second problem with participatory research relates to its applicability as a viable form of inquiry. While many might be sympathetic with its goals, the more pragmatic issue of the kinds of social contexts to which it can be applied is an important one. Most participatory research projects have been conducted in Third World countries where low income, poorly educated groups are easy targets for exploitation by multinational corporations or government agencies. In these cases, participatory research is a viable way of challenging the legitimacy of a particular sociocultural system, and of providing marginal groups with greater political clout.

In industrialized nations, however, the problem is somewhat different in that the presumption of a conflict situation may actually be detrimental to client groups. In organizations, for example, participatory research may create tensions between managers and workers that cause long-lasting damage to the climate of the organization. In addition, researchers are normally only invited into an organization at the request of management, who are usually responsible for funding projects. Under such circumstances it is very difficult to articulate an agenda that challenges the fundamental power structure of the organization. Any attempt to question the legitimacy of the status quo in an organization may result in a withdrawal of funds and termination of the project—or else implementation of another study using researchers who are more sympathetic to management concerns.

Participatory research methods have been adopted in the United States, but not always in organizational contexts. Gaventa and Horton (1981), for example, document their work with an Appalachian citizens group seeking land reform. The purpose of the study was to demonstrate to the Appalachian Regional Commission (ARC) — the government agency concerned with Appalachian development — that land ownership by absentee corporations was one of the primary reasons for the stark contrast between wealth and poverty in the region. The research was conducted by forming a task group made up of both researchers and local community members, the latter being trained in research techniques by the former. Interestingly enough, the group had great difficulty obtaining funding from the ARC, which only approved the project at the last moment. In addition, once the results of the study were formulated (showing that indeed corporate land ownership produced great hardship in the region) the ARC refused to disseminate the information, claiming that it was "unscientific" and "too subjective." Consequently, the task group published and distributed the report independently. The authors conclude that the reticence of the ARC "had more to do with political sensitivity of the information than with its accuracy" (Gaventa & Horton, 1981, p.36).

In a participatory research study conducted in a factory, Brown and Kaplan (1981), attempted to solve the problem of deteriorating labor-management relations. Requested by management to come up with solutions for the problem, the authors soon found themselves caught in the interface between opposing union and management ideologies: "As the diagnosis unfolded, difficulties emerged. Managers objected to some questionnaire items as excessively pro-union; union executives objected to other items as anti-union and threatened to prosecute the researchers for illegal influence on the workers" (1981, p.305).

As a result of this extreme polarization between the two groups, the authors decided to work exclusively with management, "in spite of their ideological sympathy for the union" (1981, p.311). As a result of this collaboration, however, a picture of the organization was constructed that reflected the diverse perspectives of the interested parties in the research program. Whereas initially managers were concerned primarily with solving specific problems, they eventually came to recognize the importance of organizational change processes and the need to incorporate divergent (including union) viewpoints into decision making. Thus:

> The resulting lists of changes and problems were presented to top management with the understanding that the information would be compiled and reported to all groups. This process engaged a broad sample of organization members in explaining past and present organization change. A variety of explanations emerged, some more pungent than others. As one ex-union executive pithily summed up previous problems: "It was just piss-poor management. Now they've started treating us like adults, and things have gotten better." (1981, p.308)

It is tempting to suggest that participatory research is applicable to all organizational contexts, but this would be a gross oversimplification of complex issues. Participatory research, like action research, is situation-specific, and must be adapted to its context of study. In the above factory study, for example, it was recognized that siding with the union as the "oppressed group" would only exacerbate tension. Accordingly, the researchers worked *with* rather than against those in power in order to change the existing power structure. On the other hand, the Appalachian study required an explicitly adversarial approach; it was obvious to researchers and community members alike that the only way to alter the power structure was to confront those who controlled it with incontrovertible evidence of inequity and exploitation. In either case, the goal of research is to provide social actors with the ability to construct alternative social realities that, by their very existence, stand in critique of dominant views of the world. Praxis occurs when social actors are able to reflect upon and transform their lived-world through the bringing together of theoretical insight and practical action.

SUMMARY AND CONCLUSION

The purpose of this chapter has been to assimilate some of the epistemological and methodological issues that arise when one conceives of a theory of organizational cultures rooted in ideology and power. Epistemologically speaking, knowledge generation is erroneously viewed as the construction of observation statements which accurately mirror an already existing, fixed world. An alternative to this positivist perspective places emphasis on the extent to which reality is socially constructed through the symbolic interaction of individuals. To this end, Rorty's notion of "conversation" reflects his disenchantment with foundational knowledge. He prefers to talk instead about the degree to which a given discourse works better than another for a given purpose; that is, how can a particular vocabulary help us to cope with the world in a fruitful way? Along similar lines, Gadamer uses the term "genuine conversation" to refer to the way in which truth is produced through the fusion of different horizons. Here, he emphasizes the importance of tradition as the grounding for a community's values—it is through the fresh articulation of this tradition that knowledge is produced.

Like Rorty and Gadamer, Habermas places language at the focal point of his theory of interests. However, he is principally concerned with the way in which language can be systematically distorted to serve as an instrument of domination. Primarily, his focus is on the way in which natural language is appropriated by technical interests to the detriment of practical-moral and emancipatory concerns. This move is important because it draws attention to the way in which language can serve an ideological function, although in Habermas's case it is principally scientific (technical) language which is viewed as distorting the relationship between the social actor and his or her humanly constructed world.

Habermas's critique of ideology is significant, but his overemphasis on rational self-reflection leads to a neglect of the interest rooted in institutional structures, and his ideal speech situation leads to the taking up of a position outside of ideology. On the other hand, Giddens's concept of structuration recognizes the degree to which institutional forms constrain the practices of social actors; at the same time, however, actors draw on the rules and resources of institutions to engage in meaningful behavior. In this context, ideology-critique does not involve taking up a perspective that transcends a particular ideology, but rather requires that insight is generated into the way that ideology constrains (deforms) sense-making to serve dominant interests. Recognition of such constraint allows for the creation of alternative forms of social reality. In Giddens's terms, the very rules and resources that constrain social practices also act in an enabling capacity as the basis for social transformation.

Methodologically, action research and participatory research have been considered as radical modes of inquiry. Emancipation occurs through praxis—theoretically informed practical action—and both methods provide ways in which organization members can actively engage in the process of social change. While both types of research are situationally contingent, action research emphasizes consensus and mutual problem solving, whereas participatory research presumes conflict and attempts to redress the inequities caused by ideological domination.

This chapter has therefore outlined the principal strengths and difficulties of a theory of knowledge that attempts to account for issues of power and ideology in meaning formation. Problems of both foundationalist and relativist positions were discussed. In the concluding chapter I will draw out the major implications of this study, and suggest ways in which a radical theory of organizational cultures can be developed further.

7

CONCLUSION: INTERPRETATION AND DOMINATION

The goal of this study has been to elucidate a theory of organizational cultures that moves beyond what I perceive as the conceptual limitations that characterize most cultural studies of organizational behavior. Extant theories of organizational culture have been consistently weak in their conceptualization of the means by which organizations produce, maintain, and reproduce their day-to-day practices. Usually this process is described in terms of intersubjectively generated understanding of the rules and beliefs that underlie judgments about appropriate and inappropriate organizing behavior. Questions about the role of power and domination in this process are rarely considered.

The reconceptualized notion of organizational cultures developed here thus explicitly considers the role of ideology, power-as-domination, and organizational symbolism in the constitution and maintenance of organizational meaning formations. I have argued that meaning does not arise spontaneously and consensually, but is rather the product of the vested interests of particular organizational groups. Power is exercised by such groups not only in the control of organizational resources (technology, information, money, etc.), but also to the degree that they are able to frame organizational reality discursively in a way that serves their own interests. Ideology serves in this capacity by producing and reproducing the subjectivity of organization members through the process of interpellation. As such, the dominant interests are taken on uncritically as the interests of all organizational groups. Ideology is thus conceived not simply as a set of beliefs, but as a materially located meaning system that *constitutes* the social actor's organizational consciousness.

In this context, a focal point of this book has been the relationship between ideology and organizational symbolism. The discursive and behavioral practices of organization members can be viewed as the material manifestation of ideological meaning formations; discourse constitutes systems of signification that both express and reconstitute the dominant ideological structure of an organization. Organizational discourse is therefore ill conceived as merely representational; that is, as a means of describing an already structured organizational system. Rather, discourse is the very medium of experience of organization members. Organizational language is therefore the principal means by which ideological meaning formations are instantiated. In Habermas's terms, language is systematically distorted (ideological) to the degree that it represents certain interests to the exclusion of other, legitimate interests. The ideological domination of one group by another is accomplished through the discursive articulation of certain meaning structures which simultaneously obscure other possible world views.

In chapter 5 I looked specifically at the way in which organizational narrative can function ideologically to produce and reproduce the forms of organizational reality required to sustain the interests of dominant groups. Stories are ideological to the extent that they privilege certain readings of organizational life while presenting themselves as reflections of the existing order of things, as "the way things are." Discursive practices such as stories do not simply reproduce dominant ideological meaning structures, however, but rather function in a complex relationship with other symbolic structures and organizational interests groups to create an intricate web of meaning. Potentially, stories articulate multiple referents, not all of which fit with the dominant ideology; but a certain ideological meaning system is reproduced to the degree that certain interest groups have the ability to make particular meanings "stick" to symbolic practices.

Chapter 6 considered the epistemological and methodological implications of the radical conception of organizational cultures developed in the previous chapters. The principal theme was that consideration of issues of ideology and domination in the creation of meaning requires extensive re-evaluation of what is taken to be true or knowable. Foundational conceptions of truth are inadequate insofar as they are based on the possibility of creating an isomorphism between the language of description and an external, objective reality. Knowledge must therefore be conceived in the context of the ability of individuals to engage in critical self-reflection, creating a situation under which conditions of domination and repression can be subject to alteration. Methodologically speaking, the adoption of a neutral, "value-free" stance by the researcher often results in the appropriation of research

findings by dominant organizational interests.[1] In contrast, the abandonment of foundational assumptions permits a view of knowledge as
a way of coping rather than as a reflection of objective reality. However,
while conceiving of theories as voices in an ongoing conversation is
fruitful, such hermeneutic-interpretive approaches are still subject to
political and institutional constraints. As such, an adequate conception
of organizational research must consider the role of vested interests in
the ongoing structuring of organizational meaning and social/discursive
practices.

THE ROLE OF INTERPRETATION

The main consequence of this reorientation is a need to examine more
closely the role played by interpretation in the construction of organizational meaning. Here, I refer to both the activity of the social actor in
interpreting events in which he or she is enmeshed, and the
reinterpretation of these events by the organizational researcher. At this
point, however, I want to focus more closely on the latter. The act of
interpretation is a fundamentally political act, especially when placed in
the context of the theoretical framework laid out in this book. Like
Thompson and others, I would argue that the interpretive act on the
part of the researcher-theorist involves an explicit attempt to reconnect
discourse to the systems of domination which it sustains. I am fairly
convinced of this relationship; that is, that in some way discourse
functions to constitute a framework for understanding and interpreting

---

[1] The tobacco industry does an excellent job of presenting "value-free" research
findings to obscure the harmful effects of cigarette smoking. For example, *Philip Morris
Magazine*, targeted at smokers, combines human interest stories ("America's Cup,"
"Spring Training," "Who Invented Spaghetti") with information about tobacco research
and legislation. Designed to protect "smokers' rights" (and the profits of the tobacco
industry), the magazine is unabashedly pro-smoking, expressing ill-concealed contempt
for "anti-smoking activists." A brief quote from an article entitled "I'm too understanding
to mind," written by an ex-smoker, provides the general tenor of the magazine:

I like the look and feel of cigarettes. They're streamlined and thin enough to look
like they're weight-conscious. There were times when they felt smooth and sexy
between my fingers. . . . Smokers and non-smokers think I'm strange because I
don't object to entering a business office where people are permitted to smoke. To
me, the smoke creates an atmosphere of industriousness, of assertiveness and
sometimes, of a macho presence. (Sandler, 1987, p. 22–23)

Focus is shifted away from health concerns, and emphasis placed on the social issues
surrounding smoking, advocating freedom from persecution for "people who choose to
smoke" (p. 23).

events that serves certain interests better than others. What is more problematic is the attempt to make explicit the connection between discourse and domination. I have explicated a theoretical model which argues that ideology is the mediating factor; that is, ideology interpellates subjects such that they are predisposed to construct reality in a way that structures relations of domination in favor of certain interest groups. However, this still leaves us with the problem of creating legitimate interpretations of discourse; in other words, it is not enough to decide that relations of domination exist, and then show how discourse serves these relations by fitting one's interpretation accordingly. Rather, one must demonstrate the validity of the interpretation that is constructed. It is the problematic issue of the interpretive act that I want to take up in the remainder of this concluding chapter.

Jameson (1981, p.17) argues that the process of interpretation is first and foremost a political process. The political interpretation of a literary text, historical narrative, and so forth, is not a residual issue that supplements other kinds of analysis. Rather, it is "the absolute horizon of all reading and all interpretations." From this perspective the process of interpretation is confronted politically, as an act which has direct implications for the way that discourse structures systems of domination in our society. From a political perspective, the goal of interpretation is not to provide some absolute reading of a text which provides a definitive explication of the relationship between that text and the world that it purports to describe. The goal is rather to draw attention to the process of interpretation itself, and to show how certain dominant readings become incorporated into texts, such that a certain view of the world is maintained and reproduced.

Culler's (1982) discussion of the process of deconstruction focuses on the act of reading itself, demonstrating the ways in which that very process can be co-opted, and hence made complicitous with the dominant ideological meaning system in a given social structure. For example, his analysis of "Reading as a Woman" (1982, pp.43–64) attempts to demonstrate the degree to which "male" literature frequently acts to co-opt the female perspective and draw women readers into identifying with anti-feminist sentiments. The primary function of feminist criticism, therefore, is not simply to interpret the world from a female perspective, or to document texts which support a feminist perspective, but rather to resist the phallocentric view of the world exhibited by both male writers and literary critics, a view which female readers are implicitly asked to adopt if they are to make a "legitimate" reading of a text. Feminist criticism thus adopts an explicitly political perspective by providing a different point of departure for the reader:

what it does above all is to reverse the usual situation in which the perspective of a male critic is assumed to be sexually neutral, while a feminist reading is seen as a case of special pleading and an attempt to form a text into a pre-determined mold. . . . The more convincing its critique of phallic criticism, the more feminist criticism comes to provide the broad and comprehensive vision, analyzing and situating the limited and interested interpretations of male critics. (Culler, 1982, pp.55–56)

This process of resistance, of creating a disjuncture between the reader and the received, dominant interpretation of the text is not exclusive to feminist criticism. The deconstruction of discourse in any context must be concerned with undermining the imposition of a veneer of reality on texts, in whatever form. Deconstructing discursive practice in this context requires that one show how it "undermines the philosophy it asserts, or the hierarchical oppositions on which it relies" (1982, p.86). Such is the case with the analysis of the IBM story in chapter 5. The ideological interpellation of organization members by this story is dependent on the hierarchical oppositions that it sets up: man vs. woman, employer vs. employee, worldly male vs. innocent bride, rule breaker vs. rule enforcer, and so forth. Such oppositions predispose listeners to the story to interpret it as an expression of the democratic nature of the corporation, in which status does not exempt one from appropriate organizational behavior. However, a dissenting, deconstructive reading of the story shows how it is these very oppositions which undermine the democratic philosophy that the story ostensibly asserts. That is, the hierarchical oppositions embodied in the narrative structure of the story are salient to the reader/listener because they embody the values implicit in IBM as a capitalist corporation. The story is only significant because the interaction produces a transcendence of the material reality of the organizational hierarchy. It attempts to co-opt the listener into the dominant reading by resolving for him or her the contradiction between the espousal of democratic values (in a democratic society) and the structural inequities built into the corporate enterprise.

Deconstruction exposes this obscuring of contradictions and demonstrates how the act of reading can create a disjuncture in the continuity of experience that ideological discourse attempts to portray. Deconstructive interpretation thus politicizes the act of reading/listening in that it problematizes the interpretive process and exposes the degree to which dominant ideological meaning structures produce a sense of experiential closure.

Interpretation from a deconstructive perspective thus exploits the disjuncture and discontinuity of experience that is always present (if only latent) in the dialectical relationship between reader/listener and text. In a sense, deconstruction recognizes the ability of all social actors to construct a text from the text being read. The politicizing of interpretation requires that this act of (re)construction explores the disjuncture inherent in the experience of the text and thus reconstitutes the dialectic between personal experience and the experience that the text presents to one (as in the case of feminist criticism). Again, to return to the IBM story, one might speculate that interpellation of the listener by the story is by no means complete, and that a distinct but latent discontinuity exists between the organizational experience the story articulates and the experience of the listener. The potential for deconstructing and reconstructing the meaning that the story presents as a fait accompli is thus present. Indeed, the story might well be recapitulated as an example of assertion of rights by organization members, and as an attempt to delegitimate the "divine right" of the corporate elite to do as they wish. Deconstructing the story can therefore make explicit the emancipatory qualities that are inherent in the narrative structure.

The legitimacy or validity of an interpretation of discourse is not tied, therefore, to issues of verifiability (i.e., whether the interpretation conforms objectively to real world conditions). Nor is an interpretation judged on its ability to reflect the "essence" of what a unit of discourse is trying to say. Rather, interpretation is legitimate to the degree that it produces social transformation; in other words, that in some way social actors are able to engage in self-reflection and to re-evaluate their conditions of existence by virtue of the deconstruction of the culture that they inhabit. In an organizational context, deconstruction of organizational practice produces discursive penetration. This involves not only knowledge of how to cope with organizational exigencies, but also points toward insight into the ideological meaning structures that frame organizational reality. Insight into those structures provides the basis for the generation of alternative organizational realities. The ultimate goal of deconstruction is thus *praxis*; that is, the attainment of both theoretical insight and practical action that is informed by such insight.

One can contextualize the development of praxis by examining the relationship between participatory research methods (see chapter 6) and the analysis of organizational symbolism. Participatory research is critically oriented, insofar as it provides organization members with the practical means for social transformation. If the thesis of this book is correct, then a prerequisite for social transformation is an understanding and critique of the way in which discourse functions. In other words, if ideology is manifested in everyday discourse, then a critique and transformation of that ideology and its concomitant power structures requires critique and transformation of organizational discourse.

Smircich describes the intent behind such critically-oriented research when she states:

> the Interpretive researcher of an organizational culture tries to uncover the structures of meaning in use in a setting and to synthesize an image of that group's reality and to make it available for consideration and reflection by the group members. I thus conceive of Interpretive research as basically a diagnostic effort in which the researcher reflects to a group a many-sided image of the meaning systems in use. (1981, pp.10–11)

I would develop this description further by suggesting that the researcher does not simply "reflect back" his or her interpretation of organizational practice. Rather, the process is one of encouraging *critique* and *innovation* through the examination of taken-for-granted meaning systems. In a sense, the goal is to make what is familiar seem strange to the social actor—to make things appear in a new light—and to use this strangeness as an incentive for critique and change.

The analysis of organizational narrative can be conceived as one potential vehicle for the application of participatory research methods in organizations. Storytelling is a pervasive aspect of organizational life, socializing members by providing the appropriate experiential base to make sense of organizational practices. Because of this pervasiveness, it becomes a useful tool for allowing organization members to engage in self-reflection and construct a clearer sense of the role of discursive practices in the creation of organizational reality. Here we can return to Deetz's (1982; Deetz & Kersten, 1983) model for examining the structuration of organizational meaning. Recall that he suggests that critical-interpretive research must incorporate the goals of understanding, critique, and education. Applied to the analysis of organizational storytelling, understanding arises when members become aware of the degree to which their organizational reality is a human, discursive construct and not simply an objective, tangible structure that transcends their own actions. Stories are therefore not viewed as mere informational vehicles about specific organizational situations, but as symbolic devices which structure organizational experience in a certain way.

Critique occurs with the recognition that the social construction of reality through storytelling is not a neutral, value-free practice, but often functions as a reproduction and privileging of certain organizational interests. For example, the "Horatio Alger" stories of organizational success might be seen as functioning to reproduce a managerial view of the world, in which success is equated with movement up the corporate ladder, higher salary, greater influence, and so forth. At the same time such stories serve to obscure the extent to which women, for example, are heavily underrepresented at upper levels of the corporate hierarchy (there are few "Harriet Alger" stories). This class of stories thus functions to privilege certain organizational interests while systematically excluding others.

Finally, education involves the enrichment of organizational discourse. Once organizational critique is achieved (i.e., the recognition of repressive forms of discourse), then social actors can begin to express their own interests in ways that escape the discursive closure inherent in systematically distorted communication. In a narrative context, the goal of education involves the formation of alternative readings of organizational discourse, reframing the way that organizational reality is conceived and experienced. The development of these rereadings is emancipatory (opening up the possibility for self-determined change) in their challenging of the accepted power relations in organizations. Stories often serve extant relations of domination by sustaining the sectional interests of hegemonic groups. Alternative readings of these stories (and the telling of different stories) question this hegemony by demonstrating the possibility for change. Using women in organizations as an example once more, one might argue that an emancipatory function is served by providing readings of stories that resist male definitions of organizational competence, and which provide narrative reinterpretations and demystification of organizational patriarchy. Thus readings which not only critique narrow male-oriented definitions of organizational competence (aggressiveness, rationality, toughness, etc.), but which also redefine what it means to competent can function in an emancipatory fashion.

The formation of new readings and new stories as the product of organizational research points out the difficulty of so-called "value neutral" research, as defined by traditional social science. Researchers actively engage with organization members in a dialectic that has social transformation as its intended outcome. In the context of Deetz's three stages, analysis of organizational narrative fulfills the ethical goal of organizational research by broadening members' experience of, and participation in, the ongoing process of organizational structuration. Such participation, however, is only realized through change in the structure of power relations. Discursive change may highlight alternative forms of organizational reality, but structural change emerges only when the connection between language and domination is made explicit (Thompson, 1984b). Organization members are required to probe beneath the discursive manifestations of organizational practice to examine the power relations that produce those practices. Discourse analysis and participatory research can fulfill this goal by providing social actors with the analytical and practical tools required to expedite social transformation.

Research within this framework might be conducted in the following manner. On entering an organization, researchers conduct open-ended interviews with a representative sample of members drawn from all levels of the organization. These interviews would elicit information relating to views of organizational philosophy, perceived problem areas, degree of job satisfaction, short- and long-range organizational goals, and so forth. Analysis of this data would reveal the kinds of stories that people use to characterize the organization, and allow the researcher to construct an interpretation of the dominant meaning systems that function in the process of organizational structuration.

The second step in the research process involves the researcher's returning to the organization members and presenting them with the constructed interpretation. It is at this stage that the dialectic between the researcher and organization members arises. In essence, it is the researcher's task to articulate a plausible interpretation of the way in which the social actors make sense of their organization. The social actors, in turn, challenge the researcher's assumptions; through the ongoing and reciprocal questioning process, both researcher and organization members are made to assess critically their sense of organizational structuration.

Responses to the researcher's construction of events may vary from claims that he or she has merely stated the obvious, through self-reflective insight, to suggestions that the researcher has got it "all wrong" (Smircich, 1981). Rejoinders to claims of stating the obvious might involve a reframing of the interpretation to make it appear more strange to organization members; this may provide insight to a practice that was previously transparently "obvious." Similarly, the researcher might respond to claims that he or she is wrong by going back to the data and reassessing the interpretation in the light of members' counter interpretation of practices. Alternatively, the researcher might request a suspension of judgment by members, and suggest a reassessment of his or her findings at a later stage in the study. One of the products of this dialectical process, however, is that organization members become highly sensitized to the constitutive power of discourse, and recognize the extent to which organizational language functions to produce and reproduce organizational reality.

In the third step organization members conduct discursive analyses of their own. In this way the organizational reality constructed by the researcher can be confronted by their own equally well-grounded view of the organization. This move allows organization members and researcher to meet on equal terms, and avoids the problems often associated with the researcher adopting a privileged standpoint regarding knowledge about lay actors. Organization members are thus not merely the objects of study, but are subjects who themselves engage in research. The dialectic that develops between researcher and organization members may produce a view of organizational reality that neither could have articulated independently.

I have no illusions about the difficulty of the research method outlined above. Nevertheless, research that is based on assumptions regarding issues of power and domination demands a high level of accountability on the part of the researcher. From an ethical perspective alone the researcher is committed to removing discursive closure and providing conditions under which constraint-free discourse can emerge. It is difficult to see how this is realizable if the researcher insists on maintaining a perspective based on dispassionate observation from afar. Participatory research is emancipatory at least in part because it bridges the gap between the researcher and the social actors being "studied." It is ethical, insofar as it attempts to reveal the fundamentally political nature of both discourse and the process of interpretation, and thus allows social actors to acquire a more active role in constituting organizational evaluation and change.

CONCLUSION

The importance of this work lies in its conception of organizational cultures as potential sites of cultural *de*formation. Organizations are not stable, fully integrated structures. Rather, they are the product of various groups with competing goals and interests. An organization serves a group's interests to the extent that it is able to produce, maintain and reproduce those organizational practices that sustain that group's needs. Part of this process involves framing organizational sense-making in a way that supports extant relations of domination, making sectional interests appear universal. In this respect, organizational ideology, as manifested in discursive practices, interpellates organization members in a certain fashion, providing a particular sense of organizational consciousness. Because of the role they play in the constitution of individual subjectivity, ideological meaning formations become naturalized and taken-for-granted; that is, they become an intrinsic part of what it means to organize.

Ironically, proponents of theories of organizational culture have helped in this process by uncritically adopting "culture" as the new by-word for organizational studies. Acceptance of "sense-making" as the dominant mode of organizing reifies culture as an organizational given. Examining the ways in which social actors generate intersubjectively meaningful behavior is important, but it must be qualified by a conceptualization of factors that distort this process. Culture produces repression and alienation as well as shared values and a sense of community. While the latter is well documented, the former is not, and it is to this area that this book has been directed.

The ultimate goal of this book is the deconstruction of structures of domination as they are manifested in human communication. This study has been conceptual in nature and is not applied to actual and specific conditions of domination. The next step in this project must therefore involve the testing of the theoretical issues developed here. This final chapter has given brief guidelines for such a project, although they are necessarily general given the context-specific nature of the research.

Finally, the legitimacy of this study rests with its invocation of a communication ethic that involves the continuous striving for the nonrealizable ideal of coercion-free discourse. The quality of community life is contingent on the application of this moral imperative. Perhaps above all others, communication scholars have a responsibility to ensure that the conditions for openly "continuing the conversation" are not eroded. This book is written with that ethic in mind.

REFERENCES

Abercrombie, N., & Turner, B. S. (1982). The dominant ideology thesis. In A. Giddens and D. Held (Eds.), *Classes, power, and conflict* (pp. 396–414). Berkeley: University of California Press.

Abrahamsson, B. (1977). *Bureaucracy or participation: The logic of organization*. Beverly Hills, CA: Sage.

Administrative Science Quarterly (1983). *28.* Special issue on organizational culture.

Althusser, L. (1970). *For Marx* (B. Brewster, Trans.). New York: Vintage Books.

Althusser, L. (1971). *Lenin and philosophy* (B. Brewster, Trans.). New York: Monthly Review Press.

Astley, W. G., & Sachdeva, P. S. (1984). Structural sources of intra-organizational power: A theoretical synthesis. *Academy of Management Review, 9,* 104–113.

Austin, J. L. (1962). *How to do things with words.* Oxford, England: Blackwell.

Bacharach, S., & Lawler, E. (1980). *Power and politics in organizations.* San Francisco: Jossey-Bass.

Bachrach, P., & Baratz, M. (1962). Two faces of power. *American Political Science Review, 56,* 947–952.

Becker, S. L. (1984). Marxist approaches to media studies: The British experience. *Critical Studies in Mass Communication, 1,* 66–80.

Benson, J. K. (1977). Organizations: A dialectical view. *Administrative Science Quarterly, 22,* 1–21.

Berger, P., & Luckmann, T. (1971). *The social construction of reality: A treatise in the sociology of knowledge.* Harmondsworth, England: Penguin.

Bernstein, R. (1983). *Beyond objectivism and relativism: Science, hermeneutics, and praxis.* Philadelphia: University of Pennsylvania Press.

Braverman, H. (1974). *Labor and Monopoly Capital: The degradation of work in the twentieth century*. New York: Monthly Review Press.

Brown, L. D., & Kaplan, R. E. (1981). Participative research in a factory. In P. Reason & J. Rowan (Eds.), *Human inquiry* (pp. 303–314). New York: Wiley.

Brown, L. D., & Tandon, R. (1983). Ideology and political economy in inquiry: Action research and participatory research. *The Journal of Applied Behavioral Science, 19*, 277–294.

Brown, R. H. (1978). Bureaucracy as praxis: Toward a political phenomenology of formal organizations. *Administrative Science Quarterly, 23*, 365–382.

Burawoy, M. (1979). *Manufacturing consent: Changes in the labor process under monopoly capitalism*. Chicago: University of Chicago Press.

Burleson, B., & Kline, S. (1979). Habermas' theory of communication: A critical explication. *Quarterly Journal of Speech, 65*, 412–428.

Burrell, G., & Morgan, G. (1979). *Sociological paradigms and organisational analysis*. London: Heinemann.

Carbaugh, D. (1982a). *Cultural communication and organizing: Toward an understanding of organizational culture*. Presented to the SCA/ICA Conference on Interpretive Approaches to Organizational Communication, Alta, UT.

Carbaugh, D. (1982b). *Some thoughts on organizing as cultural communication*. Presented at the Speech Communication Association Annual Convention, Louisville, KY.

Clegg, S. (1975). *Power, rule and domination*. London: Routledge & Kegan Paul.

Clegg, S. (1981). Organization and control. *Administrative Science Quarterly, 26*, 545–562.

Clegg, S., & Dunkerley, D. (1980). *Organization, class and control*. London: Routledge and Kegan Paul.

Cohen, M. D., March, J. G., & Olsen, J. P. (1972). A garbage can model of organizational choice. *Administrative Science Quarterly, 17*, 1–25.

Conrad, C. (1983). Organizational power: Faces and symbolic forms. In L. Putnam & M. Pacanowsky (Eds.), *Communication and organizations: An interpretive approach* (pp. 173–194). Beverly Hills, CA: Sage.

Conrad, C. (1985a). *Strategic organizational communication: Cultures, situations, and adaptation*. New York: Holt, Rinehart, & Winston.

Conrad, C. (1985b). Chrysanthemums and swords: A reading of contemporary organizational communication theory and research. *Southern Speech Communication Journal, 50*, 189- 200.

Convergence (1981). *14*(3). Special issue on participative research.

Coward, R., & Ellis, J. (1977). *Language and materialism: developments in semiology and the theory of the subject*. London: Routledge & Kegan Paul.

Culler, J. (1982). *On deconstruction: theory and criticism after structuralism.* Ithaca, NY: Cornell University Press.

Daft, R. L., & Wiginton, J. (1979). Language and organization. *Academy of Management Review, 4,* 179–191.

Dahl, R. (1957). The concept of power. *Behavioral Science, 2,* 201–215.

Dahl, R. (1958). A critique of the ruling elite model. *American Political Science Review, 52,* 463–469.

Dahl, R. (1961). *Who governs?* New Haven, CT: Yale University Press.

Dahrendorf, R. (1959). *Class and class conflict in industrial society.* Stanford, CA: Stanford University Press.

Dallmayr, F. (1984). *Language and politics: Why does language matter to political philosophy?* Notre Dame, IN: University of Notre Dame Press.

Dallmayr, K., & McCarthy, T. (1977). *Understanding and social inquiry.* Notre Dame, IN: University of Notre Dame Press.

Dandridge, T., Mitroff, I., & Joyce, W. (1980). Organizational symbolism: A topic to expand organizational analysis. *Academy of Management Review, 5,* 77–82.

Deetz, S. (1973). An understanding of science and a hermeneutic science of understanding. *Journal of Communication, 23,* 139–159.

Deetz, S. (1982). Critical interpretive research in organizational communication. *The Western Journal of Speech Communication, 46,* 131–149.

Deetz, S. (1983). Keeping the conversation going: The principle of dialectical ethics. *Communication, 7,* 263–288.

Deetz, S. (1984). The politics of the oral interpretation of literature. *Literature in Performance, 4,* 60–64.

Deetz, S. (1986). Metaphors and the discursive production and reproduction of organization. In L. Thayer (Ed.), *Organization—communication: Emerging perspectives* (pp. 168- 182). Norwood, NJ: Ablex.

Deetz, S., and Kersten, A. (1983). Critical models of interpretive research. In L. Putnam & M. Pacanowsky (Eds.), *Communication and organizations: An interpretive approach* (pp. 147–171). Beverly Hills, CA: Sage.

Deetz, S., & Mumby, D. K. (1985). Metaphors, information, and power. *Information & Behavior, 1,* 369–386.

Dreyfus, H. L. (1980). Holism and hermeneutics. *Review of Metaphysics, 34,* 3–24.

Duncan, H. D. (1968). *Symbols in society.* New York: Oxford University Press.

Eisenberg, E. (1984). Ambiguity as strategy in organizational communication. *Communication Monographs, 51,* 227–242.

Evered, E. (1983). The language of organizations: The case of the navy. In L. Pondy, P. Frost, G. Morgan, & T. Dandridge (Eds.), *Organi-*

zational symbolism (pp. 125–143). Greenwich, CT: JAI Press.

Evered, R., & Louis, M. (1981). Alternative perspectives in the organizational sciences: "Inquiry from the inside" and "inquiry from the outside." *Academy of Management Review, 6,* 385–395.

Farganis, J. (1975). A preface to critical theory. *Theory Practice, 2,* 483–508.

Finder, J. (1987). A male secretary. *New York Times Magazine,* February 22, p. 68.

Fisher, W. R. (1984). Narration as a human communication paradigm: The case of public moral argument. *Communication Monographs, 51,* 1–22.

Fisher, W. R. (1985). The narrative paradigm: An elaboration. *Communication Monographs, 52,* 347–367.

Forester, J. (1981). *Critical theory and organizational analysis.* Working paper, Department of City and Regional Planning, Cornell University, Ithaca, NY.

Forester, J. (1982). Know your organizations: Planning and the reproduction of social and political relations. *Plan Canada, 22,* 3–13.

Foucault, M. (1973). *The order of things.* New York: Vintage Books.

Frost, P. (1980). Toward a radical framework for practicing organization science. *Academy of Management Review, 5,* 501- 508.

Frost, P. (in press). Power, politics, and influence. In L. W. Porter, L. L. Putnam, K. H. Roberts & E. H. Jablin (Eds.). *The handbook of organizational communication.* Beverly Hills, CA: Sage.

Frost, P. J., Moore, L. F., Louis, M. R., Lundberg, C. C., & Martin, J. (1985). *Organizational culture.* Beverley Hills, CA: Sage.

Gadamer, H. G. (1975). *Truth and method* (G. Barden & J. Cumming, Trans.). New York: Continuum.

Gaventa, J., & Horton, B. (1981). A citizens' research project in Appalachia, USA. *Convergence, 14*(3), 30–42.

Geertz, C. (1973). *The interpretation of cultures.* New York: Basic Books.

Geertz, C. (1983). *Local knowledge: Further essays in interpretive anthropology.* New York: Basic Books.

Gergen, K. J. (1978). Toward generative theory. *Journal of Personality & Social Psychology, 36,* 1344–1360.

Geuss, R. (1981). *The idea of a critical theory.* New York: Cambridge University Press.

Giddens, A. (1976). *New rules of sociological method.* New York: Basic Books.

Giddens, A. (1979). *Central problems in social theory.* Berkeley: University of California Press.

Giddens, A. (1981). *A contemporary critique of historical materialism (Vol. 1).* London: MacMillan.

Giddens, A. (1982). *Profiles and critiques in social theory*. London: MacMillan.

Giddens, A. (1984). *The constitution of society: Outline of the theory of structuration*. Cambridge, England: Polity Press.

Gillett, E. B. (1987). Higher education's caste system: Injustice is a daily experience. *Chronicle of Higher Education*, February 4.

Goffman, E. (1959). *The presentation of self in everyday life*. New York: Doubleday.

Goldman, P., & Van Houten, D. R. (1977). Managerial strategies and the worker: A marxist analysis of bureaucracy. In J. K. Benson (Ed.), *Organizational analysis: Critique and innovation*. Beverly Hills, CA: Sage.

Goodall, H. L., Jr. (1984). The status of communication studies in organizational contexts: One rhetorician's lament after a year-long odyssey. *Communication Quarterly, 32*, 133–147.

Gramsci, A. (1971). *Selections from the prison notebooks* (Q. Hoare & G. Nowell Smith, Trans.). New York: International Publishers.

Grossberg, L. W. (1984). Strategies of marxist cultural interpretation. *Critical Studies in Mass Communication, 1*, 392–421.

Gustavsen, B. (1979). Liberation of work and the role of social research. In T. Burns, L. E. Karlsson, & V. Rus (Eds.), *Work and power* (pp. 341–356). Beverly Hills, CA: Sage.

Habermas, J. (1970a). On systematically distorted communication. *Inquiry, 13*, 205–218.

Habermas, J. (1970b). Towards a theory of communicative competence. *Inquiry, 13*, 360–375.

Habermas, J. (1970c). *Toward a rational society* (J. Shapiro, Trans.). Boston: Beacon Press.

Habermas, J. (1972). *Knowledge and human interests* (J. Shapiro, Trans.). Boston: Beacon Press.

Habermas, J. (1974). *Theory and practice* (J. Viertel, Trans.). Boston: Beacon Press.

Habermas, J. (1975). *Legitimation Crisis* (T. McCarthy, Trans.). Boston: Beacon Press.

Habermas, J. (1979). *Communication and the evolution of society* (T. McCarthy, Trans.). Boston: Beacon Press.

Habermas, J. (1982). A reply to my critics. In J. Thompson & D. Held (Eds.), *Habermas: Critical debates* (pp. 219–283). Cambridge, MA: MIT Press.

Habermas, J. (1984). *The theory of communicative action, Vol.1: Reason and the rationalization of society* (T. McCarthy, Trans.). Boston: Beacon Press.

Hall, B. L. (1981). Participatory research, popular knowledge and power: A personal reflection. *Convergence, 14*(3), 6- 17.

Hall, S. (1985). Signification, representation, ideology: Althusser and the post-structuralist debates. *Critical Studies in Mass Communication, 2,* 91–114.

Harrison, T. M. (1986). *Superior-subordinate participation: An interactional approach.* Paper presented to the Speech Communication annual convention, Chicago, November 15.

Held, D. (1980). *Introduction to critical theory.* Berkeley: University of California Press.

Heydebrand, W. V. (1983). Organization and praxis. In G. Morgan (Ed.), *Beyond method* (pp. 306–320). Beverly Hills: Sage.

Imershein, A. W. (1977). Organizational change as a paradigm shift. In J. K. Benson (Ed.), *Organizational analysis: Critique and innovation.* Beverly Hills: Sage.

Jameson, F. (1981). *The political unconscious: Narrative as a socially symbolic act.* Ithaca, NY: Cornell University Press.

Jelinek, M., Smircich, L., & Hirsch, P. (1983). Introduction: A code of many colors. *Administrative Science Quarterly, 28,* 331–338.

Jick, T. D. (1979). Mixing qualitative and quantitative methods: Triangulation in action. *Administrative Science Quarterly, 24,* 602–611.

Journal of Management (1985). 14(2). Special issue on organizational symbolism.

Koch, S., & Deetz, S. (1981). Metaphor analysis of social reality in organizations. *Journal of Applied Communication Research, 9,* 1–15.

Krefting, L. A., & Frost, P. (1985). Untangling webs, surfing waves, and wildcatting: A multiple-metaphor perspective on managing organizational culture. In P. Frost, L. Moore, M. Louis, C. Lundberg, & J. Martin (Eds.), *Organizational culture* (pp. 155–168). Beverly Hills, CA: Sage.

Kreps, G. L. (1982). *Organizational culture as an equivocality reducing mechanism.* Presented to the SCA Action Caucus on Organizational and Intercultural Communication, Speech Communication Association Annual Convention, Louisville, KY.

Kreps, G. L. (1986). *Organizational communication.* New York: Longman.

Kropowski, E. (1983). Cultural myths: Clues to effective management. *Organizational Dynamics, 12*(3), 39–51.

Kubey, R. (1986). Personal conversation, Department of Communication, Rutgers University, New Brunswick, NJ 08903.

Kuhn, T. (1970). *The structure of scientific revolutions.* Chicago: University of Chicago Press.

Kurzweil, E. (1980). *The age of structuralism.* New York: Columbia University Press.

Lakoff, G., & Johnson, M. (1980a). *Metaphors we live by.* Chicago:

University of Chicago Press.

Lakoff, G., & Johnson, M. (1980b). The metaphorical structure of the human conceptual system. *Cognitive Science, 4*, 195- 208.

Larrain, J. (1979). *The concept of ideology.* London: Hutchinson.

Larrain, J. (1983). *Marxism and ideology.* London: Macmillan.

Lemert, C. C. (1979). *Sociology and the twilight of man: Homocentrism and discourse in sociological theory.* Carbondale, IL: Southern Illinois University Press.

Louis, M. (1980). Surprise and sense-making: What newcomers experience in entering unfamiliar organizational settings. *Administrative Science Quarterly, 25*, 226–251.

Louis, M. (1983). Organizations as culture-bearing milieux. In L. Pondy, P. Frost, G. Morgan, & T. Dandridge (Eds.), *Organizational Symbolism* (pp. 37–54). Greenwich, CT: JAI Press.

Lukács, G. (1971). *History and class consciousness* (R. Livingstone, Trans.). Cambridge, MA: MIT Press.

Lukes, S. (1974). *Power: A radical view.* London: Macmillan Press.

Manning, P. (1979). Metaphors of the field: Varieties of organizational discourse. *Administrative Science Quarterly, 24*, 660–671.

March, J. G., & Olsen, J. P. (1976). *Ambiguity and choice in organizations.* Bergen, Norway: Universitetsforlaget.

Martin, J. (1985). Can organizational culture be managed? In P. Frost, L. Moore, M. Louis, C. Lundberg, & J. Martin (Eds.), *Organizational culture* (pp. 95–98). Beverly Hills: Sage.

Martin, J., Feldman, M., Hatch, M. J. & Sitkin, S. B. (1983). The uniqueness paradox in organizational stories. *Administrative Science Quarterly, 28*, 438–453.

Martin, J., and Powers, M. E. (1983). Truth or corporate propaganda: The value of a good war story. In L. Pondy, P. Frost, G. Morgan, & T. Dandridge (Eds.), *Organizational symbolism* (pp. 93–107). Greenwich, CT: JAI Press.

Mason, R. (1982). *Participatory and workplace democracy.* Carbondale, IL: Southern Illinois University Press.

McCarthy, T. (1982). *The critical theory of Jürgen Habermas.* Cambridge, MA: MIT Press.

McClellan, D. (1986). *Ideology.* Minneapolis, MN: University of Minnesota Press.

Mead, G. H. (1967). *Mind, self and society.* Chicago: University of Chicago Press.

Meissner, M. (1986). The reproduction of women's domination in organizational communication. In L. Thayer (Ed.), *Organization— communication: Emerging perspectives* (pp. 51- 67). Norwood, NJ: Ablex.

Merleau-Ponty, M. (1962). *Phenomenology of perception* (C. Smith, Trans). London: Routledge & Kegan Paul.

Morgan, G. (1980). Paradigms, metaphors, and problem solving in organization theory. *Administrative Science Quarterly, 25,* 605–622.

Morgan, G. (1983a). More on metaphor: Why we cannot control tropes in administrative science. *Administrative Science Quarterly, 28,* 601–607.

Morgan, G. (1983b). Toward a more reflective science. In G. Morgan (Ed.), *Beyond method* (pp. 368–376). Beverly Hills, CA: Sage.

Morgan, G., & Smircich, L. (1980). The case for qualitative research. *Academy of Management Review, 5,* 491–500.

Mouffe, C. (1979). Hegemony and ideology in Gramsci. In C. Mouffe (Ed.), *Gramsci and marxist theory* (pp. 168–204). London: Routledge and Kegan Paul.

Mumby, D. K. (1987). The political function of narrative in organizations. *Communication Monographs, 54,* 113–127.

Nakagawa, G. (1983). *The political function of narratives.* Unpublished paper, Department of Speech Communication, Southern Illinois University at Carbondale.

Nakagawa, G. (1987). *"Why must you reopen old wounds?" Disfiguration, refiguration and healing in stories of Japanese American internment.* Presented at the Western Speech Communication Association annual convention, Salt Lake City, UT, February 13–17.

Pacanowsky, M. (1983). A small-town cop: communication in, out, and about a crisis. In L. Putnam & M. Pacanowsky (Eds.), *Communication and organizations: An interpretive approach* (pp. 261–282). Beverly Hills, CA: Sage.

Pacanowsky, M., & O'Donnell-Trujillo, N. (1983). Organizational communication as cultural performance. *Communication Monographs, 50,* 126–147.

Parkin, F. (1982). Social closure and class formation. In A. Giddens & D. Held (Eds.), *Classes, power, and conflict* (pp. 175–184). Berkeley: University of California Press.

Pasmore, W., and Friedlander, F. (1982). An action-research program for increasing employee involvement in problem- solving. *Administrative Science Quarterly, 27,* 343–362.

Pateman, C. (1970). *Participation and democratic theory.* New York: Cambridge University Press.

Pateman, T. (1980). *Language, truth and politics: Towards a radical theory for communication.* Sussex, England: Jean Stroud.

Peters, T. J., & Waterman, R. M. (1982). *In search of excellence.* New York: Harper & Row.

Pettigrew, A. M. (1979). On studying organizational cultures. *Adminis-*

trative Science Quarterly, 24, 570–581.

Pfeffer, J. (1981). *Power in organizations.* Marshfield, MA: Pitman.

Pondy, L. R. (1983). The role of metaphors and myths in organization and in the facilitation of change. In L. Pondy, G. Morgan, P. Frost, & T. Dandridge (Eds.). *Organizational symbolism* (pp. 157–166). Greenwich, CT: JAI Press.

Pondy, L., Morgan, G., Frost, P., & Dandridge, T. (1983). *Organizational symbolism.* Greenwich, CT: JAI Press.

Putnam, L. L. (1983). The interpretive perspective: An alternative to functionalism. In L. L. Putnam & M. Pacanowsky (Eds.), *Communication and organization: An interpretive approach* (pp. 31–54). Beverly Hills, CA: Sage.

Putnam, L., and Pacanowsky, M. (Eds.). (1983). *Communication and organizations: An interpretive approach.* Beverly Hills, CA: Sage.

Ranson, S., Hinings, B., & Greenwood, R. (1980). The structuring of organizational structures. *Administrative Science Quarterly, 25,* 1–17.

Rapoport, R. (1970). Three dilemmas in action research. *Human Relations, 23, 499–513.*

Reddy, M. (1979). The conduit metaphor. In A. Ortony (Ed.), *Metaphor and thought.* Cambridge, England: Cambridge University Press.

Ricoeur, P. (1976). *Interpretation theory: Discourse and the surplus of meaning.* Fort Worth, TX: Texas Christian University Press.

Riley, P. (1983). A structurationist account of political culture. *Administrative Science Quarterly, 28,* 414–437.

Rorty, R. (1979). *Philosophy and the mirror of nature.* Princeton, NJ: Princeton University Press.

Rorty, R. (1980). A reply to Dreyfus and Taylor. *Review of Metaphysics, 34,* 39–56.

Rorty, R. (1982). *Consequences of Pragmatism.* Minneapolis: University of Minnesota Press.

Rosen, M. (1985). Breakfast at Spiro's: Dramaturgy and dominance. *Journal of Management, 11*(2), 31–48.

Sanday, P. (1979). The ethnographic paradigm(s). *Administrative Science Quarterly, 24,* 527–538.

Sandler, R. (1987). I'm too understanding to mind. *Philip Morris Magazine, 2*(4), 22–23.

Sathe, V. (1983). Implications of corporate culture: A manager's guide to action. *Organizational Dynamics, 12*(3), 5–23.

Sathe, V. (1985). *Culture and related corporate realities.* Homewood, IL: Richard D. Irwin, Inc.

Schutz, A. (1967). *The phenomenology of the social world.* Evanston, IL: Northwestern University Press.

Searle, J. (1969). *Speech Acts: An essay in the philosophy of language.*

Cambridge, England: Cambridge University Press.

Silverman, D., and Torode, B. (1980). *The material word.* London: Routledge & Kegan Paul.

Skopec, E. (1982). *Rhetorical manifestations of organizational culture.* Paper presented to the Action Caucus on Intercultural and Organizational Communication, Speech Communication Association annual convention, Louisville, KY.

Slaughter, M. M. (1985). Literacy and society. *International Journal of the Sociology of Language, 56,* 113–139.

Smircich, L. (1981). *The concept of culture and organizational analysis.* Presented at the SCA/ICA Conference on Interpretive Approaches to Organizational Communication, Alta, UT.

Smircich, L. (1983a). Organizations as shared meanings. In L. Pondy, G. Morgan, P. Frost, & T. Dandridge (Eds.), *Organizational symbolism* (pp. 55–65). Greenwich, CT: JAI Press.

Smircich, L. (1983b). Concepts of culture and organizational analysis. *Administrative Science Quarterly, 28,* 339–358.

Smith, W., & Eisenberg, E. (in press). Conflict at Disneyland: A root metaphor analysis. *Communication Monographs, 54.*

Susman, G. I., & Evered, R. D. (1978). An assessment of the scientific merits of action research. *Administrative Science Quarterly, 23,* 582–603.

Taylor, C. (1980). Understanding the human sciences. *Review of Metaphysics, 34,* 25–38.

Therborn, G. (1980). *The ideology of power and the power of ideology.* London: Verso.

Thompson, J. B. (1983a). Ideology and the critique of domination I. *Canadian Journal of Political & Social Theory, 7,* 163–183.

Thompson, J. B. (1983b). Ideology and the analysis of discourse: A critical introduction to the work of Michel Pêcheux. *Sociological Review, 31,* 212–236.

Thompson, J. B. (1984a). Ideology and the critique of domination II. *Canadian Journal of Political & Social Theory, 8,* 179–196.

Thompson, J. B. (1984b). *Studies in the theory of ideology.* Berkeley: University of California Press.

Van Maanen, J. (1979). Reclaiming qualitative methods for organizational research: A preface. *Administrative Science Quarterly, 24,* 520–526.

Vio Grossi, F. (1981). Socio-political implications of participatory research. *Convergence, 14*(3), 43–51.

Weber, M. (1947). *The theory of social and economic organization* (A. Henderson and T. Parsons, Trans.). Glencoe, IL: Free Press.

Weick, K. (1979). *The social psychology of organizing* (2nd ed.). Reading, MA: Addison-Wesley.

White, H. (1978). *Tropics of discourse: Essays in cultural criticism*. Baltimore: Johns Hopkins University Press.

White, H. (1980). The value of narrativity in the representation of reality. *Critical Inquiry, 7*, 5–27.

Wilkins, A. (1983a). The culture audit: A tool for understanding organizations. *Organizational Dynamics, 12*(3), 24–38.

Wilkins, A. (1983b). Organizational stories as symbols which control the organization. In L. Pondy, G. Morgan, P. Frost, & T. Dandridge (Eds.), *Organizational symbolism* (pp. 81- 92). Greenwich, CT: JAI Press.

Williams, R. (1977). *Marxism and literature*. Oxford, England: Oxford University Press.

Winch, P. (1958). *The idea of a social science and its relation to philosophy*. London: Routledge & Kegan Paul.

Witten, M. (1986). *Storytelling and obedience at the workplace*. Paper presented to the annual convention of the International Communication Association, Chicago, May.

AUTHOR INDEX

A

Abercrombie, N., 78, *169*
Abrahmsson, B., 50, *169*
Althusser, L., 35, 42, 72, 74, 75, 76, 77, *169*
Astley, W.G., 66, *169*
Austin, J.L., 28, 92, *169*

B

Bacharach, P., 58, *169*
Bacharach, S., 58, 66, *169*
Baratz, M., 58, *169*
Becker, S.L., 34, 169
Benson, J.K., 67, *169*
Berger, P., 11, 95, *169*
Bernstein, R., 129, 139, 142, *169*
Braverman, H., 49, 50, 87, *169*
Brown, L.D., 149, 150, *170*
Brown, R.H., 67, *170*
Burawoy, M., 37, *170*
Burleson, B., 23, *170*
Burrell, G., 5, 61, 62, 72, 128, *170*

C

Carbaugh, D., 3, 16, *170*
Clegg, S., 1, 62, 63, 89, *170*
Cohen, M.D., 1, *170*
Conrad, C., 1, 5, 20, 99, *170*
Coward, R., 74, *170*
Culler, J., 74, 105, 160, 161, *171*

D

Daft, R.L., 12, *171*
Dahl, R., 56, 57, *171*
Dahrendorf, R., 48, 49, 61, *171*

Dallmayr, F., 63, 133, *171*
Dandridge, T., 4, 12, 16, 103, *171, 177*
Deetz, S., 4, 10, 15, 18, 33, 35, 95, 97, 98, 109, 133, 163, *171, 174*
Dreyfus, H.L., 131, *171*
Duncan, H.D., 14, 68, *171*
Dunkerley, D., 1, 89, *170*

E

Eisenberg, E., 11, 12, 18, 100, *171, 178*
Ellis, J., 74, *170*
Evered, E., 9, 96, 148, *171, 178*

F

Farganis, J., 152, *172*
Feldman, M., 16, 17, 91, 103, 112, 117, 118, *175*
Finder, J., 107, *172*
Fisher, W.R., 114, *172*
Forester, J., 32, 33, 34, 48, *172*
Foucault, M., 74, *172*
Friedlander, F., 149, *176*
Frost, P., 1, 3, 4, 8, 12, 35, *172, 174, 177*

G

Gadamer, H.G., 95, 129, 138, 145, *172*
Gaventa, J., 150, 153, 154, *172*
Geertz, C., 6, 71, 144, 145, 146, *172*
Gergen, K.J., 5, *172*
Geuss, R., 73, *172*
Giddens, A., 35, 36, 42, 43, 47, 51, 81, 82, 83, 84, 86, 89, 90, 98, 105, 117, 141, 142, 144, *172, 173*
Gillett, E.B., 104, 107, *173*

Goffman, E., 113, *173*
Goldman, P., 49, *173*
Goodall, H.L., Jr., 2, *173*
Gramsci, A., 86, 123, *173*
Greenwood, R., 67, 81, *177*
Grossberg, L.W., 86, *173*
Gustavsen, B., 149, *173*

H

Habermas, J., 23, 24, 25, 26, 27, 28, 29, 30, 31, 32, 37, 38, 39, 44, 98, *171*, *172*
Hall, B.L., 150, 152, *172*
Hall, S., 46, 81, 84, 85, 93, 110, 115, 124, 135, 141, *172*
Harrison, T.M., 87, *174*
Hatch, M.J., 16, 17, 91, 103, 112, 117, 118, *175*
Held, D., *174*
Heydebrand, W.V., 147, *174*
Hinings, B., 67, 81, *177*
Hirsch, P. 11, *174*
Horton, B., 150, 153, 154, *172*

I

Imershein, A.W., 67, *174*

J

Jameson, F., 105, 106, 109, 114, 129, 134, 160, *174*
Jelinik, M., 11, *174*
Jick, T.D., 9, *174*
Johnson, M., *174*, *175*
Joyce, W., 12, 16, 103, *171*

K

Kaplan, R.E., 150, 154, *170*
Kersten, A., 33, 36, 163, *171*
Kline, S., 23, *170*
Koch, S., 18, *174*
Krefting, L.A., 8, *174*
Kreps, G.L., 10, 13, 103, *174*
Kropowski, 7, *174*
Kubey, R., 75, *174*
Kuhn, T., 129, 130, *174*
Kurzweil, E., 74, *174*

L

Lakoff, G., 18, *174*, *175*
Larrain, J., 39, 40, 44, 74, 77, *175*
Lawler, E., 66, *169*
Lemert, C.C., 74, *175*
Louis, M., 3, 4, 6, 9, 12, *172*, *175*
Luckmann, T., 11, 95, *169*
Lukács, G., 87, 123, *175*
Lukes, S., 59, 60, *175*
Lundberg, C.C., 3, 4, 12, *172*

M

Manning, P., 16, *175*
March, J.G., 1, *170*, *175*
Martin, J., 3, 4, 7, 8, 12, 16, 17, 91, 99, 103, 112, 117, 118, *172*, *175*
Mason, R., 87, *175*
McCarthy, T., 37, 42, 43, 45, 46, 63, 140, *171*, *175*
McClellan, D., 71, *175*
Mead, G.H., 14, *175*
Meissner, M., 107, *175*
Merleau-Ponty, M., 95, *176*
Mitroff, I., 12, 16, 103, *171*
Moore, L.F., 3, 4, 12, *172*
Morgan, G., 4, 5, 12, 61, 62, 72, 128, 136, *170*, *176*, *177*
Mouffe, C., 86, *176*
Mumby, D.K., 18, 98, 102, 105, *171*, *176*

N

Nakagawa, G., 105, 109, *176*

O

O'Donnell-Trujillo, N., 10, *176*
Olsen, J.P., 1, *170*, *175*

P

Pacanowsky, M., 3, 10, 137, *176*, *177*
Parkin, F., 78, *176*
Pasmore, W., 149, *176*
Pateman, C., 87, 98, *176*
Peters, T.J., *176*
Pettigrew, A.M., 16, *176*
Pfeffer, J., 1, 63, 64, 65, 66, 83, *177*
Pondy, L., 4, 12, 18, *177*
Powers, M.E., 99, 103, 121, *175*
Putnam, L.L., 3, 5, *177*

R

Ranson, S., 67, 81, *177*
Rapoport, R., 148, *177*
Reddy, M., 14, *177*
Ricoeur, P., 115, *177*
Riley, P., 105, *177*
Rorty, R., 4, 128, 129, 130, 131, 132, 134, 135, 138, *177*
Rosen, M., 100, *177*

S

Sachdeva, P.S., 66, *169*
Sanday, P., 6, *177*
Sandler, R., 159, *177*
Sathe, V., 7, 8, *177*
Schutz, A., 95, *177*
Searle, J., 28, 92, *177*
Silverman, D., 74, *178*
Sitken, S.B., 16, 17, 91, 103, 112, 117, 118, 175
Skopec, E., 15, *178*
Slaughter, M.M., 111, *178*
Smircich, L., 5, 9, 11, 16, 103, 163, 165, *174, 176, 178*
Smith, W., 11, 12, 18, *178*
Susman, G.I., 148, *178*

T

Tandon, R., 149, 150, *170*
Taylor, C., 131, *178*
Therborn, G., 78, 79, 80, 86, *178*
Thompson, J.B., 97, 98, 100, 101, 102, 109, 116, 117, 119, 164, *178*
Torode, B., 74, *178*
Turner, B.S., 78, *169*

V

Van Houten, D.R., 49, *173*
Van Maanen, J., 9, *178*
Vio Grossi, F., 150, 151, *178*

W

Waterman, R.M., *176*
Weber, M., 62, *178*
Weick, K., 1, 2, 10, 65, 95, 103, *178*
White, H., 110, 114, *179*
Wiginton, J., 12, *171*
Wilkins, A., 7, 16, 102, 103, *179*
Williams, R., 87, *179*
Winch, P., 129, 145, *179*
Witten, M., 112, 113, *179*

SUBJECT INDEX

A

Abnormal Discourse
role in scientific knowledge, 131, 132
Action
human, and organizational structures
dialectical nature, 65, 67
social, and ideology dialectical nature,
78
Action research approach
limitations, 149, 150
to organizational research, 148–150
Agency
human, role in organizational
structures, 51, 52
Althusser's approach
limitations, 78
positivist nature, 77
to ideology, 74–78
Ambiguity
role in meaning formation, 100
Authority structures
role of interest, 49

B

Behavioral theories
of power, 56–58
Behaviorist approach
limitations to power, 59, 60
"Black" (as term of identity)
and discursive consciousness, 84, 85
and ideological struggle, 85
Bureaucracy
and ideology, 91

C

Capitalist society
technical rationality, 39
Capitalism
critical theory approach, 38
Class interests
and technical rationality, 42
Communication
and organizational power, 33, 35
and power, relationship, 3
Habermas' theory, 23–31
organizational
critical theory approach, 35, 36
role in meaning production, 14, 15
role in organizational culture, 12
systematically distorted
discursive penetration, 142
role in normative power, 34
as model for ideology, problematic
nature, 44, 45
impossible discourse, 98
Communicative competence
and double structure of speech, 28, 29
and universal pragmatics, 28
Habermas' theory, 28–31
Competence; see Communicative competence
Complexity
and organizational stories, 16, 17
and organizational symbolism, 16
Conflict
latent, role in power, 60
role in power, 59
Consciousness
and ideology, 72, 77
discursive

Consciousness, discursive (*continued*)
  and "black" (as term of identity), 84,
    85
  and taken-for-granted knowledge, 84,
    85
  practical consciousness, 83, 84
  practical
  and discursive consciousness, 83, 84
  and taken-for-granted knowledge, 84
Consensus
  false, role in power, 59, 60
  problematic nature of concept in organi-
    zational culture, 48
  role of ideal speech situation, 48
Contradiction
  and ideology, 87
Conversation
  radical, and organizational research,
    137–143
  role in scientific knowledge, 133, 134
Conversational approaches
  to organizational research, limitations,
    136, 137
Corporate images
  of IBM, 33
  of McDonald's restaurants, 33
Critical approach
  to organizational research, 147
Critical theory
  and managerial perspective, incompati-
    bility, 31, 32
  differences from interpretive paradigm,
    36, 37
  differences from psychoanalytic theory,
    42, 43
  role of psychoanalytic theory, 37, 38
  role of self-reflection, 36
Critical theory approach
  to capitalism, 38
  to organizational communication, 35, 36
Cultural deformation
  and organizational symbolism, 104
Cultural pragmatist view
  of organizational culture, 7, 8
Cultural purist view
  of organizational culture, 8, 9
Culture
  and Gramsci's hegemony, 86
  and organizing as key terms in organi-
    zational culture research, 6, 7
  organizational
    ideological role of stories, 158, 161, 162

  role of ideology, 157
  role of interpretation, 159–166
  role of power, 157
  and ideology, 89–93

D

Decision Making
  and power, 57
  organizational, symbolic functions, 65
Deconstruction
  as means for analysis of organizational
    narratives, 105, 106, 109
  of discourse, 160, 161, 162
Deep Structure
  as alternative concept for organizational
    communication research, 20, 21
Deformation
  cultural–organizational symbolism, 104
Descriptive approach
  to organizational symbolism, 15
Dialectic
  of understanding and truth, 138
Dialectical nature
  of human action and organizational
    structures, 65, 67
  of social action and ideology, 78
Discourse, 97; *see also* Language
  abnormal, role in scientific knowledge,
    131, 132
  deconstruction, 160–162
  impossible
    and systematically distorted communi-
      cation, 98
    organizational symbolism, 98
  organizational
    ideological nature, 98, 99
    and ideology, 101
  role in
    domination, 160
    ideology, 162
    organizational reality, 97
    organizational sense making, 158
    power, 97
Discursive analysis
  as alternative method for organizational
    research, 165, 166
  of ideology, 117, 119, 120
Discursive Change
  role in organizational change, 164
Discursive consciousness

and "black" (as term of identity), 84, 85
and practical consciousness, 83, 84
and taken-for-granted knowledge, 84, 85
Discursive model of rationality; see Discursive rationality
Discursive penetration
    and systematically distorted communication, 142
Discursive rationality
    and ideal speech situation, 29, 30
    and political relations, 32
    discursive model of rationality, 29
Disneyland
    organizational reality, 11, 12
Domination
    role in organizational structures, 63
    role of discourse, 160
Double structure
    of speech and communicative competence, 28, 29
Duality
    of structure and ideology, 82

E

Emancipatory interests
    and self-reflection, 27
    role in knowledge formation, 25, 26, 27
Empirical-analytic sciences
    role of technical interests, 24, 25
Epistemology
    and ideology, 127
Ethnographic approach
    to organizational symbolism, 100

F

False consensus
    role in power, 59, 60
Functionalism
    as dominant philosophy in organizational research, 4
    differences from interpretive paradigm, 5, 6
    limitations in organizational research, 6
Functionalist approach
    to social science, 144

G

Gadamer's approach
    to scientific knowledge, 137–140
Giddens' approach
    theory of structuration, 82, 90
    to ideology, 82–88
    to understanding and ideology, 141, 142
Gramsci's hegemony
    and culture, 86
Group interests
    and power, 60

H

Habermas' critical theory
    critique, 39–47
Habermas' theory
    of communication, 23–31
    of communicative competence, 28–31
    of interests, 24–28
Habermas' view
    of understanding, 139
Hegel's theory
    of knowledge formation, limitations, 26
Hegemony
    Gramsci's, and culture, 86
Hermeneutic science
    role of *Verstehen*, 25
Hierarchy
    and reification, 88
Human action
    and organizational structures, dialectical nature, 65, 67
Human agency
    role in organizational structures, 51, 52
Humanism, 72; see also Radical humanism

I

IBM
    analysis
        of organizational narrative, 118, 120–124
        of an organizational narrative, 119
    corporate images, 33
Ideal speech situation
    and discursive rationality, 29
    as model for ideology, problematic nature, 45–47
    discursive rationality, 30
    limitations, 141
    role in consensus, 48
Ideological functions
    of organizational narratives, 102–124

Ideological interpretation
  of texts, validity problem, 115, 116
Ideological nature
  of language, 98
  of organizational discourse, 98, 99
  of organizational narratives, 105
  of organizational stories, 101
Ideological state apparatuses
  and societal superstructure, 75
Ideological structures
  role of time clocks, 79, 80
Ideological struggle, 86
  and "black" (as term of identity), 85
Ideology
  Althusser's approach, 74–78
  and bureaucracy, 91
  and consciousness, 72, 77
  and contradiction, 87
  and duality of structure, 82
  and epistemology, 127
  and legitimation of organizational mean-
    ing structures, 73
  and material practices, 75
  and normative power, 30, 31
  and organizational culture, 89–93
  and organizational discourse, 101
  and organizational interests, 81
  and organizational symbolism, 95–125,
    158
  and power, synonymous nature, 51
  and reification, 87
  and social action, dialectical nature, 78
  and social reality, 79
  and subjectivity, 77
  and understanding, Giddens' approach,
    141, 142
  as descriptive, 73
  as pejorative, 73
  as positive, 73
  as problematic concept, 71
  as technical rationality, problematic na-
    ture, 39, 40, 41
  discursive analysis, 117, 119, 120
  Giddens' approach, 82–88
  imaginary nature, 76
  interpretive analysis, 117, 120
  materialistic nature, 79
  means of analysis, 116, 117
  model
    ideal speech situation, problematic
      nature, 45–47
    psychoanalytic theory, problematic

    nature, 42–44
  systematically distorted communica-
    tion, problematic nature, 44, 45
  pejorative view and ideology-critique,
    80
  radical humanism approach, 72
  radical structuralist approach, 72
  role in organizational culture, 157
  role of discourse, 162
  social analysis, 116–119
  Therborn's approach, 78–82
Ideology-Critique
  and pejorative view of ideology, 80
Impossible discourse
  and organizational symbolism, 98
  and systematically distorted communi-
    cation, 98
Institutionalization
  and power, 64
Interests
  and worker participation, 50
  class — technical rationality, 42
  emancipatory
    role in knowledge formation, 25, 26,
      27
    and self-reflection, 27
  group — power, 60
  Habermas' theory, 24–28
  organizational — ideology, 81
  problematic nature of concept, 39–42
  role in organizational structures, 48
  role of — in authority structures, 49
  technical
    quasi-transcendental nature, 25
    role in empirical-analytic sciences, 24,
      25
  vested
    role in organizational sense-making,
      35
  and organizational reality, 50
Interpretation, 109; see also Sense making
  political nature, 159, 160
  role in organizational culture, 159–166
Interpretive analysis
  of ideology, 117, 120
Interpretive paradigm
  and organizational symbolism, 95
  differences
    from critical theory, 36, 37
    from functionalism, 5, 6
  language as focus of study, 95
  of organizational research, 3

Interpretive paradigm approach
  to knowledge, 128
  to organizational research, 147
  to social science, 144, 145
Interpretive-functionalist debate
  in organizational communication, 4
Intersubjective nature
  of meaning, 10
Intersubjectivity
  role in sense-making, 10–12

K

Knowledge
  and scientific paradigms, 129
  and scientific revolutions, 129
  interpretive paradigm approach, 128
  positivist view, 127, 128
    limitations, 128
  scientific
    Gadamer's approach, 137–140
    Kuhn's View, 129–130
      limitations, 130
    role of abnormal discourse, 131, 132
    role of conversation, 133, 134
    Rorty's view, 130–135
      limitations, 135
  taken-for-granted
    discursive consciousness, 84, 85
    organizational structures, 67
    practical consciousness, 84
  theories, 129–137
Knowledge formation
  Hegel's theory, limitations, 26
  Marx's theory, limitations, 26
  role of emancipatory interests, 25, 26, 27
Knowledge generation
  problematic role of researcher, 143
Kuhn's view
  of scientific knowledge, 129, 130
    limitations, 130

L

Language, 97; see also Discourse
  as focus of study of interpretive para-
    digm, 95
  ideological nature, 98
  representational view, limitations, 102
  role in organizational reality, 96
  role in social reality, 96, 97
  role in understanding, 138, 139

Language in organizations, 18; see Organi-
    zational language
Latent conflict
  role in power, 60
Legitimation
  of organizational meaning structures
    and ideology, 73

M

Managerial perspective
  and critical theory, incompatibility, 31,
    32
  and organizational stories, 101
  of organizational communication theory,
    1
  role in organizational reality, 93
  role in organizational research, 2
Marx's theory
  of knowledge formation, limitations, 26
Mass media
  role as ideological state apparatus, 75
Material practices
  and ideology, 75
Materialistic nature
  of ideology, 79
McDonald's restaurants
  corporate images, 33
Meaning
  intersubjective nature, 10
Meaning formation
  and meaning deformation, 73
  organizational narratives, role, 102
  role in organizational structures, 90
  role of ambiguity, 100
  role of power, 48, 49
Meaning production
  role of communication, 14, 15
Meaning structures
  organizational, legitimation ideology, 73
Meaning-centered approach
  to organizational culture, 19, 20, 21
Meetings
  symbolic nature, 68
Metaphors
  and organizational language, 18
  role in organizational culture, 18, 19
Methodology
  social science, political nature, 144
Moral functions
  of organizational narratives, 111

N

Narrative structure
  and sense making, 109, 110
Narratives, 105; *see also Stories*
  organizational
    deconstruction as means for analysis, 105, 106, 109
    ideological functions, 102–124
    ideological nature, 105
    moral functions, 111
    role in organizational reality, 114
    role in sense making, 108
    and power, 114
    and reification, 121, 122
    in meaning formation, role, 102
Non-decision making
  and power, 58
Normative power
  and ideology, 30, 31
  role of systematically distorted communication, 34

O

Organizational change
  role of discursive change, 164
Organizational communication
  critical theory approach, 35, 36
  interpretive-functionalist debate, 4
Organizational communication research
  deep structure as alternative concept, 20, 21
Organizational communication theory
  concept of power, 1
  managerial perspective, 1
Organizational culture, 3; *see also* Interpretive paradigm
  and ideology, 89–93
  and sense-making, 9–12
  as alternative method for organizational research, 3, 4, 6
  cultural pragmatist view, 7, 8
  cultural purist view, 8, 9
  ideological role of stories, 158, 161, 162
  meaning-centered approach, 19, 20, 21
  perspectives, 6–9
  problematic nature of concept of consensus, 48–50
  role of
    communication, 12
    ideology, 157

  interpretation, 159–166
  metaphors, 18, 19
  organizational symbolism, 12–19
  power, 157
Organizational culture research
  key terms, organizing and culture, 6, 7
Organizational decision making
  symbolic functions, 65
Organizational discourse
  and ideology, 101
  ideological nature, 98, 99
Organizational interests
  and ideology, 81
Organizational language
  and metaphors, 18
Organizational meaning structures
  legitimation ideology, 73
Organizational narratives
  and power, 114
  and reification, 121, 122
  deconstruction as means for analysis, 105, 106, 109
  ideological functions, 102–124
  ideological nature, 105
  in meaning formation, role, 102
  moral functions, 111
  role in organizational reality, 114
  role in sense making, 108
Organizational power
  and communication, 33, 55
  role of organizational symbolism, 66, 67, 68, 92
Organizational reality
  and organizational stories, 81
  and organizational symbolism, 12
  and vested interests, 50
  of Disneyland, 11, 12
  role of
    discourse, 97
    language, 96
    managerial perspective, 93
    organizational narratives, 114
    stories, 16–18
  social nature, 8, 9
Organizational research
  alternative method
    discursive analysis, 165, 166
    organizational culture, 3, 4, 6
  and radical conversation, 137–143
  and rationality, 2
  conversational approaches, limitations, 136, 137

critical approach, 147
dominant philosophy, functionalism, 4
interpretive paradigm, 3
interpretive paradigm approach, 147
limitations of functionalism, 6
limitations of positivist approach, 5
participatory research approach, 148,
    150–155
role of
    Verstehen in, 4
    managerial perspective, 2
    story analysis, 163, 164
sense making as concept, 3
Organizational sense-making
role of discourse, 158
role of vested interests, 35
Organizational stories
and complexity, 16, 17
and managerial perspective, 101
and organizational reality, 81
and self-presentation, 113
functions, 103
ideological nature, 101
Organizational structures
and human action, dialectical nature,
    65, 67
and taken-for-granted knowledge, 67
role of
    domination, 63
    human agency, 51, 52
    interests in, 48
    meaning formation, 90
    power, 63
    rationality, 62, 63
    rules, 90
    sense making, 90
Organizational symbolism
and complexity, 16
and cultural deformation, 104
and ideology, 95–125, 158
and impossible discourse, 98
and interpretive paradigm, 95
and power, 83
and women, 107, 108
descriptive approach, 15
ethnographic approach, 100
limitations of previous theories, 99, 100
representational view, 13, 14
role in
    organizational culture, 12–19
    organizational power, 66–68, 92
    sense making, 92

Organizations
concept of power, 61–68
rationality myth, 2
role of storytelling, 108–113
symbolic nature of power, 66
technical rationality, 41
Organizational research
action research approach, 148, 149, 150
Organizing
and culture as key terms in organiza-
    tional culture research, 6, 7
role in systematically distorted commu-
    nication, 35

P

Paradigms
scientific, knowledge, 129
Participatory research approach
limitations, 151–155
to organizational research, 148, 150–155
Pejorative view
of ideology and ideology-critique, 80
Political nature
of social science methodology, 144
of interpretation, 159, 160
Political relations
and discursive rationality, 32
Positivist approach
limitations to organizational research, 5
Positivist nature
of Althusser's approach, 77
Positivist view
of knowledge, 127, 128
    limitations, 128
Power
and communication, relationship, 3
and decision making, 57
and group interests, 60
and ideology, synonymous nature, 51
and institutionalization, 64
and non-decision making, 58
and organizational narratives, 114
and organizational symbolism, 83
and rationality myth, 2
behavioral theories, 56–58
concept in
    organizational communication
        theory, 1
    organizations, 61–68
    structural-functionalist paradigm, 61,
        62

Power, concept in (*continued*)
  limitations of behaviorist approach, 59, 60
  normative
    ideology, 30, 31
    role of systematically distorted communication, 34
  organizational
    role of organizational symbolism, 66, 67, 68, 92
    and communication, 33, 35
  role
    in meaning formation, 48, 49
    in organizational culture, 157
    in organizational structures, 63
    in social relations, 48
    of conflict, 59
    of discourse, 97
    of false consensus, 59, 60
    of latent conflict, 60
    of social structure, 59
  structural nature, 55
  symbolic nature in organizations, 66
Practical consciousness
  and discursive consciousness, 83, 84
  and taken-for-granted knowledge, 84
Pragmatic view, 8; *see also* Cultural pragmatist view
Pragmatics, 28; *see also* Universal pragmatics
Psychoanalytic theory
  as model for ideology, problematic nature, 42–44
  differences from critical theory, 42, 43
  role in critical theory, 37, 38

Q

Quasi-transcendental nature of technical interests, 25

R

Radical conversation
  and organizational research, 137–142, 143
Radical humanism approach
  to ideology, 72
Radical structuralist
  structuralism, 72

Radical structuralist approach
  to ideology, 72
Rationality
  and organizational research, 2
  discursive
    and ideal speech situation, 30
    and political relations, 32
    ideal speech situation, 29
    role in organizational structures, 62, 63
  technical
    ideology, problematic nature, 39–41
    and class interests, 42
    in capitalist society, 39
    in organizations, 41
Rationality myth
  and power, 2
  in organizations, 2
Reality, 79; *see also* Social reality
  organizational
    role of discourse, 97
    role of language, 96
    role of managerial perspective, 93
    role of organizational narratives, 114
    organizational stories, 81
    vested interests, 50
  social
    role of language, 96, 97
    ideology, 79
Reification
  and hierarchy, 88
  and ideology, 87
  and organizational narratives, 121, 122
Representational view
  of language, limitations, 102
  of organizational symbolism, 13, 14
Repressive state apparatuses
  and societal superstructure, 75
Researcher
  problematic role in knowledge generation, 143
  role in thick description approach, 146
Revolutions
  scientific, knowledge, 129
Role
  of technical interests in empirical-analytic sciences, 24
Rorty's view
  of scientific knowledge, 130–135
  limitations, 135
Rules
  role in organizational structures, 90

S

Science
  role as opposition to ideology, 76
  social
    functionalist approach, 144
    interpretive paradigm approach, 144,
      145
    thick description approach, 144, 145
    methodology, political nature, 144
Scientific knowledge
  Gadamer's approach, 137–140
  Kuhn's view, 129, 130
    limitations, 130
  role of
    abnormal discourse, 131, 132
    conversation, 133, 134
  Rorty's view, 130–135
    limitations, 135
Scientific paradigms
  and knowledge, 129
Scientific revolutions
  and knowledge, 129
Self-presentation
  and organizational stories, 113
Self-reflection
  and emancipatory interests, 27
  role in critical theory, 36
Sense-making
  and narrative structure, 109, 110
  as concept in organizational research, 3
  organizational
    role of discourse, 158
    role of vested interest, 35
  role
    in organizational structures, 90
    of organizational symbolism, 92
    of organizational narratives, 108
    of intersubjectivity, 10, 11, 12
Social action
  and ideology, dialectical nature, 78
Social analysis
  of ideology, 116–119
Social nature
  of organizational reality, 8, 9
Social reality
  and ideology, 79
  role of language, 96, 97
Social relations
  role of power, 48
Social science

functionalist approach, 144
interpretive paradigm approach, 144,
  145
thick description approach, 144, 145
Social science methodology
  political nature, 144
Social structure
  role in power, 59
Societal superstructure
  and ideological state apparatuses, 75
  and repressive state apparatuses, 75
Speech
  double structure communicative compe-
    tence, 28, 29
Stories, 105; see also Narratives
  ideological role in organizational cul-
    ture, 158, 161, 162
  organizational
    functions, 103
    ideological nature, 101
    and managerial perspective, 101
    and organizational reality, 81
    and self-presentation, 113
  role in organizational reality, 16–18
Stories in organizations, 16; see also Orga-
    nizational stories
Story analysis
  role in organizational research, 163, 164
Storytelling
  role in organizations, 108–113
Structural nature
  of power, 55
Structural-functionalist paradigm
  concept of power, 61, 62
  limitations, 61, 62
Structuralism, 72; see also Radical structur-
    alist
Structuration
  theory, Giddens' approach, 82, 90
Structure
  duality ideology, 82
  narrative, and sense making, 109, 110
Structures
  ideological, role of time clocks, 79, 80
  organizational
    role of domination, 63
    role of human agency, 51, 52
    role of meaning formation, 90
    role of power, 63
    role of rationality, 62, 63
    role of rules, 90

Structures, organizational (*continued*)
    role of sense making, 90
        human action, dialectical nature, 65, 67
Struggle
    ideological, 86
    and "black" (as term of identity), 85
Subjectivity
    and ideology, 77
Superstructure
    societal
        and ideological state apparatuses, 75
        and repressive state apparatuses, 75
Symbolic functions
    of organizational decision making, 65
Symbolic nature
    of meetings, 68
    of power in organizations, 66
Symbolism
    organizational
        ethnographic approach, 100
        role in organizational power, 66–68
Symbolism in organizations, 12; *see also*
    Organizational symbolism
Systematically distorted communication
    and discursive penetration, 142
    and impossible discourse, 98
    as model for ideology, problematic nature, 44, 45
    role in normative power, 34
    role in organizing, 35

T

Taken-for-granted knowledge
    and discursive consciousness, 84, 85
    and organizational structures, 67
    and practical consciousness, 84
Technical interests
    quasi-transcendental nature, 25
    role in empirical-analytic sciences, 24, 25
Technical rationality
    and class interests, 42
    ideology, problematic nature, 39–41
    in capitalist society, 39
    in organizations, 41
Text interpretation
    validity problem, 115
Texts

ideological interpretation, validity problem, 115, 116
Theory
    of structuration, Giddens' approach, 82, 90
Therborn's approach
    to ideology, 78–82
Thick description approach
    difficulties, 145
    role of researcher, 146
    to social science, 144, 145
Time clocks
    role in ideological structures, 79, 80
Truth
    and dialectic of understanding, 138

U

Understanding
    and ideology, Giddens' approach, 141, 142
    dialectic truth, 138
    Habermas' view, 139
    role of language, 138, 139
Universal pragmatics
    and communicative competence, 28

V

Validity problem
    in ideological interpretation of texts, 115, 116
    in text interpretation, 115
Verstehen
    role in hermeneutic sciences, 25
    role in organizational research, 4
Vested interests
    and organizational reality, 50
    role in organizational sense-making, 35

W

Women
    and organizational symbolism, 107, 108
Worker participation
    and interests, 50

Z

Zweckrational, 62